Human   s

Human Universals

Donald E. Brown

Department of Anthropology
University of California–Santa Barbara

McGraw-Hill, Inc.
New York St. Louis San Francisco Auckland Bogotá
Caracas Lisbon London Madrid Mexico Milan
Montreal New Delhi Paris San Juan Singapore
Sydney Tokyo Toronto

For Carrie, Barry, and Rosminah

Human Universals

Copyright © 1991 by McGraw-Hill, Inc. All rights reserved. Printed in the United States of America. Except as permitted under the United States Copyright act of 1976, no part of this publication may be reproduced or distributed in any form or by any means, or stored in a data base or retrieval system, without the prior written permission of the publisher.

567890 DOC/DOC 998

ISBN 0-07-008209-X

This book was set in Zapf Book Light by the College Composition Unit in cooperation with Ruttle Shaw & Wetherill, Inc.
The editors were Phillip A. Butcher, Lori Pearson, and Scott Amerman; the production supervisor was Kathryn Porzio.
The cover was designed by Eric Baker.
R. R. Donnelley & Sons Company was printer and binder.

Library of Congress Cataloging-in-Publication Data

Brown, Donald E. (Donald Edward), (date).
    Human universals / Donald E. Brown.
        p.   cm
    Includes bibliographical references and index.
    ISBN 0-07-008209-X
    1. Culture.   2. Cultural relativism.   3. Physical anthropology.
4. Human behavior.   5. Sociobiology.   I. Title.
GN357.B76   1991
306—dc20   90-22171

Contents

Preface   *vii*
Introduction   *1*

CHAPTER 1
Rethinking Universality: Six Cases   9

Color Classification   *11*
Samoan Adolescence   *14*
Male and Female among the Tchambuli   *20*
Facial Expressions   *23*
Hopi Time   *27*
The Oedipus Complex   *32*
Conclusion   *37*

CHAPTER 2
Conceptualizing, Defining, and Demonstrating Universals   39

CHAPTER 3
The Historical Context of the Study of Universals   54

CHAPTER 4
Explaining Universals   88

Explaining a Universal with a Universal   *89*
Cultural Reflection or Recognition of Physical Fact   *92*
Logical Extension from (Usually Biological) Givens   *94*

v

Diffusionist Explanations that Rest upon the Great Age of the
    Universal and, Usually, Its Great Utility   95
Archoses   96
Conservation of Energy   98
The Nature of the Human Organism, with Emphasis on the Brain   98
Evolutionary Theory   99
Interspecific Comparison   111
Ontogeny   112
Partial Explanations   113

CHAPTER 5
Incest Avoidance   118

CHAPTER 6
The Universal People   130

CHAPTER 7
Universals, Human Nature, and Anthropology   142

Bibliography   157
Index   203

Preface

This book is a reflection on human universals and what they imply. Some of the implications are far reaching. I conclude, for example, that what we know about universals places clear limits on the cultural relativism that anthropologists have developed and disseminated widely. Furthermore, what we know about universals suggests the need to revise a conception of human nature that anthropologists have helped to shape and that has spread so far beyond the social sciences that it is now embedded in what Robin Fox (1989:24) calls "the whole secular social ideology" of our time. Because these conclusions are far from trivial, it may be worth recounting the experiences that initially stimulated my interest in universals and led, ultimately, to this book. Since this book is only an imperfect step along the way toward the fuller assessment that human universals deserve, I will also point to its shortcomings.

In 1974 Donald Symons and I co-taught a seminar on primate and human sexuality. Symons presented an early draft of his book *The Evolution of Human Sexuality* (1979), in which he argued that there are certain pan-human sex differences. On the occasion that he discussed a list of these differences—it then contained, if I recall correctly, some five to seven items (such as the quicker and more visually-cued sexual arousal of males)—I bet him that I could find a society in which each of the alleged sex differences was reversed. As a typical sociocultural anthropologist trained in the 1960s, I had absorbed the lesson of Ruth Benedict's *Patterns of Culture* (1934) and many other anthropological classics and textbooks that stressed the inherent variability and autonomy of culture. I was willing to accept the idea of certain kinds of widespread regularities or tendencies, but I thought it highly unlikely that sex differences in temperament or behavior would show any complex similarities in all societies. The latter smacked of rigid biological determinism. But I did not win the bet—and I began to think more carefully about human universals, cultural relativism, and, especially, about the role that human biology plays in human affairs.

vii

Sometime thereafter I glanced through E. O. Wilson's *On Human Nature* (1978). My views were still so conditioned by the sociocultural perspectives in which I was trained that I was not inspired to read the book, but I noticed that Wilson quoted a list of human universals that had been compiled by the anthropologist George P. Murdock. The "sociobiology" controversy, galvanized by Wilson's book of that title, was very much in the air at the time, and it struck me that sociobiologists might be more convincing if they confined their explanations to universals rather than attempting to show that virtually everything that humans do somehow maximizes their reproductive success. While I no longer accept a simplistic formulation in which human invariants may plausibly be explained in biological terms, while the variables demand cultural explanations, that formulation did keep me thinking about universals.

A few years later, the books by Freeman, Malotki, and Spiro that are described in Chapter 1 were published. These books convinced me that the issues surrounding universals, especially the questions they raise about cultural relativism, needed more attention than they were receiving. I considered the prospect of writing this book, and I began to offer seminars and ultimately a lecture course on human universals.

When I began to write, I had in mind something relatively uncomplicated that might stand in opposition to Benedict's *Patterns of Culture* and draw attention to the existence and seemingly obvious implications of invariants in human affairs. But the issues turned out to be more complicated than I had realized, and the resulting book is a compromise between a popular essay and a more scholarly work. Moreover, once I felt that the main points had been articulated, I stopped searching for and digesting further materials on universals. I am confident that this book is the most exhaustive study of human universals to date, but I know that I have not covered the entire literature. (Although I have ceased to look for them, some 50 or so references on universals have piled up on my desk in the last year.) In spite of the compromises I have made, I am sure that many readers will find consolation in one reviewer's observation that this book is only half as long as it could be.

There are some parts of the book that almost certainly will benefit from a more thorough thinking through than I now provide. Consider, for example, the definitions of universals: while I employ only a few of them, I cite a number of others that probably can be reduced to a shorter and more orderly list. And although I put considerable thought and effort into the explanation of universals, the issues sometimes require expertise that I do not possess. Finally, I should note the obvious: no anthropologist can be an authority on more than a handful of universals. The reader who wants to know whether a particular feature that I have accepted as being a universal really is so will have to go beyond this book. Although the future may allow me to correct some of the flaws, I must express the hope now that the persons I will thank below for their many thoughtful comments on this book will be credited for some of its strengths—to which they surely contributed—but not blamed for its shortcomings—for which I just as surely am responsible.

Acknowledgments

The entire manuscript or very substantial portions of it were read by my departmental colleagues Napoleon A. Chagnon, Elvin Hatch, A. F. Robertson, and Donald Symons; by the other anthropologists George N. Appell, Robin Fox, Derek Freeman, Barry Hewlett, Allen R. Maxwell, Raymond Scupin, M. G. Smith, and John Tooby; by the linguists R. McMillan Thompson and Sandra A. Thompson; by the psychologists Leda Cosmides, Martin Daly, and Margo Wilson; by the sociologists Suzanne Retzinger, Thomas J. Scheff, and Pierre van den Berghe; and by a dozen or more students, of whom I would particularly like to thank Helen (Yonie) Harris, Walter Lehmann, Reed Wadley, and Tracy Wise. I received very helpful comments on specific aspects of the book from Ralph Bolton, Richard Chacon, Matthea Cremers, Alan J. Fridlund, Ward H. Goodenough, Thomas Harding, Douglas Hayward, Hsiu-Zu Ho, Brijitte Jordan, Gwendolyn Lauterbach, Jack N. Loomis, Paul Mattson, Susan Mies, Mattison Mines, Douglas Mitchell, J. Tim O'Meara, Craig Palmer, Douglas Raybeck, Melford Spiro, Lawrence Sugiyama, and Janice Timbrook. Jean-Claude Muller, Robert Netting, and Ronald P. Rohner very kindly supplied me with materials too ample or too late to be properly incorporated in the book. At a very late stage I received encouragement and advice from the historian Carl Degler. I expect that his forthcoming book, *In Search of Human Nature*, which is a history of Darwinian thought in the social sciences, will expand and deepen the analysis presented in my chapter on history. In addition to the departmental colleagues already mentioned, I should also note the unfailing encouragement from other colleagues, particularly Manuel L. Carlos, William Madsen, and Phillip L. Walker, whose comments passed on in the hallways are much appreciated. To the scholars and students whose suggestions I have used but whose names now escape me, and to those whose advice I failed to take, I offer apologies.

Although I have mentioned my colleague Donald Symons twice already, it would be remiss not to note that he did more than start me thinking about universals and more than merely read my manuscript. He read several versions of it and many sections over and over, patiently providing detailed written comments each time. Just as patiently, he explained evolutionary theory and provided numerous references. His writings on evolutionary psychology have been a considerable influence on me and this book and will, I think, have a considerable influence on the study of human nature well into the future.

David Hume characterized the study of human nature as a subject of "unspeakable importance." Evolutionary psychology, informed by the comparative study of the constant as well as the variable in human affairs, is one of the most important theoretical frameworks currently available to advance the study of human nature. I have no doubt about the importance of human nature, nor about the relevance of universals in illuminating it; I can only hope that this book will convince others that the study of human universals should loom larger in the attempt to understand humanity and human affairs.

Donald E. Brown

Introduction

Many anthropologists, probably most of them, are skeptical of statements that generalize about what all peoples do. But are there not generalizations of that sort that really do hold for the wide array of human populations? There are—and not enough has been said about them. This skepticism and neglect of human universals is the entrenched legacy of an "era of particularism" in which the observation that something *doesn't* occur among the Bongo Bongo counted as a major contribution to anthropology (Erasmus 1961:387). The truth of the matter is, however, that anthropologists probably always take for granted an indefinite collection of traits that add up to a very complex view of human nature. Let me give some examples.

In a course that I teach on the peoples and cultures of Southeast Asia I have often illustrated the cultural elaboration of rank that is found in many Southeast Asian societies—and certainly among the Brunei Malays with whom I did my doctoral research—with the following anecdote. In the course of my research I was once seated with two young men on a wooden bench at the front of the house that my wife and I rented in a ward of the Brunei capital. A third young man was seated just a few feet away on the rung of a ladder but at the same height as the rest of us. There was no one else around. Tiring of sitting on the bench, I slipped down from it to sit on the walkway. I was followed almost instantly by all three of the young men. Just as quickly I realized that they had done it not because they too were uncomfortable on the bench (I had been there longer than they) but because in the Brunei scheme of things it is not polite to sit higher than another person, unless you considerably outrank that other person. So I protested, urging them to please remain seated on the bench. They said it wouldn't look nice. I said there was no one but us around to notice. One of them closed the matter by noting that people across the river—to which he gestured (it was about a quarter mile away)—just *might* see what was going on. The clear implication was that he and his fellows weren't about to let anyone see them apparently breaking one of the important rules in the etiquette of rank, even though they knew they wouldn't be offending me.

I always told this story to illustrate difference, to show the extremity to which Bruneis concerned themselves with rank, and it always seemed to be a very effective message. As a teacher of anthropology I know very well that cultural differences elicit some sort of inherent interest. Ruth Benedict's *Patterns of Culture* (1934) is an all-time anthropological best-seller, and its essential message is the astonishing variability of human customs. No one teaching anthropology can ignore the way students

1

react to revelations about the amazing ways other peoples act and think. And no one teaching anthropology can fail to sense the wheels turning in students' minds when they use these revelations to rethink the ways people act and think in their own society. Teachers of anthropology not only see this in students, they cultivate it. But are the differences all that should be of concern to anthropology? Does an emphasis on differences present a true image of humanity?

I now realize that the story I have told my students is pervaded with evidence of similarities: above all, the young men were concerned with what other people would think about them; they were also concerned with politeness in particular, rules in general; even their concern with rank was only a matter of difference in degree. I could go on, mentioning their use of language and gestures; the smooth conversational turn taking; the concepts of question, answer, explanation; the use of highness/lowness to symbolize rank; and much more.

At a more subtle level, I believe, some amazing things were happening that I took no note of. Without my explaining things in detail, in my broken Malay, the young men had instantly grasped my point: the setting was informal and I wanted them to treat me as they would treat each other (they would not have moved down or up in unison for each other in those circumstances); furthermore, it was "not my custom" to be offended by people sitting higher than me. I think that my companions sized up these aspects of the immediate situation just as I had.

But they also saw a wider context in which their behavior could be misinterpreted by others, and with what seemed like a few words and a gesture, they explained their position to me and closed the matter. There were more than a few words and gestures: there were tone of voice, facial expressions, body language, and an enormously complex context of past, present, and future. And there were four human minds, each observing, computing, and reacting to the "implicature" (Scheff 1986:74) of the bare words so silently and automatically as to occasion no notice. All this—from the conscious concern with what others would think to the unconscious assessments of implications—formed a plainly human background, from which I in my lectures had pulled out a quantitative difference as the focus of attention.

I use the word "quantitative" because, although it may not be *my* custom to think that the height of one's seat should match one's rank, the idea is not foreign to western culture. There are some wonderful examples of the equation between seating height and rank, or dominance, in Charlie Chaplin's film "The Great Dictator." What distinguishes the Bruneis from us is the greater frequency of day-to-day contexts in which the equation is observed among Bruneis.

Now it might be objected that the Brunei Malays are so westernized that of course they are similar to us in many ways; one needs a pristine, uncontacted people to see the real exceptions. This is an assumption that I would have taken quite seriously at one time, and that was acted upon by my university schoolmate Lyle Steadman (1971). Like me, he received his anthropological training in the 1960s and was steeped in cultural determinism. In order to fully explore the consequences of having a nonwestern worldview, he did his work among a New Guinean people, the Hewa, who had had no more than the most fleeting and widely spaced contacts with European patrols. At the time Steadman studied the Hewa they lived in one of the last "restricted" areas of New Guinea. This meant that the area was "uncontrolled," and Europeans, including missionaries, were forbidden to enter it. One of the reasons the Hewa were essentially uncontacted was that they lived so sparsely on the land that from one family's household to another was typically a grueling 2-hour walk over a rugged terrain covered by dense rain forest.

Steadman had to learn the Hewa language in the field, but long before he was conversant in it he discovered—somewhat to his surprise, because it didn't jibe with his assumptions about the influence of differing world views—that he and the Hewa "could understand each other well enough to live together" (1971:26–27). As time went by, and he learned more about the ways in which the world is put together differently in Hewa than in English, he was led to observe that the differences were largely superficial: "This fact of experiencing the world in a similar way," in spite of its being carved up differently in different languages, "became increasingly obvious as I acquired greater proficiency in the language" (1971:27). At the deeper level of why language might be used in the first place, at the level of motives, the similarities were just as evident: "Living, travelling, working and hunting with the Hewa, made it clear to me that their basic concerns, the concerns motivating their behaviour, were similar to my own" (1971:26). I think that anyone who watches the film "First Contact" and is keeping an open mind about similarities will see that New Guineans who were first contacted by Australian prospectors in the 1930s showed many generic human traits. The differences between the natives and the prospectors are numerous, but the similarities are there too.

Lest anyone think that an anthropologist who takes cultural differences seriously would not make the kinds of assumptions that Steadman and I would, let me give a final illustration from one of the most famous essays by Clifford Geertz, an anthropologist who makes no secret of his emphasis on cultural differences. His essay, "Deep Play: Notes on the Balinese Cockfight" (1971), begins with a description of how he and his wife achieved rapport with the Balinese villagers they were to study. Although the Geertzes had gained official entrée into a village, the villagers were treating them pretty much as though they didn't exist: "everyone ignored us in a way only a Balinese can do" (1971:1). On the next page we are also told that a Balinese is an "always precisely controlled person."

One page later, however, the Geertzes and the villagers, all attending an illegal cockfight at which armed police made a sudden and unexpected appearance, engage in somewhat less controlled behavior: "People raced down the road, disappeared head first over walls, scrambled under platforms, folded themselves behind wicker screens, scuttled up coconut trees.... Everything was dust and panic." The village chief ran to a river where he pretended to be innocently bathing; the Geertzes followed a villager into his yard, where all pretended, when a policeman arrived, to have been sipping tea and engaging in legitimate ethnographic discourse.

After this event, the Geertzes were "in" with the villagers, who never tired of gently mimicking the panicked flight of the Geertzes or of wondering why they had not just stood their ground on the basis that they were foreigners who had been mere bystanders. Geertz comments that this event gave him "the kind of immediate, inside-view grasp of an aspect of 'peasant mentality' that anthropologists not fortunate enough to flee headlong with their subjects from armed authorities normally do not get" (1971:4).

But how important is the "peasant mentality," or even Balinese culture, for understanding this story? Not very. After the scene is set with some explanatory local details (which are not remarkable), the rest of the episode requires and receives no interpretation whatsoever because it is completely intelligible to a nonpeasant, non-Balinese reader. It is, for the most part, simply human: panicked flight from armed outsiders (nearly all police on Bali at that time were Javanese), attempts to deceive authority or deny wrongdoing, mimicking and teasing, rehashing an exciting and amusing event, trying to make sense of people's behavior, asking questions, laughing, etc.[1] Even the most Balinese element—the initial apparent indifference of the villagers to the Geertzes—was only a surface difference. Beneath the surface, the villagers were—as one would expect—paying a great deal of attention to the strangers in their midst: they were "watching every move we [the Geertzes] made" (1971:1). Thus, 5 minutes after the Geertzes followed the man, whom they had never met before,

---

[1]Again, compare the New Guineans in the movie "First Contact." Their behavior, captured on film both in the 1930s and many years thereafter when they reminisce about the events of the 1930s, also shows fear of armed outsiders, attempts to deceive them, mimicking and teasing of each other and themselves, relished rehashing of the past, attempts to make sense of others' behavior, asking questions, laughter, etc. These similarities to us, and the Balinese, neither require nor receive explanation in the film.

into his yard, he was explaining to the police who the Geertzes were in a manner so "detailed and so accurate" that Geertz was "astonished" (1971:3).

I could go on with the similarities between the Balinese and everybody else (and will in chapter 6), but let me instead express a suspicion that *nowhere* in the ethnographic literature is there *any* description of what real people really did that is not shot through with the signs of a universal human nature. By virtue of this fact, anthropologists and the people they study—and then the readers of ethnography—share a vast reservoir of interpretive principles. As Sperber (1982:179–180) notes, anthropologists routinely conduct research that can only be done because in crucial ways the differences between us and the peoples we study are not in fact very great; yet because *everybody* likes to hear that "they" are different from "us," anthropologists dwell on the differences. Quite a number of anthropologists have registered similar complaints. That humans share so many similarities, and that many if not most anthropologists have left them in the background—or even denied them—points to some anthropological issues that need to be discussed.

If they hold not merely for Bruneis, Balinese, New Guineans, and Americans but for all peoples, similarities of the sort referred to above are called human universals. They are not confined to the more or less psychological phenomena that I have so far described but include the use of fire and tools, a division of labor by sex, and much more. This book explores a series of general questions about human universals. How many are there? What are the different kinds of universals? What is their importance? How can we be sure that something is a universal? How does one explain universals? What part do they play in the anthropological enterprise, or in understanding human affairs?

Although I address an anthropological audience, what I have to say is relevant in wider circles. This is so because the task of anthropology is too large for professional anthropologists alone to deal with, so that a series of disciplines—notably sociology, psychology, linguistics, history, economics, political science, geography, biology, and philosophy—are important players in the anthropological enterprise. Besides, anthropology is by definition focused on humans in general, so humans in general may have some interest in its results.

There are five central theses to this book. The first is that universals not only exist but are important to any broad conception of the task of anthropology. Among those anthropologists who have overcome their skepticism about the very existence of universals, some have argued that such universals as exist are not important. Insofar as their argument is not merely the expression of a value judgment, it is wrong.

Second, universals form a heterogeneous set. A great many, for example, seem to be inherent in human nature. Some are cultural conventions that have come to have universal distribution. Others fall under different headings.

Third, the study of universals has been effectively tabooed as an unintended consequence of assumptions that have predominated in anthropology (and other social sciences) throughout much of this century. From 1915 to 1934 American anthropologists established three fundamental principles about the nature of culture: that culture is a distinct kind of phenomenon that cannot be reduced to others (in particular, not to biology or psychology), that culture (rather than our physical nature) is the fundamental determinant of human behavior, and that culture is largely arbitrary. This combination of assumptions made universals anomalous and very likely to be rare; to admit or dwell upon their existence raised troubling questions about anthropology's fundamental assumptions. These assumptions also led many anthropologists to conclude or argue that anthropology should be narrowed from the study of humanity to the study of culture.

Fourth, human biology *is* a key to understanding many human universals. It has long been assumed that insofar as universals exist it makes sense to think that they must in some rather direct fashion reflect human biology rather than human culture. Conflict as it may with the assumptions of the preceding paragraph, this assumption is correct, and its consequences must be incorporated into any currently acceptable understanding of the anthropological enterprise.

Fifth, evolutionary psychology is a key to understanding many of the universals that are of greatest interest to anthropology. The feature of human biology most of interest to anthropology is the human mind. A theoretical understanding of the process that shaped the human mind, Darwinian selection, provides the most inclusive theoretical framework for the illumination of the human condition.

To answer the questions raised above and to defend my main theses, the materials are presented as follows. Chapter 1 summarizes several studies that raise serious questions about anthropology's skepticism toward universals—and about anthropology's faith in cultural relativism. Some of these studies have been seen as revolutionary; collectively they are even more so. If they do not definitively settle the issues of universality that they address, they nonetheless indicate that some anthropological rethinking of universals is in order and is underway.

Chapter 2 explores the ways in which universals are conceptualized, defined, and demonstrated; chapter 3 presents a history of the study of universals; and chapter 4 examines the means of explaining universals. By summarizing recent attempts to explain incest avoidance, chapter 5 looks in greater detail at the means of explaining universals. Chapter 5 also suggests that ways of doing anthropology that were abandoned early in this century deserve a reexamination. Chapter 6 presents a series of universals in the form of statements true of all societies.

The last chapter examines the relationships that link the nexus of universals, human nature, and the human mind on the one hand with the structure of anthropological thought on the other. Finally, an annotated bibliography presents a large sample of writings that deal in one way or another with universals.

1

Rethinking Universality: Six Cases

In 1983 the anthropological community was convulsed by reactions to Derek Freeman's *Margaret Mead and Samoa: The Making and Unmaking of a Myth*. Remarkably, two books with a very similar message but by different authors attacking different myths were published within a year of Freeman's. One was Melford Spiro's *Oedipus in the Trobriands* (1982); the other was Ekkehart Malotki's *Hopi Time* (1983). Each of these books refutes or questions one of the centerpieces of anthropological relativism.

In *Coming of Age in Samoa* (1928) Margaret Mead argued that adolescence among Samoans was not the time of storm and stress that it is in the West and, hence, that the Western conception of adolescence is strictly cultural—something that we could change. Freeman shows that adolescence was just as stressful in Samoa as in the West and that in other ways Samoa was not so different from Western societies as Mead had led us to believe.

No less influential than Mead's classic on Samoa was Bronislaw Malinowski's *Sex and Repression in Savage Society* (1927), in which he argued that the Oedipus complex was peculiar to what he called "patriarchal" societies. Among the matrilineal Trobriand Islanders, he purported to show, a different complex emerged—one in which a boy felt hostility not to his father but rather to his mother's brother (who in matrilineal societies occupies a position in various ways analogous to a father in a patrilineal, or patriarchal, society). This was a weaker form of relativism, but again it showed, or seemed to show, that what some Westerners considered natural or universal wasn't. Yet Spiro (1982)—by reanalyzing Malinowski's own data, which are renowned for their volume and accuracy—now argues persuasively that the Trobrianders did have an Oedipus complex and that the "family complex," as Malinowski preferred to call it, is not as variable as Malinowski's analysis seemed to show.

A decade after Malinowski wrote *Sex and Repression*, Benjamin Lee Whorf, a gifted and largely self-taught amateur anthropological linguist, formulated his argument either that the Hopi had no sense of time or that their sense of time was very different from ours. The problem of Hopi time is intimately linked to what came to be called the Sapir-Whorf hypothesis. Edward Sapir was an anthropological linguist who had been Whorf's mentor. Their hypothesis is that the categories of language shape perceptions of the world. As Sapir (1929:209) put it, "the 'real world' is to a large extent unconsciously built up on the language habits" of a society, and insofar as each society has its own language the "worlds in which different societies live are distinct worlds." In other words, if the speakers of a given language have no terms for something, it is not a part of their thought or worldview and in some sense is scarcely perceived. Since the Hopi language, Whorf said, has no conceptions of time built into it— or embodies very different conceptions of time—the Hopi therefore perceive the world in a radically different way than we do. This was an extreme conceptualization of cultural relativism. But it now appears, insofar as it rests upon the Hopi case, to be quite wrong. Malotki (1983) amply documents the richness of Hopi conceptions of time and their essential similarities to ours.

Although Freeman's, Spiro's, and Malotki's works are remarkable for their temporal contiguity, they do not stand alone. A few years earlier another refutation of one of Mead's arguments was published by Deborah Gewertz (1981), almost 15 years earlier the universality of certain facial expressions was demonstrated (Ekman et al. 1969; Izard 1971), and at the same time another outstanding refutation of cultural relativism was presented in Brent Berlin and Paul Kay's *Basic Color Terms: Their Universality and Evolution* (1969).

In another of Mead's classics, *Sex and Temperament in Three Primitive Societies* (1935), she attempted to show that the Tchambuli, a New Guinean people, had male and female temperaments that were the reverse of what we consider normal. In the 1970s Gewertz restudied the Tchambuli, whom she calls the Chambri, and found that Mead had misinterpreted the situation among them. Thus Gewertz effectively smashes another of the icons of relativism.

Psychologists had long debated whether the facial expressions of emotions were universal or culturally relative. The one anthropologist to participate in the debate, Weston La Barre (1947), favored relativism. But by the early 1970s two independent lines of psychological research, culminating in studies conducted among preliterate peoples of New Guinea, had shown that there are universal facial expressions of emotions.

Berlin and Kay's (1969) attack on relativism was the first to be published. This work does not overthrow any particular famous anthropological study, but it certainly overthrows an entrenched prejudice. I, and no doubt most anthropologists over a number of decades, had been taught and saw no reason to doubt that color classification was largely arbitrary. The spectrum of color from red through violet is a range of continuous variation with no natural divisions from the standpoint of the physics of light. Therefore, the number of terms for colors, and the boundaries between them, were considered arbitrary—no two peoples' color terms would necessarily be the same. Berlin and Kay show that although color classification does vary, it also shows remarkable uniformities: particularly in the sequence in which basic color terms are added to the lexicon. The revolutionary nature of their findings has not escaped notice. Let us look at each of these cases in more detail, beginning with the two that are best known in anthropology.

COLOR CLASSIFICATION

Anthropologists and linguists had long known that the way colors are classified varies from language to language. Careful studies conducted by anthropologists after World War II, such as Harold Conklin's (1955) study of Hanunóo color words, made the point very clearly. Many anthropologists, in accordance with the "prevailing doctrine" of "extreme linguistic relativity," interpreted these findings as showing that there were no semantic universals in the domain of color terms, that the lexical coding of color was arbitrary (Berlin and Kay 1969:1–2). Berlin and Kay (1969:159–160) quote a number of sources to illustrate their point. I will quote from the same sources. This is from a prominent textbook (and one that I used as a student):

> Language...is the mold into which perception must be fitted if it is
> to be communicated. Any single language imprints its own 'genius'
> on the message.... Probably the most popular, because it is the
> most vivid, example for describing cultural categories that the
> necessity to communicate creates in human perception is to
> compare the ways in which different peoples cut up color into
> communicable units. The spectrum is a continuum of light waves,
> with frequencies that...increase at a continuous rate.... But the
> way different cultures organize these sensations for communica-
> tion show some strange differences. (Bohannan 1963:34–35)

The following is a stronger statement by an anthropologist, though not in a textbook:

> [T]here is no such thing as a natural division of the spectrum.
> Each culture has taken the spectral continuum and has divided it
> upon a basis which is quite arbitrary. (Ray 1952)

The views of many linguists were the same. A very influential linguistics textbook (again, one that I was taught from) puts the matter this way:

> There is a continuous gradation of color from one end of the
> spectrum to the other. Yet an American describing it will list the
> hues as red, orange, yellow, green, blue, purple, or something of
> the kind. There is nothing inherent either in the spectrum or the
> human perception of it which would compel its division in this
> way. (Gleason 1961:4)

Bearing in mind that many sociocultural anthropologists conceive their task as a kind of translation from other cultures to ours, the views of a linguist described as "perhaps the leading American authority on translation" (Berlin and Kay 1969:159) were quite influential:

> *The segmentation of experience by speech symbols is essentially
> arbitrary.* The different sets of words for color in various languages
> are perhaps the best ready evidence for such arbitrariness. For
> example, in a high percentage of African languages there are only
> three "color words," corresponding to our *white, black* and *red,*
> which nevertheless divide up the entire spectrum. In the
> Tarahumara language of Mexico, there are five basic color words,
> and here "blue" and "green" are subsumed under a single term.
> (Nida 1959:13, italics in original)

This conception of the relationship between language and color was not confined to anthropologists and linguists. Berlin and Kay (1969:160) quote "an experimental social psychologist addressing a general audience of humanists" in a popular scientific journal: "Our partitioning of the spectrum consists of the arbitrary imposition of a category system on a continuous physical domain" (Krause 1968:268). Nor was the conception confined to color terms. "The non-existence, *in principle*, of semantic universals" had "become a dominant article of faith in much of social science" (Berlin and Kay 1969:160).

On the basis of their experience with the relative ease of translation between color terms in a variety of unrelated languages, Berlin and Kay began to doubt the validity of the doctrine of extreme relativism. They did not doubt that "to understand the full range of meaning of a word in any language, each new language must be approached in its own terms, without *a priori* theories of semantic universals" (1969:1), but they did not think this necessarily meant there were no semantic universals.

To test the doctrine of extreme relativism in the categorization of colors Berlin and Kay assembled lists of color terms from informants speaking 98 different languages representing a wide selection of unrelated major linguistic stocks. Although the number of color terms in each language did vary, they found that no more than eleven colors accounted for the basic color terms found in each language. The main defining features of a basic color term are that it is monolexemic (containing a single irreducible unit of meaning, such as "red," not two or more lexemes as in "reddish" or "dark blue"), is not included in another color term, is general in application, and is psychologically salient to its users. The eleven basic colors are white, black, red, green, yellow, blue, brown, purple, pink, orange, and gray. Nonbasic colors, such as "pumpkin-colored," "like the tail of a peacock," "bluish," "bluish-purple," and the like were excluded from analysis.

Once the basic color terms for each language had been determined, native speakers of those languages were asked to outline the boundaries of the colors on a color chart. The chart was composed of 329 color chips arranged along one axis in order of hue (the spectrum of colors) and along the other axis in order of brightness (brighter colors at the top, dimmer at the bottom; all at maximum saturation). To the side of the main chart were nine more chips of neutral hue, grading from white through gray to black. The informants drew a line around the chips that fit each of their basic color categories and designated the chip that was its best or most typical representative (the focal point of the color term).

Although the boundaries of color terms vary—by and large, the fewer the terms the wider their bounds—the focal point of each basic color is substantially the same from one language to another. For example, people whose languages contain only two basic color terms tend to include the darker hues with their "black," and the lighter hues with their "white." Given the broad designation of these terms, they might just as well be glossed as "dark" and "light," but their focal points are the black and white chips. When "red" is added, to make a classification with just three basic terms, the third category typically includes some oranges, yellows, browns, pinks, and purples along with the red chips that are the focus of the category. As each basic term is added—moving to languages with four, five, six basic terms, and so on—less and less of the chart remains without a basic color term label and each of the areas designated by the new terms still tends to have a common focal point from one language to another. Considerable areas of the chart remain without designations in terms of basic colors. This definitively falsified the doctrine of total arbitrariness of color classification: color classification does not arbitrarily slice a continuum.

But Berlin and Kay found a further surprising result. The *order* in which basic color categories enter languages is not arbitrary either. If a language has only two colors—and all languages have at least two—they are always white and black; if a language has three colors, the one added is red; if a fourth is added, it will be either green or yellow; when a fifth is added, it will then include both green and yellow; the sixth added is blue; the seventh added is brown; and if an eighth or more terms are added, it or they will be purple, pink, orange, or gray. Considerable subsequent research on color classification has necessitated modifications in this sequence, yet basic color terms apparently evolve in a largely universal pattern (Witkowski and Brown 1978). Berlin and Kay (1969:159) dismiss "extreme linguistic-cultural relativism," at least with respect to basic color terms, as a "myth created by linguists and anthropologists."

Berlin and Kay's findings have been placed "among the most remarkable discoveries of anthropological science" (Sahlins 1976:1). Much of what makes them remarkable is the effect they have had on anthropological prejudices and the new channels for research they made sensible. For example, the psychological saliency of basic color terms has been explored cross-culturally in a variety of ways (Bolton 1978; Heider 1972), attempts have been made to explain *why* humans perceive colors uniformly (e.g., Ratliff 1976; Boynton and Olson 1987), studies of the classification of botanical and zoological life forms have revealed evolutionary sequences similar to those that Berlin and Kay found in the classification of basic colors (Brown 1977b, 1979; Witkowski and Brown 1978), and the discovery of cross-culturally stable focal points for color (and other) categories gave rise to new conceptions of how humans categorize and reason (Rosch 1975, 1983).

SAMOAN ADOLESCENCE

Coming of Age in Samoa was Margaret Mead's most famous book. It was written to provide part of the answer to the questions "What is human nature? How flexible is human nature?" (Mead 1928:ix). Mead, her mentor Franz Boas, and other anthropologists,[1] suspected that "much of what we ascribe to human nature is no more than a reaction to the restraints put upon us by our civilisation" (Boas 1928:n.p.). More specifically, Mead and Boas suspected that the difficulties of adolescence were not inherent. These difficulties, Mead thought, were less due to "being adolescent" than to "being adolescent in America" (1928:5). To put her ideas to the test, in 1925–26 Mead studied young women in three villages in Samoa, among whom there were 25 adolescents. She found that for them adolescence was neither stressful nor marked by abrupt changes other than

---

[1]Ruth Benedict, a graduate student working with Boas when Mead began her studies with him, was a particularly potent influence. This is discussed further in chapter 3.

the purely physiological. She concluded that "adolescence is not necessarily a time of stress and strain, but that cultural conditions [may] make it so" (1928:234). There was, thus, nothing natural about the American or Western conception of adolescence. She explained the stress-free character of adolescence in Samoa in terms of the differing cultural and social arrangements of the Samoans, in particular a "general casualness":

> For Samoa is a place where no one plays for very high stakes, no
> one pays very heavy prices, no one suffers for his convictions or
> fights to the death for special ends. Disagreements between parent
> and child are settled by the child's moving across the street,
> between a man and his village by the man's removal to the next
> village, between a husband and his wife's seducer by a few fine
> mats.... No implacable gods, swift to anger and strong to punish,
> disturb the even tenor of their days. Wars and cannibalism are
> long since passed away and now the greatest cause for tears, short
> of death itself, is a journey of a relative to another island. No one is
> hurried along in life or punished harshly for slowness of
> development.... And in personal relations, caring is slight. Love
> and hate, jealousy and revenge, sorrow and bereavement, are all
> matters of weeks. From the first month of its life, when the child is
> handed carelessly from one woman's hands to another's, the
> lesson is learned of not caring for one person greatly, not setting
> high hopes on any one relationship. (1928:198–199)

Most important was the "lack of deep feeling" that was the "very framework" of Samoan "attitudes toward life." Samoa was "kind to those who... learned the lesson of not caring, and hard upon those few individuals who...failed to learn it." The latter were "delinquent, unhappy misfits" (1928:199, 200).

Also to the advantage of the Samoan adolescent was a casual sexual code, limited only for the daughters and wives of chiefs. (It is not clear whether Mead is referring to "chiefs" in general, whose wives and "daughters" would include almost all women, or only high-ranking chiefs. Though she appears to say the former, it would vitiate her argument [Tim O'Meara, personal communication].) Missionaries were not supporters of any such casualness, but their protests were "unimportant" (1928:202). The Samoan Church (London Missionary Society) took a "laissez faire attitude" and did not press youth too hard for participation that would curb their sexual freedom. The less bewildering choices of creeds and careers in Samoa made adolescence less stressful too, as did the slower pace of sociocultural change.

These differences between Samoan and Western civilizations paid off not only for adolescents but for Samoans in general: according to Mead,

Samoans lacked the neuroses we have in great numbers and in particular lacked frigidity and psychic impotence. Mead thought that child-rearing practices and attitudes toward sex accounted for much of this. Particularly important was the presence in the household of numerous adults (and numerous children too) so that children did not form such close attachments to their own parents. Also important was the greater knowledge of sexuality, birth, and death that Samoan adolescents readily acquired. The definition of the "normal" in sexuality was wider among the Samoans, and a "satisfactory sex adjustment in marriage" was always attainable (Mead 1928:223). Sexual jealousy was all but absent; rape, as we understand it, was foreign to Samoan thought.

Another factor in producing the well-adjusted Samoan was a tendency to penalize the precocious child and pace activities to the standards of the "laggard" or "inept" (Mead 1928:223). This toned down individualism and minimized the jealousy and rivalry so productive of difficulty for Westerners.

Mead's book was published in the midst of a debate over the relative importance of biological and cultural determinants of behavior—the nature-nurture controversy—and was hailed as a definitive demonstration of the importance of culture or nurture. It was an immediate success and became one of the best selling anthropological books of all time, having almost incalculable influence (Freeman 1983). In subsequent publications Mead not only repeated the points made above but often stated them in starker terms or embroidered them. Mead's study of Samoa and the conclusions drawn from it have been cited approvingly in almost all anthropological texts for a long period (see, e.g., Aceves and King 1978; Barnouw 1978; Benderly et al. 1977; Haviland 1983; Hoebel 1972; Honigmann 1959).

Mead's book was based on 9 months of fieldwork in Samoa, conducted when she was 23 years old. Derek Freeman, who conducted 6 years of fieldwork in Samoa, mostly in the 1940s and 1960s, finds Mead wrong on many points, certainly in her main conclusion. His book, which he describes as a "study of a major twentieth-century myth," is a formal refutation of Mead's. Although Freeman's work was done some time after Mead's, a number of factors allow him insight into the Samoa of her time and much earlier.

To begin, Samoa is an unusually well documented society, having been carefully observed and reported upon from early in the nineteenth century. The islands Mead lived on were administered by the United States, so that various reports and archival sources describe Samoa of the 1920s. Persons alive when Mead worked in Samoa were still alive when Freeman did his research and could well remember the 1920s. Finally, a number of anthropologists besides Freeman worked in Samoa in the post–World War II period, and they provide alternative views of Samoan society. From these various sources it is obvious that Mead's principal conclusion, and much else in her description of Samoa, is seriously wrong.

Her picture of Samoan adolescence as a stressless period is contradicted by her own data. Four of Mead's 25 female adolescent informants were delinquent, by her own account. Two of them committed acts of delinquency during Mead's brief visit. What Mead failed to realize was that this percentage of delinquents and frequency of delinquent acts was actually quite high. The rate of delinquent acts, for example, was "ten times higher than that which existed among female adolescents in England and Wales in 1965" (Freeman 1983:258). Since Mead classified three further girls as "deviants upwards" (those who constructively sought to escape from traditional patterns), the percentage of maladjusted adolescents was even greater than is indicated by the delinquents. Freeman's informants denied that adolescence was free of stress, and comparative statistics, generally from more recent times, show a cross-culturally typical pattern of first convictions for criminal offenses in Samoa to peak in the adolescent years.

These observations alone dispose of Mead's main conclusion, but Freeman also shows that the various reasons Mead gave for the stress-free character of Samoan adolescence were more often than not equally groundless. The Samoans do not have a casual attitude toward sex; in fact, they have a rather extreme double standard. As Mead herself noted, the Samoans possessed a cult of virginity. She reconciled this with their supposed pattern of adolescent free love by arguing, as was mentioned earlier, that only a relatively small number of high-status girls needed to remain virgins; even if they didn't, it was simple to fake the blood of a ruptured hymen. Freeman shows that not only was the cult of virginity a prominent element in traditional Samoan culture, but that it had been further encouraged by Samoan Christianity. In early times a girl who was expected to be a virgin but who failed to be one might be beaten to death. In Christian times, formal church membership—and, contrary to Mead, adolescent girls were strongly urged to join—strictly forbids fornication.

On the other hand, to obtain a virgin is a strong male goal, and Samoan males are not above achieving their goal by illegal means. Freeman describes two culturally prescribed patterns of Samoan rape, one surreptitious ("sleep crawling"), the other forceful. Mead was aware of the former pattern but treated it as an abnormality in which a boy might deceptively pass himself off as a lover who was expected in the dark; to Mead it added "zest to the surreptitious love-making" conducted in girls' homes (1928:95–96). In the surreptitious pattern of rape a boy or man tries to sneak up on a sleeping virgin and thrust two fingers into her va-

gina (this was the standard, public method of deflowering virgins in traditional Samoa). Thus despoiled, the girl is then expected to have no alternative but to elope with her rapist. Those who attempted this form of
getting a virgin might be violently dealt with by the girl's kin, and of course
it was a crime. In forceful rape the rapist attempted to knock his victim
out with a blow to the solar plexus; once unconscious she was deflowered
in the usual way, and this might be followed by penile intromission. These
patterns of rape have been described from early in the nineteenth century; rape was the third commonest crime in Samoa in the 1920s and
was routinely reported in the press at that time. Freeman argues that the
Samoans have one of the highest rates of rape in the world. He also argues that fear of rape produces the frigidity of Samoan women that another anthropologist (Holmes 1958:55) reports is sometimes the source
of familial strain.

It is beyond the scope of this essay to retrace all of Freeman's refutations, showing that Samoans do and have fought for strongly held beliefs, do show completely expectable sexual jealousy, do not and have
not taken their religion lightly, and so on. But one further point must be
discussed, because it is central to the stresses and strains of Samoan adolescence and to the formation of adult Samoan psyche and behavior.
Samoans do not spare the rod; they punish their children severely. At an
early age a child is forced to submit to severe corporal punishment from
parents and elder siblings; the child is expected to sit and take the punishment without struggling or talking back. Harsh physical punishment
may be meted out even to adults. Most children learn to restrain themselves when punished and grow up with the ability to be polite in front
of authority figures while cursing them behind their backs. The price paid
for outward politeness and submissiveness includes a not unexpected
array of psychic problems and a tendency to violent behavior. This violence has been noted from early times to the present.

Given the discrepancies between Mead's account and the realities
of Samoan life, it is no surprise that her account has been pretty consistently condemned by Samoans, which Freeman has no difficulty docu-
menting. One can only ask how Mead could have been so wrong. It is
not easy to do justice to Freeman's answers to that question. But the main
outlines are as follows: First, Mead went to Samoa without a knowledge
of the language and with unfortunate gaps in her familiarity with the extensive literature on Samoa. Since she had, in fact, a greater familiarity
with the literature on other parts of Polynesia, such as Tahiti, where the
patterns of religion and sexuality were very different, she probably had
expectations that biased her from the start. When she reached Samoa
she did not undertake a general study of the Samoan ethos and culture
but launched directly into her study of adolescence.

Her informants were adolescent girls; neither boys nor adults were studied. Modern Samoans have for some time suspected that the girls amused themselves by pulling her leg—a suspicion confirmed by the recently recorded testimony of one of Mead's original informants (Freeman 1989). This is a standard form of psychic aggression in Samoa, says Freeman.[2] Since Mead chose not to live with a Samoan family, she limited her means of checking what her informants told her with the way people actually behaved or with what others might say.

Finally, as Freeman cogently argues, Mead went to Samoa hoping to show that culture was more important than nature, and wrote up her research under continuing intellectual pressure to maintain this position. While she did not intentionally distort, her biases quite clearly shaped her interpretations.

Mead never returned to Samoa to double-check her findings, even though it was not many years before dissent was voiced. Eventually Mead (1969) admitted that perhaps she had visited Samoa during a period when by good fortune its usual strict patterns had been relaxed—she knew by then that her account was not corroborated by other sources or authorities. But the myth that Samoan conditions offer proof that adolescent behavior is essentially conditioned by culture, and behind it the larger myth that culture does, but biology does not, shape human behavior, retained a vigor that is readily gauged by the vociferous dismissal of Freeman's book when it received the public notice deserved by a work designed to demolish one of anthropology's hoariest myths.[3]

I hasten to add that Freeman did not say we should affirm the position of the extreme naturists of the 1920s whom Boas, Mead, and others sought to refute (see chapter 3). But he did say that human behavior is the product both of human biology and human culture and that to continue to argue that for all practical purposes the former may be ignored is a position that will retard the understanding of culture as well as human nature.

Freeman's restudy does not show that adolescent stress is a uni-

---

[2]It is called *taufa'alili* or *taufa'ase'e*. Tim O'Meara (personal communication) calls it "recreational lying," and notes that it is one of the most common forms of humor and recreation in Samoa. Among other things, he adds, its prevalence in all age groups shows how widespread aggressive feelings are in Samoa (see also Freeman 1989).

[3]Early in 1983, the membership of the Northeastern Anthropological Association voted to direct its executive board to criticize the publisher of Freeman's book, and the *New York Times*, for the book's publicity campaign. Later in the same year, the American Anthropological Association, at its annual meeting, voted to express its dismay that the magazine *Science 83* had recommended Freeman's book for holiday gift-giving (Caton 1990: 228–229). These votes were fairly direct measures of the anthropological commitment to cultural determinism and the tabula rasa view of the mind that will be discussed in subsequent chapters.

versal, or that sexual jealousy is. But it seriously questions Mead's contention that Samoan data prove that neither of these is a universal. Other lines of evidence suggest that both *are* universals, and we have some good ideas as to why they should be.

MALE AND FEMALE AMONG THE TCHAMBULI

The Chambri, better known as the Tchambuli, the name Margaret Mead used for them in *Sex and Temperament in Three Primitive Societies* (1935), live on an island in a lake near the Sepik River in Papua New Guinea. They are famous in anthropology for purportedly showing the flexibility of male and female temperaments. In *Sex and Temperament* Mead described three societies representing three different patterns of male and female temperament. In one case, both the sexes conformed to our ideal of a man; in another, both sexes conformed to our ideal of a woman. In the third society, the Chambri, Mead found something no less strange, "a genuine reversal of the sex-attitudes of our culture, with the woman the dominant, impersonal, managing partner, the man the less responsible and the emotionally dependent person" (1935:279). Mead concluded from her study that the sex-linked characteristics of behavior and psyche that we think are "normal" are in fact arbitrary: "We are forced to conclude that human nature is almost unbelievably malleable, responding accurately and contrastingly to contrasting cultural conditions" (1935:280). The Chambri case did not present the neat pattern that this last sentence suggests, however, for there was a "contradiction at the root of Tchambuli society" (Mead 1935:263).

Kinship was patrilineal, polygyny was normal, wives were bought by men, men were stronger than women and could beat them, and men were considered by right to be in charge. These ideals flew in the face of a very different reality: "it is the women in Tchambuli who have the real position of power in society" and "the actual dominance of women is far more real than the structural position of the men" (Mead 1935:253, 271).

The roots of female dominance were threefold. First, the women were the economically productive element among the Chambri. Women did nearly all the fishing, and they traded fish with bush peoples in the hills for sago and other foodstuffs. Women also wove mosquito nets, which were important items of trade. Female productivity provided the Chambri with the exchange valuables needed for ceremonies, wife purchases, and other transactions. Women went about their business in a self-assured, matter-of-fact, and competent way. Second, women exhibited considerable solidarity. Third, women seemed relatively untroubled emotionally.

In contrast, men were de facto dependents, forced to wheedle foodstuffs and money from women. While Chambri men were supposed to be headhunters, they in fact bought their victims. Men spent almost all their time in artistic activities: painting, dancing, and the like. Pleasant though men's activities might be, they were games, insubstantial or a sham. Men constantly bickered in a petty and peevish fashion with one another; they preened in a way that can only be called prissy. They made "catty" remarks to one another (Mead 1935:252). Indulged by their women, men went on shopping trips like women in the West. Finally, men were prone to psychological problems. The "unadjusted" among them might even try to act aggressively toward women (1935:271–272).

Mead attributed many of the Chambri male's characteristics to child rearing. While boys and girls were raised alike up to the age of six, at that point little boys entered a difficult period. While their sisters were inducted quickly and easily into the women's world and activities, for three to four years the boys were left at loose ends: they weren't welcome in the older boys' and men's world, nor could they remain at home in the female world. At this point boys also began to ponder the discrepancy between Chambri ideals and the sad truth that females were in fact in charge. Men had to purchase wives, or have them purchased for them, but only if women gave them the purchase price. Men could have more than one wife, but this was because more than one woman might choose some man as husband.

In many ways Mead's study of the Chambri and the two societies she compared them with was even more startling in its results than *Coming of Age in Samoa*. It is no surprise that Chambri women were to become an "icon" of women's studies (Gewertz 1981:94). But the implications of the Chambri case were toned down in anthropology at least in part because Mead later, in the 1962 introduction to *Male and Female*, took more of a universalist approach to male and female temperaments. However, Mead's description of Chambri temperaments, along with the conclusions she drew from studying them, are summarized with few reservations in various recent anthropological textbooks (Aceves and King 1978; Benderly, Gallagher, and Young 1977; Harris 1980; Selby and Garretson 1981).

Gewertz restudied the Chambri in 1974–75. She was primarily interested in trade and exchange but noted that the picture of male and female given by Mead was no longer applicable, if it ever had been. Gewertz reconstructs the Chambri and Margaret Mead's view of them as follows: In traditional Chambri conceptions, men are aggressive and women submissive. In their interactions with each other they generally conform to this conception and have apparently done so for as long as there is evidence (i.e., back to about 1850). True, Chambri women were the breadwinners, but they "have never controlled the relations of production, for

they have had little access to the political arena in which more significant transactional decisions are made" (Gewertz 1981:99–100). Although
Chambri women were the productive element in their society, their husbands and fathers controlled the fruits of female productivity, and used
them to enhance their (the men's) status. Gewertz saw no reason to think
the matter had been different when Mead studied the Chambri. Although
Mead (1935:254) explicitly states that it is a woman's choice to hand over
the proceeds of her activities, she gives no example of a woman asserting
herself by withholding valuables or even of allocating them as she chose.
Gewertz says flatly that Chambri women "have never been free to determine to whom or in what circumstances their produce will be given"
(1981:100). Rather, women were under the pressure of conflicting demands
from the different men in their lives—husbands and fathers—each of
whom might use force on his wife or daughter. If Chambri women were
dominant, they did not dominate Chambri men. They might challenge
men, but such were "the challenges of subversives who have no direct
access to political decision making" (Gewertz 1981:100).

There was, however, a context in which Chambri women were dominant: it was vis-à-vis *other women*, the women who traded sago to
Chambri women for their fish. The sago suppliers were bush people who
lived in scattered small communities throughout nearby hills. They were
considered inferior by the Chambri and, in various senses, were to
Chambri as Chambri women are to Chambri men: the Chambri were dependent on the bush people for sago (the bush people could have got
fish on their own), the bush people were submissive in the face of Chambri
dominance, the bush people were politically vulnerable. Thus there were
contexts in which Chambri women acted like men—Mead's observations
were to a degree accurate—but the contexts did not include Chambri
women dominating Chambri men.

Another way in which context was critical to Mead's observations
was the temporal context. As Mead noted, the Chambri had only recently
returned to their island after a lengthy exile resulting from defeat by neigh-
bors. Mead failed to see the impact this unusual situation had on the
Chambri. In their period of exile the Chambri had taken up residence
among their inferiors, the bush-dwelling sago suppliers. Some Chambri
men had even married women from these groups. In the Chambri scheme
of things, wife-giving groups are superior to wife-takers—so that Chambri
men by marrying bush women had in effect nullified Chambri dominance.
On returning to their island it was up to Chambri women to reassert their
old pattern of superiority over bush women, so that the barter of fish for
sago could resume its traditional pattern. Without access to sago, Chambri
men would not be able to compete successfully with the men they considered their equals—the other fisherfolk of the region (among whom were

the enemies who had once expelled them). The "strain" and "watchfulness" that Mead had reported in Chambri men were quite explicable in this circumstance: they were not yet certain that they would succeed in reestablishing the old pattern (and may perhaps have wondered if the white man's protection would be adequate).

Chambri men's artistic activities had a temporal explanation too. When driven from their islands the Chambri's physical structures and all their ritual paraphernalia had been burnt. Chambri men were still busy in the 1930s rebuilding all that had been lost.

Thus Mead saw a temporary condition in which normal male activities, male-male competition especially, were muted. She credited Chambri women with an aggressiveness and dominance that they did have in some spheres but not over and against their men.

We might note in closing this section that the myth of the onetime existence of a society in which females dominated men in the public arena is ethnographically widespread. In recent years there has been a diligent search for such societies, or the reliable record of them, but none has been found (Bamberger 1974). It seems fair to say that Mead's *Sex and Temperament* contributed substantially to the myth.

FACIAL EXPRESSIONS

Facial expressions have rarely been examined anthropologically, and yet I think a great many anthropologists would consider them to be culturally determined. To support their opinions they could cite La Barre (1947) and Birdwhistell (1963, 1970).

La Barre writes about both facial expressions and gestures and does not clearly distinguish between them. As an anthropologist he is "wary" of any claims that they may be instinctive, and his discussion is almost entirely confined to cultural differences. Although he notes that "the physiologically conditioned response and the purely cultural one" are typically mixed in the language of gesture throughout the world (1947:57), the cultural component is sufficient to ensure that "there is no 'natural' language of emotional gesture" (1947:55).

When Birdwhistell began, in 1945, to plan his research into what he calls "kinesics," i.e., "patterned and learned aspects of body motion which can be demonstrated to have communicational value" (1963:125), he assumed that there were universal expressions of "primary emotional states" (1963:126). But his research led him to the opposite conclusion: the emotional states that he had considered natural are in fact culturally defined, and "there are probably no universal symbols of emotional state or tone" (1963:126).

Birdwhistell partially refined his views later, noting that no ethnographer had reported a people among whom the smile does not occur as an indicator of a situation that is "pleasurable, friendly, benevolent, positive, and so on" (1970:33). And the word he underlines in the following also suggests caution: "there are no universal...facial expressions...which provoke *identical* responses the world over" (1970:34). Nonetheless, he rejected the propositions that there are any facial expressions that are "closer to the biological base than others" and that any expressions "in isolation" transculturally indicate particular emotional states (1970:38). It follows that facial expressions are as essentially arbitrary as indicators of emotions as are the various linguistic labels given them in one language or another.

On the other hand, there were psychologists who, in agreement with Darwin (1872), found certain facial expressions of emotion to be universal. Until the 1970s the debate was inconclusive, and the "predominant view within psychology" was "against universals" (Ekman 1972:210). But by the early 1970s two independent lines of research, both by psychologists—Carroll E. Izard (1971) and Paul Ekman and his associates (see especially Ekman et al. 1969; Ekman 1972, 1973)—had provided persuasive evidence that the facial expression of emotions was both culturally relative *and* universal.

The main element in these research programs consisted of "judgment" studies: experiments in which persons from different cultures are shown photographs of persons with particular expressions on their faces (happy smiles, frowns of sadness, etc.) and asked to judge what emotion is being shown. Generally the respondents are asked to choose from a list of emotion words in their own language. In some cases the respondents were asked to link little stories with the facial expressions they would produce. Alternatively, persons in one culture were photographed when they were asked to show the expression that particular events would produce, and then respondents from another culture were asked to link the photographs with the hypothetical events. With few exceptions (the exceptions attributed to faulty research design, particularly language problems), raters from all cultures were substantially in agreement on which emotions were indicated by various expressions.

One study, designed to elicit facial expressions more naturally, is particularly striking (Ekman 1972:239–260; 1973:214–218). Japanese and American subjects—the former chosen because of their alleged tendency to mask facial expression of emotions—were asked to watch two types of films under two experimental conditions. One type is stressful (showing, for example, a bloody eye operation), one is not. In one experimental condition the subject was alone in a room, in the other condition there was another person present asking questions. In each condition the subject was misled as to the precise nature of the research, and in each condition the subject's face was actually being filmed.

Once the films were obtained, the ones taken with the subjects alone in the room were shown to Japanese and American subjects who were asked to judge when the persons being filmed were watching the stressful film and when not. Japanese and Americans did not differ in their ability to link persons of their own or the other culture to the films they responded to. Moreover, when the films were examined frame by frame by trained raters, employing a method for analyzing the component parts of the face into its various elemental expressive configurations (the "components" as opposed to "judgment" method), they found no significant difference between the kinds of expressions made by Japanese and Americans to the two films (the components method is described in Goleman 1981).

However, there was one significant difference between the Japanese and Americans. Upon examining the films taken when another person accompanied the subject as he or she watched the stressful films, it was found that the Japanese smiled more frequently than the Americans. In short, when on stage, so to say, the Japanese masked expressions or substituted one for another. But when offstage, the Japanese and Americans responded alike.

To understand what these experiments show, Ekman posits two general determinants of facial expression. One is a "facial affect program" that is a part of every individual's nervous system and that links emotional states with particular movements of facial muscles to produce universal expressions of certain basic emotions. The other determinant consists of "display rules," culture-specific standards about the display of emotions. He links the two into a "neuro-cultural" theory of facial expressions. To fully understand or interpret facial expression, we must posit both universals and cultural variants.

In spite of the experiments just described, there remained a substantial objection to claims for universality of facial expression: all the subjects were in direct or indirect visual contact with each other. Was it not possible, therefore, that they had *learned*—via motion pictures, television, and more direct observation—to interpret each other's expressions, even though the expressions were different? Or was it not possible that all the subjects had acquired familiarity with an essentially arbitrary and cultural, but increasingly international *language* of facial expression? Even though uniformly recognized from culture to culture, might this language not have been acquired through John Wayne movies rather than facial affect programs? In order to eliminate these possibilities it was necessary to conduct research among preliterate peoples who had experienced as little contact as possible with those outside influences that might promote a culturally imperialistic set of facial expressions.

Accordingly, two such societies were studied: the Fore of Papua New Guinea and the Grand Valley Dani of West Irian, which is in the Indonesian part of the island of New Guinea (Ekman 1972:269–276; 1973:210–214). In the former case, Ekman's research team conducted the study; in the latter case it was done by two anthropologists (Karl and Eleanor Heider), who are reported initially to have been skeptical of claims for universal emotional expressions. Each of the peoples studied had only recent contact with Euro-American culture, and from among them, subjects were chosen who had never seen motion pictures, visited westernized communities, worked for Europeans, etc. The results—which were based on the natives' judgments of photos of Euro-Americans and then the latters' judgments of photos of the natives—were essentially the same as when all the subjects were from literate cultures. The conclusion seems inescapable: there are universal emotional expressions.

There is some controversy concerning which and how many basic (primary, elementary, or "coarse") emotions are indicated by distinct facial expressions. Happiness (or joy), sadness (or grief), disgust, surprise, fear, and anger are usually mentioned; contempt has also been claimed (Ekman and Friesen 1986; cf. Izard and Haynes 1988). The study of emotions is complicated by the fact that they are expressed in various degrees of intensity and because many expressions are blends resulting from mixed emotions and from the interaction of facial affect programs with display rules. Moreover, people may attempt to imitate facial expressions for various reasons and with varying degrees of success, and culturally specific ways of caricaturing facial expressions have to be considered, too. Clearly, the face does more than express emotions.

Indeed, one critic (Fridlund n.d.) argues that the primary function of human (and animal) facial expressions is not to express emotions but to communicate *intention* in a social setting. There may be emotions that typically accompany particular intentions in particular settings, but in the causal pathway, so to say, the emotions are secondary to the intentions. Fridlund does not deny cross-cultural commonalities in facial displays, but he is critical of the existing explanations both for the similarities and the differences. He also criticizes the methods that have been used to test or support those explanations.

My own assessment is that communicating intention and expressing emotion are not mutually exclusive explanations, but that fine-grained analyses of the functions of human behavior cannot help but be salutary. Getting to where we presently are in such analyses clearly required breakthroughs in the objective study of facial displays and careful cross-cultural comparisons. It will take more of the same to move further ahead.

HOPI TIME

Benjamin Lee Whorf was the principal modern architect of what came to be known as the Sapir-Whorf hypothesis. Edward Sapir, a distinguished anthropological linguist, had been Whorf's teacher. Sapir had written influentially on the relationship between culture and language and had drawn attention to the ways in which language and culture interact. For example, the Eskimos are said (incorrectly, as it turns out [Martin 1986]) to have an elaborate terminology for differing kinds of snow, some East African cattle-herding peoples have similarly elaborate terms for cattle, and so on. These cases of linguistic differences at the lexical level make good sense in terms of the cultures in which they occur.

Whorf is the person most frequently associated with an extreme version of this argument, in which our language or its categories shape our thoughts and worldview. What our language does not classify, we don't see, don't readily see, or don't attend to. Whorf stated his position in both extreme and more reasonable forms; it is the former that are of interest here. The less extreme forms of the Whorfian hypothesis have a degree of plausibility, and some supporting evidence, but the argument remains unsettled (Haugen 1977; Witkowski and Brown 1982).

Whorf studied the Hopi language and by 1936 had come to a startling conclusion: one of the fundamental categories of Western thought—time—is culturally relative:

> After long and careful study and analysis, the Hopi language is seen to contain no words, grammatical forms, constructions or expressions that refer directly to what we call "time," or to past, or future, or to enduring or lasting. (Carroll 1956:57)

> [T]he Hopi language contains no reference to "time," either explicit or implicit. (Carroll 1956:58)

Whorf did not hesitate to draw the relativist conclusion:

> I find it gratuitous to assume that a Hopi who knows only the Hopi language and the cultural ideas of his own society has the same notions, often supposed to be intuitions, of time and space that we have, and that are generally assumed to be universal. In particular, he has no general notion or intuition of TIME as a smooth flowing continuum in which everything in the universe

proceeds at an equal rate, out of a future, through a present, into a past. (Carroll 1956:57)

Since these quotations are from a posthumously published paper, it should be noted that in a paper published in 1940, while he was yet alive, Whorf also described the Hopi verb and the Hopi language as "timeless" (Carroll 1956:216, 217).

But in other places Whorf took a different position: not that the Hopi had no sense of time as we (or a physicist) might understand it but that the Hopi conception of time was very different from ours. He said that the Hopi recognized "psychological time" but that this was quite different from time as a physicist understands it. For example, Whorf says that the Hopi language does not objectify time. Units of time, in Hopi, are not aggregated in the plural. The Hopi do not say "ten days" as they might say "ten men." In Hopi one says "they left after the tenth day" rather than "they stayed ten days." "Plurals and cardinals are used only for entities that form or can form an objective group" (Carroll 1956:140), and units of time are not such entities. As a consequence, Whorf argued, the Hopi would not think of ten days as ten different entities forming an "assemblage" (in the sense that they would think of ten men) but would see them as "successive visits" of the "same" entity (Carroll 1956:148).

Whorf said that the Hopi, unlike almost all other known peoples, did not use spatial metaphors to talk about time (i.e., they would not talk about a *long* time). "The absence of such metaphor from Hopi speech is striking. Use of space terms when there is no space involved is NOT THERE— as if on it had been laid the taboo teetotal!" (Carroll 1956:146).

Whorf said that the Hopi verb lacked tense, and he implies that the Hopi, in contrast to Westerners with their objectified sense of time, have little interest in "exact sequence, dating, calendars, chronology" (Carroll 1956:153).

Moreover, Whorf thought that profound philosophical and practical lessons were to be drawn from Hopi (and other American Indian) conceptions of time. In this and other respects Hopi was a decidedly superior form of communication and thought: "The Hopi actually have a language better equipped to deal with...vibratile phenomena than is our latest scientific terminology;...in the formal systematization of ideas... English compared to Hopi is like a bludgeon compared to a rapier" (Carroll 1956:55, 85).

Generally, Whorf was quite clear in his illustrations of how Westerners think of time, but he was often much less clear about how it was that the Hopi did it. Much of the literature on Hopi time was subsequently devoted to figuring out just what Whorf had meant. Given the striking nature of his claims, it was "inevitable," says Malotki (1983:4), that Whorf and those who expounded extreme versions of his ideas, should "spawn a number of myths." Malotki (1983) cites some of the more outlandish extrapolations from Whorf's contentions (fortunately, few if any recent anthropological textbooks repeat Whorf's extreme claims, except with substantial reservations, e.g., Barnouw 1975). A serious problem was that neither Whorf nor anyone else had published much in the way of Hopi texts, dictionaries, and grammars—without which the accuracy of Whorf's claims could not be determined.

Beginning in the 1970s, Ekkehart Malotki undertook a study of Hopi time (and space). The opening page of the resulting book on time (Malotki 1983) quotes a Hopi sentence, translates it literally, and then rephrases the translation as follows:

> Then indeed, the following day, quite early in the morning at the hour when people pray to the sun, around that time then he woke up the girl again.

This sentence alone, assuming it did not include terms and ideas only recently borrowed by Hopi, would seem to be enough to dispose of any contention about the absence of time concepts among the Hopi. But Malotki goes on with more than 600 pages of documentation of Hopi temporal metaphors; units of time (including days, day counts, segments of the day, yesterday and tomorrow, days of the week, weeks, months, lunation, seasons, and the year); the ceremonial calendar; timekeeping devices; pluralization and quantification of time expressions; such miscellaneous time words as "ancient," "quick," "long time," "finished," and so on; the Hopi tense system; and even more. But since Whorf's own writings refute the idea that the Hopi language was timeless, it is his more specific claims about the ways in which Hopi time differs from ours that require attention.

With respect to the objectification of time, Malotki shows that the Hopi do talk about aggregated units of time and do use cardinal numbers in counting days. Whorf's claim (Carroll 1956:140) that such "an expression as 'ten days' is not used" in Hopi is "utterly false" (Malotki 1983:526). Malotki documents his refutation not only with materials he gathered but with published Hopi texts that predate Whorf's interest in linguistics. Thus "an objectification of time units is not in the least foreign to Hopi" (Malotki 1983:529).

Malotki (1983:15) finds in Whorf's own unpublished Hopi-English dictionary an entry in which a spatial term is used metaphorically for time and concludes that Whorf "must have been aware that a spatialized vision of time was not alien to the Hopi language." Malotki goes on to demonstrate just

> how greatly Whorf erred....We shall see that the technique of
> spatio-temporal metaphorization is...ubiquitous...in Hopi. It
> involves not only countless postpositions and adverbs of place but
> also a number of verbs and nouns, among them a direct equation
> of the noun *qeni* 'space' with the notion 'time.' (1983:16)

Whorf had originally described Hopi as having tense and only in his later writings repeatedly denied that it did. Malotki brands this as one of the particularly tenacious myths about Hopi. The issues are complicated, and Malotki does not give a full account (he refers to a previously published analysis of the Hopi verb by other linguists). In essence, he finds that Hopi is no more free of tense than is English: both have only two formal tenses to express past, present, and future. English has past and present (we do not form the future by changing the form of the verb but by adding other words) and Hopi has future and nonfuture. Any analysis of the consequences of formal tense alone would find English as timeless as Hopi. Through the use of the Hopi aspect system (divided into the perfective and imperfective), and through other linguistic devices, "Hopi speakers never consider themselves at a loss in determining whether a particular utterance refers to past, present, or future time" (Malotki 1983:625).

Contrary to Whorf's views, Malotki (1983:482) finds Hopi culture "favorably bent to the keeping of records" and "developed on a very sophisticated level" with respect to chronology, calendars, and dating. Malotki describes for the Hopi a "horizon-based sun calendar"; "exact ceremonial day sequences"; "knotted calendar strings"; "notched calendar sticks"; and time keeping by means of marks on walls, by "alignment of sun holes in a house wall," and by means of "shadow observation." Information on each of these items is hard to obtain, since most of the practices have long been out of use or involve knowledge that Hopi do not wish to share. In some cases Malotki documents the use of these time-keeping devices and systems before Whorf's research.

Malotki's (1983:530) overall conclusion is that "Whorf's claim about Hopi time conception being radically different from ours does...not hold" (Gipper [1976] drew a similar conclusion).

So how and why did Whorf go astray? The most serious problem seemed to Malotki (1983:526) "that Whorf based his observations on an extremely incomplete corpus of linguistic data. As far as the domain of time is concerned, he seems to have barely scratched the surface." Perhaps as a consequence, Whorf failed to grasp a Hopi linguistic element that means "times" and which is used to form aggregated units of time (so that a literal phrase "five times day" translates as "five days"). In other cases Whorf oversimplified or overinterpreted by taking grammatical features out of their sentential context and by failing to examine them in a sufficiently comparative perspective. His treatment of tense in the Hopi verb was a case in point. In some cases, of course, Whorf was at least partly correct. For example, it is true that some units of time in Hopi are not pluralized. But Malotki likens these instances to English nouns that do not get pluralized (e.g., "two dozen eggs," "three yoke of oxen," "few," and "several"): they do not seem to alter our worldview.

Beyond these problems lies another: did Whorf have a motive for distorting his findings or exaggerating his claims? The linguist Haugen (1977) draws attention to Whorf's long-term interests in the mystical as an explanation for Whorf's "enthusiastic advocacy." Many of Whorf's papers appeared in a theosophical journal published in Madras. In one of these papers Whorf advocated linguistic research as a path to Yoga with "therapeutic value" (Carroll 1956:269). Haugen (1977:23) also argues that the early students of American Indian languages needed a justification for their researches, something more than an argument based on "the mere accumulation of knowledge." The hypothesis of relativism provided such a justification, and any demonstration of extreme relativism in language and culture had still greater impact. Whorf's argument that language shapes how we think and even what we think about helped to popularize linguistics (Carroll 1956:18).

This argument can be traced through Boas to the mostly German thinkers, particularly Wilhelm von Humboldt, who laid the foundation for linguistic and cultural relativism (Hoijer 1954; Haugen 1977). Haugen (1977:19) outlines this intellectual line of descent in a paper entitled "The Cult of Relativity," but perhaps the title is overly strong language, too.

Neither Haugen, Malotki, nor any other linguist fully rejects the notion of relativity. As Malotki notes, the Hopi did not use their calendar to record the passage of time as we do; the Hopi have not been affected as strongly as we have by the invention and spread of timepieces. What must be rejected, therefore, is not relativism in general but, rather, extreme forms of relativism, such as the notion that the concept of time as we understand it is *essentially* relative and absent from Hopi. In some contexts even Whorf rejected extreme versions of relativism: "My own studies suggest, to me, that language, for all its kingly role, is in some sense a superficial embroidery upon deeper processes of consciousness which are necessary before any communication, signaling, or symbolism whatsoever can occur" (Carroll 1956:239). That view of the relationship between mind and language is perhaps the predominant view among linguists today.

Unlike Freeman's refutation of Mead's account of Samoa, Malotki's refutation of Whorf's analysis of Hopi occasioned little notice. Linguists had already given Whorf's analysis of Hopi a "decent burial" (Haugen 1977:12).

THE OEDIPUS COMPLEX

Malinowski's claim that the Oedipus complex is not universal was perhaps the least challenged of the similar claims discussed here. In part this stemmed from the very considerable authority of Malinowski, but perhaps more important were the intrinsic probability that his argument could be correct and the limits he often placed on relativism. In the very work in which he argued for the relativity of the Oedipus complex, he frequently reiterated his opinion that innate dispositions shape human behavior in many ways. While he thus denied the universality of the Oedipus complex in particular, he did so by affirming, in effect, the universality of family complexes in general.

Since Freud had developed his concept of the Oedipus complex on the basis of clinical experience with European peoples—and they predominantly from delimited strata—it seemed to Malinowski that it would be of interest to examine the complex, and related phenomena such as the unconscious, in the very different setting provided by the matrilineal Trobriand Islanders. Malinowski reported striking differences. Whereas "in the Oedipus complex there is the repressed desire to kill the father and marry the mother,…in the matrilineal society of the Trobriands the wish is to marry the sister and to kill the maternal uncle" (1961:76).

In Malinowski's formulation, the Freudian Oedipus complex was part of "a theory of the influence of family life on the human mind" (1961:17). It followed, so Malinowski reasoned, that different family systems might produce different complexes, different patterns of "mental attitudes or sentiments," conscious or unconscious, between the members of the family. Since he found the Oedipus complex culture-bound, Malinowski employed the more neutral terms "family complex," "nuclear complex," or "nuclear family complex."

The Oedipus complex was the feature of the family complex that most impressed Freud. It manifests itself in the psychic orientation of a male toward his mother and father. In the normal case the young boy desires to possess his mother and eliminate his father, but these desires are repressed (or extinguished) as the boy matures. If repressed, they remain a part of the boy's (or man's) psyche, but unconscious. In abnormal cases, the childhood desires work psychological mischief. The complex of a female was the opposite of the Oedipus complex—but it received much less attention from Freud and almost none from Malinowski (or Spiro).

In his conception of the Oedipus complex, Malinowski placed great emphasis on the superiority of the patriarchal husband over his wife, the coolness of the father toward his son, and the economic dependence of both wife and children on the breadwinning father. By contrast, the Trobriand wife was not subservient to her husband, for she derived much of the family's wherewithal from her brother. The husband was not even considered the procreator of her children, for the Trobrianders believed that children entered their mother's womb as spirits.

Nonetheless, the tie between father and children was warm. Compared to the Trobriand father, the European father was brutal. A Trobriand woman's son would inherit property and position not from his father but from his mother's brother. Relations between a boy and his mother's brother—who possessed authority over the boy that was the matrilineal counterpart of *patria potestas*—were comparatively cool. Relations between a boy and his sister were also strained, since a rigid taboo required their separation at an early age and the utmost propriety in their subsequent interactions.

As an additional contrast, Trobriand youth were allowed to experiment freely with sexuality—barring, of course, any contact between brother and sister.

Under these conditions, which do indeed differ markedly from conditions in the West, Malinowski found that the counterpart of the Oedipus complex in the Trobriands was a boy's desire to possess his sister and eliminate his mother's brother. Malinowski's finding became "the cornerstone for the thesis propounded by relativists of all persuasions—anthropological and nonanthropological, Freudian as well as anti-Freudian—that...the Oedipus complex...is a product of Western institutions and, more particularly, of the Western 'patriarchal' family structure" (Spiro 1982:x).

> Thus, the Trobriand case is offered as disproof of the universality
> of the Oedipus complex not only in anthropology textbooks (Beals
> 1979:345; Ember and Ember 1973:322–323; Hoebel 1972:43;
> Honigmann 1967:273–274; Kottak 1978:19; Richards 1972:228), but
> also in the works of psychological...and psychoanalytic...
> anthropologists, as well as of classical...and neo-Freudian...
> psychoanalysts (Spiro 1982:1; citations partially omitted).

There were those who were skeptical. Kathleen Gough (1953), for example, who worked with the matrilineal Nayar, reported that they had a normal Oedipus complex. And the first anthropologist to restudy the Trobriand Islanders, H. A. Powell (1957; 1969), disputed Malinowski's analysis of the Oedipus complex. But Malinowski's analysis, according to Spiro (1982:174ff), had become a "scientific myth," repeated endlessly and very rarely questioned. Powell was ignored on the point. Had Malinowski's analysis not achieved mythical status, Spiro argues, it would have been questioned, for Malinowski's logic and evidence were far weaker in the case of the Oedipus complex than in other matters on which his claim to fame was based.

Spiro stresses that for Freud the Oedipus complex is triangular: the boy's hatred of his father and desire to possess his mother are connected, in that the two males are rivals. The boy is sexually jealous of the father. Malinowski treated the complex as two dyads: the boy desired his mother for the usual reason but hated his father because of the authority he exercised over the boy. If the father exercised little authority, and was warm and loving, as in the Trobriands, then the boy would hate his mother's brother who did have authority over him. This formulation, says Spiro, has many difficulties, but because of it Malinowski ignored lines of investigation that would have borne more directly on whether there was an Oedipus complex among the Trobrianders.

First of all, Malinowski himself said that a little Trobriand boy has an intense passion for his mother. This is quite understandable, because for the first two years of his life he has virtually exclusive possession of her. He sleeps with her at night, she nurses him on demand, and since the Trobrianders have a lengthy postpartum sex taboo, his father is no rival for two full years. The father, Spiro says, goes to sleep elsewhere during this period.[4] Without a sexual outlet it is understandable that—whether consciously or not—the mother may be specially "seductive" to her son during the period of the postpartum sex taboo.

This pleasant period in the Trobriand boy's life is interrupted when the father resumes sexual relations with his wife—more or less in full view of the child, for the Trobrianders live in one-room houses. At about this time, or a year or two later, the child is weaned, too.

Spiro asks, sensibly enough, is it not likely in these circumstances that a little boy would be jealous of his father, no matter how warm and loving the father might be? There is, unfortunately, no direct evidence on the point.[5] Malinowski asserted that the boy's attachment to his mother dissipates spontaneously and smoothly—childhood sexuality being free and easy—but he provides no supporting evidence, other than the observation that adult Trobriand males have no conscious sexual interest in their mothers. As Spiro rightly observes, this tells us nothing about a *repressed* interest: unless they are abnormal, adult males in the West have no conscious sexual interest in their mothers either.

Malinowski also provided very little evidence for the onerousness of the demands of mothers' brothers on their nephews. Consequently, just as the lack of jealousy of the boy toward his father is mysterious, so too is the alleged intensity of the boy's hostility toward his mother's brother.

A solution to these mysteries, first argued by Ernest Jones (1925), is that the boy's erotic fixation on his strongly tabooed sister is a displacement of his desire to possess his mother; his hostility to his mother's

[4]Actually, Malinowski is vague on this point, and a recent fieldworker among the Trobrianders, Weiner (1985), denies that the father sleeps elsewhere.
[5]Weiner (1985:761) seems to indicate that the weaning is "traumatic."

brother is, likewise, a displacement of his hostility toward his father. Rather than having no Oedipus complex, the Trobriand male has a particularly strong one, one that has undergone more stringent repression than in the West. Given the loving nature of the Trobriand father, any hostility toward him would be particularly painful. Who could possibly be a better substitute target for the hostile feelings generated by the father than the fatherlike mother's brother? Given the particularly strong attachment to the mother, when it must be repressed, who could better stand for her than her daughter?

Without the vital information on the reaction of boys to their fathers' resumption of sexual relations with their mothers, Spiro turns to whatever other kinds of data and lines of reasoning might substantiate his suspicions. Whereas Malinowski found no "traces" of the Oedipus complex, Spiro finds them in abundance. Indeed, it was the existence of what he deemed to be traces of the Oedipus complex that first turned Spiro to consideration of whether Malinowski might have been wrong. In addition, Spiro shows that Malinowski's reasoning on many points was deficient.

To illustrate the latter point, Spiro notes that easy sexual outlets among his peers does not allow the boy raised in an Israeli *kibbutz*[6] to achieve a quick or natural extinction of his fixation on the mother, even though the *kibbutz*-raised boy has far less reason to be attached to her (until recent reforms, *kibbutz* children were reared collectively by specialists—parents were minimally involved). Malinowski was wrong to think that the availability of sexual playmates in itself would replace the infant boy's fixation on his mother.

The centerpiece of the traces of the Oedipus complex is what Spiro calls the "absent-father pattern": the curious absence of the father from myths, dreams, and reproductive beliefs. Malinowski's (1929) analysis of Trobriand reproductive beliefs, which include the startling assertion that men play no necessary part in reproduction, is anthropologically famous.

In Spiro's interpretation, the absence of the father from these domains is the consequence of repressed hostility toward the father, hostility rendered particularly painful because of the understandable and conscious warm regard for fathers. Given that, on the conscious level, fathers are so well thought of, their absence from myths and dreams with a family content is indeed most striking. Spiro says that in terms of a strictly structural analysis the father *is* present, though in disguised form. In the myth that Malinowski singled out as underpinning the matrilineal Trobriand family there are four actors: the culture hero Tudava, who was

---

[6]A *kibbutz* is a utopian socialist commune. The *kibbutz* movement began in 1910. There are now hundreds of *kibbutzim* in Israel, but their inhabitants account for only a very small percentage of the country's total population.

born of a virgin; his mother; his mother's brothers; and a cannibalistic ogre. As Spiro interprets it, the ogre is the disguised father. Malinowski had himself hit upon this interpretation, but he saw it as a remnant from a patriarchal period in Trobriand history: the father had been turned into an ogre to discredit patriarchy. Malinowski chose not to pursue this bit of conjectural history (generally, by the way, he condemned conjectural history). There are further reasons to support Spiro's interpretation. We know from other matrilineal societies that their mere constitution does not eliminate hostility between a boy and his father, and Malinowski at one point said that when a man dies, and the cause is not obvious, suspicion falls on his wife and children, including, presumably, his sons.

Spiro suggests that the father is absent from Trobriand dreams for the same reason (though why he should be absent from females' dreams is not explained). Malinowski said that the Trobrianders dreamed very little. Spiro suggests that they dream as much as anyone, but remember less because their Oedipal content is exceptionally repressed.

Spiro argues that Malinowski misstated and misunderstood Trobriand "ignorance of physiological paternity." Until recently no people in the world had an understanding of this microscopic activity. What characterized the Trobrianders was an active *denial* of the connection between a macroscopic activity—insemination—and reproduction. The Trobriand huffiness on this point was made very clear by Malinowski: it was not, therefore, a matter of knowledge or ignorance but of ideology. If Spiro is correct, it was a matter of psychology too:

> [A]ny exception to a near-universal ethnographic belief or practice which cannot be explained as a response to ecological conditions, adaptive requirements, and other determinants of a "rational" type is most likely to find an explanation in motivational determinants of an "emotional" type. (Spiro 1982:61)

The denial of the role of the father in reproduction is an ultimate solution to the Oedipus complex. Moreover, in place of the notion of reproduction through insemination, the Trobrianders believe that a spirit child enters the mother's womb. Symbolically, this achieves both goals of the Oedipal boy at once: possession of his mother and elimination of his father.

Spiro provides further evidence of a repressed wish for a boy to possess his mother. One line of evidence is provided by magic associated with the *kula* ring, a system of interisland exchange of valuables and other goods conducted by men. The main valuables, objects of endless fascination for men, are "female" arm bands and "male" (pendant-shaped) necklaces. Their exchange is explicitly described in sexual and marital terms (e.g., the armband "clinches" the necklace; the latter "pierces" the former; the two are "married" in exchange). As Spiro reads some of the texts of *kula* magic, the two partners in *kula* exchanges are symbolically equated with a mother and her young son, the older partner to the exchange being the mother.

Another line of evidence is found in the pattern of adultery. When it is possible, as in the case of sons of chiefs who are polygynous, the particular target of the adulterous male is often his own father's wives (though not the real mother). Spiro finds this an "extreme example" of the man acting out his Oedipal desires and the most serious of Malinowski's failures to recognize the traces of the complex.

For these and other reasons that Spiro presents, it seems safe to say that Malinowski's famous demonstration of the mutability of the Oedipus complex has been overstated. While the structure of the complex theoretically could be different—if the boy, his mother, and her consort(s) were *not* constant elements—empirically it never is different (as a societal norm). Structurally, therefore, the Oedipus complex is an apparent universal.

In two other respects, however, the complex can and does vary: in its strength and outcome. As Spiro tries to show, its strength was greater in the Trobriands than in the West. Its outcome may be that it is extinguished, that it is repressed, or that it is imperfectly repressed. Spiro goes on to show that these different outcomes have quite different repercussions for society and culture. Thus in many New Guinean societies marked by incomplete repression of the Oedipus complex, boys are either expelled from the family at puberty or earlier, or undergo severe puberty rituals that bring them firmly under elder male control and separate them from their mothers. These rites are at times terrifying and brutal, allowing men, so Spiro avers, an outlet for their own Oedipal hostilities toward their sons. Spiro also suggests that the sheer quotient of magic to knowledge in these societies is raised damagingly by the unconscious mischief of unresolved Oedipal urges.

Spiro concludes his discussion with the comment that Malinowski's argument was so weak, and involved such anomalies, that it could only have stood the test of time if it, like any myth, served an important function for those who believed it. The "will to believe" must have been a factor. Spiro leaves it to some historian of ideas to determine who sustained the myth and why.

CONCLUSION

The cases just summarized vary in the degree to which they successfully defend their respective theses or demonstrate universality. From the viewpoint of appropriate method and data, Berlin and Kay's treatment of basic color terms is commendable, and it is directly relevant to universality, yet their work has not gone uncriticized. From the viewpoint of intimate familiarity with the ethnographic particulars, Freeman's work is all but peerless, but he does not attempt to demonstrate a universal, and the critics of his work are numerous (see, e.g., Samoa Controversy 1983; Holmes 1987; and footnote 3, above).   .

Against the thesis that the Hopi have no concept of time, Malotki's compilation of evidence to the contrary is hard to refute, but was this really Whorf's thesis? Against the thesis that the Hopi sense of time was fundamentally different from ours, Malotki's data and arguments are clearly substantial, but the issues are complicated and it may take some time for the dust to settle on the debate over Hopi time. Furthermore, even if Hopi time or Samoan adolescence are much like ours, may not evidence from other societies still provide a case in support for the essential relativity of adolescence and the sense of time? The same question can be asked of facial expressions: sound as the existing research may be, are there not numerous other societies yet to be examined to test the universality of emotional expression? Other objections to the facial expression research were stated earlier.

The evidential bases of Gewertz's and Spiro's works are not greatly different from those of the persons they criticize, and there is every reason to think that as many people who believe Gewertz and Spiro will persist in believing Mead and Malinowski on the relevant issues. It might be worth noting that Annette Weiner, who has done recent fieldwork with the Trobriand Islanders, and who is generally critical of Spiro's analysis, finds the argument for the universality of the Oedipus complex to have a "convincing ring" (1985:761). A great many other anthropologists will not be so convinced because they are skeptical or hostile toward psychology in general and Freudian analyses in particular.

In short, none of the studies above *proves* that something is a universal—which may be impossible anyway—nor is it certain that any of them conclusively demonstrates universality. It is also worth noting that all these cases together offer no reason to question the very notion of cultural relativity. But each of them casts serious doubt on important earlier arguments against the universality of the phenomena they treat, and they raise anew the need to look more carefully at human universals and at extremist conceptions of cultural relativity.

The frequency with which the authors of these studies use the word "myth" to describe the views they attempt to refute indicates their awareness of a propensity in anthropology to accept purported rejections of universality on the basis of flimsy evidence. In chapter 3 I attempt to explain this propensity. But the more immediate task, taken up in the next chapter, is to define universals and examine the means available to demonstrate universality.

2

Conceptualizing, Defining, and Demonstrating Universals

Universals may be found in the individual, in society, in culture, and in language—though in many cases it is neither useful nor reasonable to consider these phenomenal realms in isolation from each other. At the level of the individual, universals may be found in every (normal) individual—or in every individual of a particular sex and/or age range—and can often be understood from the perspective of a single individual. Some emotions and their facial expressions are examples. Features that are thought to be straightforwardly anatomical or physiological are rarely if ever included in anthropological discussions of universals, so that universals at the level of the individual are generally confined to patterns of action, thought, and feeling. Universals at this level must underlie social, cultural, and linguistic universals, since society, culture, and language ultimately have no source that excludes individuals and their capacities. Stated differently, all societies, cultures, and languages are the products of individuals and their interactions with each other and with their environments.

To illustrate social universals, all societies are structured by statuses and roles and possess a division of labor. These phenomena lie near the core of the social realm, which consists in essence of social statuses and their relationships but also of the interrelationships between the individuals (who "inhabit" statuses). Although individuals are normally affected by them, anthropologists probably think of social universals most frequently as traits or complexes attached to and defining collectivities rather than individuals. But certain mental and behavioral mechanisms, present in all normal individuals, are undoubtedly also involved in hu-

39

man sociality. Since statuses are also cultural, and generally possess linguistic labels, social phenomena touch upon the individual at one end and culture and language at the other.

Although most anthropologists are comfortable talking about societies in the plural, as though they were discrete and countable entities, attempts to specify the boundaries of societies pose many difficulties. There are, for example, societies within societies, and there are individuals who belong to more than one society at a time. In important senses, societies transmute themselves from one into another as time passes. (I will continue to write about "peoples" and "societies" in spite of these difficulties.)

Culture consists of the conventional patterns of thought, activity, and artifact that are passed on from generation to generation in a manner that is generally assumed to involve learning rather than specific genetic programming. Besides being transmitted "vertically" from generation to generation, culture may also be transmitted "horizontally" between individuals and collectivities. Examples of culture are tools, kinship terminologies, and worldviews—which in each case may take distinct forms among peoples who are genetically indistinguishable. Culture is divisible into "traits" (single items) and "complexes" (more or less integrated collections of traits) and typically is thought of as though it were attached to collectivities rather than isolated individuals. This deemphasis of the individual stems not from an anthropological belief that individuals do not create culture but from the observation that any given individual receives more culture than he or she creates. Because so much culture is imposed upon rather than created by any particular individual, anthropologists (and others) often think of culture as a sort of supraindividual entity in itself, or as something dictated by that supraindividual entity called "society."

Since conventional social arrangements are by definition a part of culture, this further confounds the social and the cultural. There are, thus, many contexts in which "social" and "cultural" are used interchangeably (particularly when stressing a contrast with things "biological"). Furthermore, anthropologists often use "a culture" and "a society" as synonyms, stressing by the former the entire collection of cultural traits and complexes associated with a particular society or people. Some parts of culture are not very profitably understood in social terms—some items of material culture, for example—and it is these nonsocial elements that are understood when one contrasts culture and society.

Because any language possesses many conventional traits that are transmitted within populations much as culture is transmitted, and because the lexicon of any language has a close relationship to the culture of its speakers, language has often been thought of as closely related to or even a very important part of culture. At any rate, all peoples use one or more particular languages; all languages have phonemes, morphemes, and syntax[1]; and each of these aspects of the structure of language contains further universal elements. In terms of its structure, language is normally understood as a more or less closed system whose parts are defined or understood in relation to one another; few parts of any particular language are normally understood as phenomena connected to the individual. But social factors are often important in understanding the syntax and semantics of particular languages, and some features of language (such as the "marking" that will be discussed later) can only be understood when it is borne in mind that individual organisms employ and shape it. Thus sociolinguistics and psycholinguistics have emerged as subdisciplines within, or adjuncts of, linguistics.

Although anthropology literally means the "study of man(kind)" in the widest sense, twentieth-century anthropology—at least in the English-speaking world—has been primarily concerned with the social and cultural aspects of human affairs. As I noted earlier, human anatomy and physiology, identified as "biological" in contradistinction to the "social" and "cultural" realms, have been left to other disciplines or given a somewhat marginal existence within anthropology. Moreover, as a matter of practice in anthropology—at least until the 1960s—if a universal was to be of interest it usually could not be too obviously or completely determined by human biology, nor could it be a "lower" mental function; "higher" mental functions have been a bit more acceptable as topics of anthropological concern. What is probably the most famous list of universals in anthropology—George P. Murdock's list published in 1945 (quoted and discussed in the next chapter)—is specifically a list of cultural universals.

All humans breathe, and yet no list of universals mentions the fact: the linkage to biology is too close, the sociocultural influence too negligible, the distance from "higher" mental functions too great. This is not to say that anthropologists are never professionally interested in breathing: the effects on the human body of life at high altitude—generally resulting in increased lung capacity—is, for example, an area of research for physical anthropologists. But most of the remaining anthropologists would find breathing of interest only to the extent that it is modified by social or cultural conditions (as in yogic practices).

To explore a more complicated example, sexual activity is, in some senses, as physical as breathing. Sexual activity occurs in all societies, but it too does not appear on most lists of universals. Unlike breathing,

---

[1]Deaf sign languages—which *are* languages, which do possess syntax and morphemes, and which are found in every community of deaf people—do not possess phonemes; however, they do possess structural units below the morphemic level and analogous to phonemes (Sandra Thompson, personal communication).

however, sexual activities show many obvious social and cultural modifications, and the anthropological literature on human sexuality is considerable. From the viewpoint of anthropological interest in universals, however, it has not been sex itself that has been of most interest (actual descriptions of coitus are quite rare), but certain phenomena associated with it, such as incest regulations and male-female differences in temperament and behavior.

Universals may in fact be linked to human biology—and this is sometimes stated as an anthropological assumption (e.g., Sahlins 1976; Shepher 1983; and discussions in subsequent chapters). But to judge by much of the existing practice, universals must not be so closely linked to biology that there is nothing left to say about them from the perspective of social and cultural anthropology.

For a considerable period the term "universal" was used without anyone thinking it needed to be defined. During that period the implicit definition was approximately as follows: a trait or complex present in all individuals (or all individuals of a particular sex and age range), all societies, all cultures, or all languages—provided that the trait or complex is not too obviously anatomical or physiological or too remote from the higher mental functions.[2]

I repeat that this is a definition that fits much existing practice; it may not prove to be useful in the future. One of the reasons why it will probably require revision is the difficulty of making useful distinctions between biology and culture. I write at, and am a product of, a time when the distinction remains fundamental to most anthropologists—even though it is vaguely and falsely conceived. *Nothing* in human culture comes into being or gets transmitted without consideration of the specifically human genetic makeup. Yet significant aspects of human anatomy and physiology can only be fully understood with some consideration of human culture, which always and everywhere is a crucial part of the environment that interacts with human genes to produce human organisms. Any hypothetically conceived boundary between the "thoroughly genetically determined" and the "not too obviously biological" is more likely to be a boundary between what has and what has not been interesting to anthropologists. An anthropology less concerned with the opposition of culture to biology, and more concerned with their interaction, may well arrive at many new conceptions, including new conceptions of universals.

For example, consider the views of two of the most important present-day contributors to understanding universals, Noam Chomsky in linguistics and Robin Fox in anthropology. Both distinguish "substan-

[2]As will be seen below, more sophisticated definitions are employed by linguists. Note also that linguistic universals are often omitted from anthropological discussions of universals.

tive" universals (Fox 1989:113; Chomsky 1965:27–30; Chomsky and Halle 1968:4), which are what anthropologists usually mean by universals, from universals at a deeper level. For Chomsky these are "formal"; for Fox they are universals at the level of "process" (examples will be given below). Both Chomsky and Fox assume or find that these deeper and more significant universals, which on the "surface" do not necessarily or even typically manifest themselves in substantive universals, are rooted in human neurobiology. Fox (1989) goes on to argue that the distinctions between the individual, society, and culture are entirely artificial and a barrier to the development of social science.

But, as I said, I write at a time when these distinctions are still fundamental to the way social scientists think. Furthermore, my discussion follows anthropological practice in giving serious weight to substantive universals—even though it does not exclude formal or processual universals that may lie at deeper levels.

In addition to the distinctions Chomsky and Fox make between substantive and deeper universals, there are quite a number of other *kinds* of universals that must be examined. To begin with, some anthropologists draw attention to the distinction between universals and "near universals," generally to argue that the distinction is not important.[3] Various lines of reasoning support this position. One is that, given the quality of ethnographic reporting, the distinction could reflect error of reporting. We know for certain that many of what we expect to be universals could not be shown to be present in all societies from the ethnographic record as it presently stands. But the reason the trait or complex appears to be absent in some society or societies is either that the record is silent on the matter or that the record is wrong. If, for example, the rate of murder were a constant in all societies, those of very small scale might not have a murder in several generations. Under these circumstances the members of the society might very well say that they never murder, and the anthropologist might find no contrary evidence. But both anthropologist and native could be wrong in saying murders don't occur in the society in question. As a concrete example, Roberts and Sutton-Smith (1962:167) originally concluded from a broad-ranging study of games that they were not universal. But in a later publication (Sutton-Smith and Roberts 1981:437), they decide that the adequacy of the reports of societies without competitive games should be "questioned seriously."

Another line of reasoning is that human behavior is so complex and malleable that any trait or complex can only approach universality. Thus men nearly universally find lighter skin pigmentation attractive in women

---

[3]A linguist, Comrie (1981:19), makes a parallel distinction between "absolute" universals and tendencies. His tendencies include both near universals and the statistical universals discussed below.

(van den Berghe 1986). Van den Berghe provides an evolutionary explanation for this preference, and yet Western societies—where tanned skin has had an appeal—indicate that it is not universal. Presumably, a countervailing tendency—to admire signs of high status, such as tanning indicated—can override a tendency for men to prefer lighter-skinned women. This line of reason presumes that there are so many human tendencies (each of which, by the way, may be a universal at some deep level) that few if any can override all the others to manifest itself as a (substantive) and absolute universal. Even if a trait or complex had a universal distribution, the argument goes, we can imagine the conditions (unusual though they might be) that would eliminate it in some particular case.

Closely related is the argument that universals lie at the end of a continuum: traits and complexes can be scaled all the way from those that are unique to a particular individual, society, culture, or language up to those found everywhere. The distinction between a near-universal and a universal (or absolute universal), then, is not significant, or imposes an artificial break in an unbroken natural continuum. A near-universal is universal enough.

The dog, for example, was absent from some cultures, probably less than 5 percent of those known to ethnography. If, however, it had spread everywhere, what difference would it make in our understanding the dog-human relationship? If some people really did get along without fire—and it is possible that some branches of early *Homo sapiens* did not have it—we wouldn't understand the uses of fire or its apparent universality any the less. It is certainly fair to say that many universals and near-universals are likely to have very similar explanations.

No one seems yet to have thought about where to place the cutoff that distinguishes near-universals from merely widespread traits and complexes. Perhaps a cutoff at a 95 percent distribution, by analogy with the 5 percent rule for statistical significance, might make sense in some cases. In the case of the distribution of cultural traits or complexes, such as the domestic dog, it would.

A trait or complex more widespread than chance alone can account for is called a "statistical universal" (Greenberg 1975:78). The near-universal is, in a sense, an extreme form of the statistical universal. A remarkable example of a statistical universal is the use of words with meanings closely related to "little person" to label the pupil of the eye—as indeed is the case in English. This occurs in approximately one-third of all world languages (Brown and Witkowski 1981)—far beyond what is expected, given that the alternatives are limitless. Words for small animals are disproportionately represented as the sources of words for muscles—again English is an example since "muscle" is from the Latin for mouse, and of course "calf" is a further example. Some such label for muscles occurs in almost 20 percent of a sample of world languages (Brown and Witkowski 1981). The obvious reason for "pupil" and its semantic analogues is that close scrutiny of the pupil reveals a "little person" looking out at you: your own reflection. The apparent reason for "muscle" and its analogues lies in the similarity of motions: small animals dart about in a manner analogous to the motion of muscles under the skin.

Another conception of universals distinguishes "implicational" or "conditional" universals from "unrestricted" or "non-conditional" universals (Greenberg 1966; 1975:77–78). An implicational universal is a trait or complex that always appears when certain conditions obtain. It takes the form "if A then B," in which A is not an individual, society, culture, or language and is not itself a universal. It is a rule that is universally applicable. An example is that "all societies possessing paved highways possess centralized government." Rules of this sort are common in anthropology, and are often convincingly demonstrated. Implicitly they are even more widely used, as Hempel (1942) has shown for historical explanations in general.

But this conception of universals presents a sort of optical illusion in that it illustrates relativity when looked at in one way and universality when viewed from another angle: some peoples have paved highways, but some don't; some have centralized government, but some don't (relative statements); yet all that have one have the other (universalistic). When one examines the causes of universals, it is apparent that the relativistic image that results from implicational universals is a surface appearance; fundamentally there is little difference between unrestricted and implicational universals.

Implicational and statistical universals in combination are particularly common. That is, statements of the sort "if A then a tendency to B," in which A is not an individual, society, culture, or language, probably constitute the single most common form of cross-cultural generalization. That particular kinds of kinship terminologies tend to be found in matrilineal societies while alternative kinship terminologies tend to be found in patrilineal societies are but two of the no doubt hundreds of generalizations of the sort that are familiar in anthropology. If anthropologists typically thought of these as kinds of universals, universalistic thinking would be far more prevalent than it is. But because of the optical illusion mentioned above, and because of the statistical rather than absolute form of these statements, their kinship with universals is rarely noted.

Generally, I provide little discussion of implicational or statistical universals that are little more than conventional cross-cultural generalizations. But it is important to be aware of the extent to which these kinds of generalizations imply a connection with universals or universalistic perspectives.

An important variant of the implicational universal consists of universal evolutionary sequences. These take various related forms. They may be "if *A* then *B*" statements in which it is asserted that *A* can only emerge after *B*, as when it is asserted that the locomotive can only emerge after the wheel; or they may be the same form of statement in which it is asserted that both *A* and *B* emerge in tandem as the result of some prior factor *C*. Alternatively, they may take the form of "if at developmental stage *A*, then trait or complex *B* will be found." The various "unilineal" schemes of sociocultural development proposed by nineteenth- and twentieth-century anthropologists are cases in point (a lengthy quotation of A. V. Kidder in the next chapter is a good illustration). The evolutionary stages in which color terminology develops, as noted earlier, are further examples. Closely related sequences have been posited for the development of botanical and zoological life forms (Brown 1977b, 1979).

What is perhaps another variant of the implicational universal posits what might be called a universally fixed "pool" of sociocultural elements, from which all traits or complexes of a given type are formed. Linguists, for example, find that all phonemic systems are based on a finite list of possible speech sounds or contrasts of speech sounds (Jakobson, Fant, and Halle 1967). Any particular language employs a selection from the universally given possibilities. The International Phonetic Alphabet, thus, is meant to have universal applicability.

Similarly, Kroeber (1909) found that just eight semantic elements (including those that distinguish sex, generation, and lineal from collateral kin) structure the kinship terminologies—diverse though they be—of many different societies. For example, the English terms "brother" and "sister" are distinguished by sex, "mother" and "grandmother" by generation, "son" and "nephew" by the distinction between lineal and collateral kin. Other elements have since been added; collectively they form a universal pool from which all kinship terminologies are drawn. The universal-pool kind of universal takes the form of "if *A* then some selection from *B*, *C*, *D*,...*N*," in which *A* is any individual, society, culture, or language.

Hale (1975) discusses a kind of universal that has affinities both to those forming a universal pool and to near-universals. He gives counting as an example: peoples may have a very elementary system of numbers and yet have a full-blown ability to count (which allows them very quickly to adopt complex number systems when they become available and prove useful). Theoretically, he argues, numbers and counting could be absent among a given people (he gives no example), particularly if they had no need to count. And yet the ability to count is universal as an innate (and presumably specific) capacity of the human mind. Hale gives further examples from linguistics, where certain patterns are near-universals that probably result from innate tendencies that are only rarely blocked by unusual conditions.

Contrasting with "innate" universals are those that are "manifest" (Tooby and Cosmides 1989), and this is a distinction that must be borne in mind to make sense of some of the most influential statements on universals, such as those of Chomsky and Fox that were noted earlier. Consider the following: "Though the device of metathesis, like all linguistic universals, is in principle available to speakers in any language, it does not, of course, follow that every language must actually present examples" (Chomsky and Halle 1968:361). For Chomsky the interesting universals lie below the surface. Fox (1980:7) has taken an analogous position in anthropology. Thus the nuclear family, which is manifest on the "substantial, institutional level" rather than "at the level of *process*," is not universal, while "the bonding processes on which it is based" are (Fox 1980:7). Most explicit anthropological discussions of universals are, as Fox also notes, heavily weighted toward those that are manifest.

Yengoyan (1978) suggests another contrast, by distinguishing the innate universals that Hale describes from "experiential" universals. An example of the latter is that all people have the experience of seeing that blood is red and, hence, that symbolic equations of red with blood are very widespread if not universal.

Another conception of universals is embodied in the "universal framework" or "universal model." In this usage the universal or universals are not of central research interest but rather are tools for research on phenomena connected with them. The universal framework consists of abstract, analytical definitions, assumptions, and procedures that guide research on selected topics—in any and all societies. Malinowski's (1944) framework for the analysis of cultures was probably the most famous in anthropology, but behind it was Wissler's (1923) earlier and cruder model and perhaps one presented by Warden (1936). (Malinowski's and Wissler's models are described in chapter 3). Another example was Robert Redfield's (1953) framework for the cross-cultural analysis of worldviews. Kearney (1984:39) summarizes most of the framework in a three-dimensional diagram whose parts are formed by such distinctions as that between self and other, we and they, human and nonhuman, nature and divinity— distinctions likely to give order to any people's worldview. As the framework for his analysis of human kinship and marriage systems, Fox (1967:31) identifies four "principles" that underlie and give order to them all: (1) "The women have the children," (2) The men impregnate the women," (3) "The men usually exercise control," and (4) "Primary kin do not mate with each other."

The features of a universalistic framework are discussed by G. N.

Appell (1973), who has developed one for the analysis of social structure in terms of the property relations that define and relate social statuses of all kinds. The validity of this kind of a framework rests upon the universality of its starting points: Appell's framework rests upon the universality of social statuses and property. Universalistic frameworks are often proposed, used for a time, and discarded in favor of others.

Related to the conception of the universalistic framework is the distinction between "universals of classification" and "universals of content." Such broad categories as religion or government are extreme versions of the former. To some anthropologists such categories seem meager in the face of the complexity to which they refer. Wissler's (1923) "Universal Pattern," discussed in the next chapter, consists mostly of universals of classification. A universal of content, on the other hand, is one in which the details of the phenomenon are themselves universal. Facial expressions of emotions and the coyness display (discussed later) are good examples of universals of content. Many universals stand between those that are purely classificatory and those whose content is specified in detail, precisely because it has been the aim of anthropological research to fill in at least part of the universal content of universals that initially were little more than delineated categories of research. The currently burgeoning studies subsumed under the heading of "gender" rest very largely on a universal of classification—the division of labor by sex—but have shown that there is at least a slender content to the universal. The low repute that universals of classification sometimes have, due to the variability of their contents, should be balanced against consideration of their fecundity or open-ended nature. The enormous range of what humans do with language, for example, in no way leads us to undervalue it.

Universals are importantly distinguished as either emic or etic. In anthropology, "etic," by analogy with phon*etic* analysis in linguistics, refers to analyses in terms of cross-culturally valid, scientific frameworks (universalistic frameworks).[4] "Emic," by analogy with phon*emic* analysis, refers to the way the natives conceptualize things. In English, to illustrate the original linguistic conceptions, the *p* of "pin" and "spin" are phonemically the same. English speakers, unless they are also phoneticians, do not meaningfully distinguish them. But to a phonetician, these are two different sounds: the *p* in "pin" is aspirated (accompanied by a puff of air), the other is not. (Hold a thread or thin strip of paper closely in front of your mouth while pronouncing these two words, and the difference between the *p*'s will be readily apparent.)

---

[4]What is sometimes called an "etic grid," the collection of etic distinctions found to lie behind some universal or cross-culturally valid domain, is a universal pool. The semantic components that Kroeber (1909) found in the domain of kin terms are an example.

To say that a universal is an emic universal, then, is to say that it is a part of the conceptual system of all peoples. It is a part of their culture that is meaningful to them and that is probably more or less integrated into their worldview. Applying this standard to religion, Hockett (1973) denies that it is universal: the Menomini Indians (and no doubt many other peoples) do not conceptualize religion as a distinct sphere of their culture. It is a commonplace in anthropology that institutionally distinct spheres in one culture may be merged in others. In general, and to simplify, sociocultural evolutionary advance has been marked by the progressive emergence of, say, distinctive governmental, religious, and economic spheres from an originally diffuse kinship sphere. In cases where this institutional proliferation and specialization have not occurred, we usually say that economic functions, for example, are discharged by kinship institutions; we do not usually say that economic functions do not exist if the category "economy" is not a part of the native system of categories (even though we do want to note this, and it may well be a significant factor in understanding native life).

By the same token, it would be an unusual linguist who would say that if a people does not have a conception of grammar they or their language has no grammar. Hockett is a linguist, and in most cases I treat universals the way he would treat grammars: if it is there it is there, whether the natives are aware of it or not. For example, chapter 4 is entitled "Incest Avoidance" rather than "The Incest Taboo" because the former is an etic concept that may well be universal, whereas incest taboos have numerous emic variants and pretty certainly are not universal. In short, I generally define universals etically, but at times they are also conscious, verbalized, emic parts of culture. Emic universals may be of special interest, but there is no reason to confine the discussion of universals to them alone. (Failure to realize that one party is speaking of emics and the other of etics is a fertile source of disagreement among anthropologists.)

A distinction not currently in the anthropological literature, but that I believe will be useful, divides universals of "essence" from those of "accident." "Intrinsic" and "extrinsic" universals might also be suitable terms. Chomsky and Halle (1968:43) use the terms "essence" and "accident," and they appear to overlap with the distinctions noted earlier between formal and substantive universals. Universals of essence are those that could not be eliminated except by unnatural interventions (e.g., by genetic engineering, or in concentration camps). Universals of accident are those that we can more easily (and realistically) imagine not being universal. The purest examples of the former are those strictly biological features of the species that do not generally receive much anthropological attention (Malinowski and Fox providing notable exceptions). Spiro illustrated the latter by arguing that if the Oedipus complex is universal, it is so in part by accident: we just never find the (easily imaginable) conditions that would eliminate it. Fire and cooking also illustrate the latter type.

Universals of essence at the level of the individual collectively constitute human nature, or at any rate would be important ingredients in its definition. Universals of essence at the level of society and culture—if such universals exist—constitute the nature of society and the nature of culture and would probably express the *logic* of sociocultural integration and development. Possible examples at the cultural level would be provided by those implicational universals that in a generalized form assert that wholes do not precede parts (an example, previously mentioned, is that the locomotive does not precede the wheel). Perhaps it will prove more useful to see the distinction between essential and accidental universals as parts of a continuum of more or less fixed universality. I take it that much of the current debate concerning male and female differences turns round the issue of whether certain of the universal differences are essential or accidental.

Another term that needs to be introduced is "new" universals: those traits or complexes that were not present in all the societies known to ethnology but that have become universal in all extant societies. Tobacco is a very likely candidate (Aginsky and Aginsky 1948). The dog and metal tools are among the equally likely candidates, and such items as plastic containers, phosphorus matches, and machine-manufactured clothing do not (alas for the romance of anthropology) seem far behind. With each decade the new universals must swell in numbers, as the once rich diversity of cultures is steadily eroded.

It might also be useful to designate "former universals" for all those experiences that were once the common lot of humanity but have since been eliminated in some populations. A few related examples are high infant mortality, relentless childbearing and nursing for most women, and relatively rare experiences of menstruation (Harrell 1981; Ward 1963:37), but one could also note transportation by foot only, the virtual absence of impersonal relationships—and very much more. Since many former universals were part of the environment in which human nature evolved, keeping them in mind will be particularly useful in any attempt to understand that human nature.

Finally, it should be noted that universals are sometimes stated in the negative. Thus it is said, for example, that no society is a matriarchy (Bamberger 1974) and that no society's music is composed exclusively of notes of equal length (Nettl 1983:40). This list could also go on for quite some length. Chomsky often states universals in the negative and with the implication that at some deep level there not only are no exceptions but could not be exceptions (see, e.g., Chomsky and Hampshire 1968).

The first and most obvious point about the demonstration of universals is that it is never done by exhaustive enumeration, showing that a phenomenon exists and existed in each known individual, society, culture, or language. There are too many known peoples to make this feasible, and there are too many shortcomings in the descriptions of "known" peoples. Thus all statements of universality are hypotheses or arguments based on various limited kinds of evidence (this is not to say that confidence in the validity of the hypotheses or arguments does not vary).

One way of constructing an argument for universality results from wide reading in the anthropological literature, which gives weight to statements that one has never seen reliable reference to an exception to some proposed universal. This is often coupled with the stated or tacit view that no convincing reason is known as to why the trait shouldn't be universal. The anthropologist best illustrating this kind of argument was George Peter Murdock, founder of the Human Relations Area Files (HRAF). These files contain coded information on a wide range of societies and were specifically designed to sample and quantify the range of ethnographic traits and complexes (the sample size was originally 400, which was thought to be slightly more than 10 percent of all societies known to ethnography and history [Murdock 1975:xii]). Murdock's broad command of ethnographic literature lent authority to his list of human universals (1945).

Murdock's feat can now be duplicated by use of the HRAF to test the hypothesis that something is universal (for an example, see Otterbein 1987). The result is not to show that it occurred in all societies but that in none of the societies sampled is it found not to exist, which allows the reasonable inference that if not universal it is at least nearly universal. The larger the sample of societies from the HRAF, the stronger the inference.

Most anthropologists, it should be noted, do not have that overall familiarity with ethnography that Murdock possessed, and they don't use the HRAF either. Yet on some specific topic they may read as widely as Murdock did, so that on that topic their assessments of universality carry considerable weight.

Another quite different kind of argument rests on a few, sometimes only two, ethnographic observations—but the observations are carefully conducted. In this argument the societies must be very different in most respects, so that when some trait or complex is shown to be present in each, one suspects that it may well be common to all societies. When Paul Ekman and his associates (1969), for example, wanted to provide a particularly convincing test of the idea that the emotional meanings or determinants of certain facial expressions are universal, they visited tribal peoples of New Guinea who had only recently made their first contact with Westerners and showed them photos of Western persons displaying various emotions through facial expression. As noted in the previous chapter, Ekman's team found that most of the natives could accurately identify several emotional expressions. Ekman labels these emotions as "basic" and posits that they are universal. Most anthropologists, by virtue of their experience with other peoples, can confirm this universality, and Ekman's claim has not been challenged in spite of the extremely limited sample he used (though it should be recalled that he had previously tested his findings among several more accessible peoples).

The recent film "First Contact," compiled from footage produced in the 1930s when numerous New Guinean natives first met the white man (Australian prospectors), allows almost anyone to re-create the sort of experiment Ekman's team conducted. The New Guineans and Australians had strikingly contrasting cultures—as the film amply documents—and yet the attentive viewer can see numerous ways in which the two peoples were fundamentally the same: facial expressions, gestures, and aesthetic appreciation being only a few of the obvious examples (see also Connolly and Anderson 1987).

Eibl-Eibesfeldt's (1979) photos of a coyness display by an African native woman is a persuasive demonstration of the universality of the display, even though it provides evidence from only a single people, which of course we implicitly compare with the evidence provided by ourselves and other peoples we may know. Given the complexity of the display and the conditions that elicit it, the odds are simply too heavily against it developing independently and by chance in the same form among disparate peoples. (It is as if we discovered that in unrelated languages people expressed *the idea of* "I love you" with phrases that actually *sounded like* the English "I love you.")

Another mode of arguing for universality consists of dispensing with those cases that have been set forth as evidence against universality. Several examples were given in the last chapter.

A potent kind of argument for universality might come about as a byproduct of a determined but unsuccessful attempt to show that a trait or complex is not universal. Feminist interests, for example, led to diligent searches for examples of female-dominated societies. When feminist anthropologists now say that there is no substantial evidence that such societies ever existed (Bamberger 1974, Ortner 1974), their conclusion carries a certain weight.

An important ingredient in some arguments for universality consists of providing a convincing explanation for the universal. When we can understand the conditions that produce a universal, and get a sense for the ubiquitousness of those conditions, we then more readily accept the universality of the trait or complex.

Even if all methods of demonstrating the universality of a trait or complex have been employed, it bears repeating that universality has still not been proven. However, the likelihood that the phenomenon is at least a near-universal, and for that reason a significant part of human nature or the human condition, may then be very great. Most of the phenomena I discuss (particularly in chapter 6) have not been demonstrated to be universal by all available means, and renewed or continued attempts at such demonstration are now in order.

3

The Historical Context
of the Study
# of Universals

Some anthropologists write about universals with little or no sense that they are controversial, but other anthropologists—some very prominent (e.g., Geertz 1965)—maintain that universals have little significance if they exist at all. The roots of this anthropological ambivalence toward universals have to be sought in the wider history of anthropological thought, where the scientific concerns of discovery, method, and theory interact with the ideology and politics of anthropologists and others. In important respects, the history of the study of universals is more an indirect reflection of wider anthropological concerns than of the direct concerns of those who might wish to understand universals.

Although the attention they have received has been far from constant, universals have long been a part of the conceptual framework of anthropology.[1] Consider the views of E. B. Tylor, who is generally regarded as the founder of academic anthropology in the English-speaking world. He developed a distinctively *cultural* anthropology, as opposed to an anthropology that would explain the differences between peoples in racial terms. To support the doctrine of the psychic unity of humanity he noted the detailed similarity of "gesture-language" in all parts of the world and the uniformity in stages of cultural development (1870:370). In his *Prim-*

[1]A concern with universals in some senses of the term is ancient in both West and East. Plato's "forms" are the most familiar example, but for further examples see Koepping's (1983) discussion of the Stoic conceptions that gave rise to Bastian's "elementary ideas" (described below) or Staal's (1988) comparison of ancient Indian with Western universals of logic.

itive Culture (1891) Tylor stated that human culture is pervaded by "uniformity," due to the "uniform action of uniform causes," the "general likeness of human nature," and "general likeness in the circumstances of life." Tylor considered his pages to be so "crowded with evidence of...correspondence among mankind" that he did not dwell on the details in any one place. As a specific example he noted the universality of language and its fundamental similarity among all peoples (1891:1, 6, 7, 161).

But Tylor's conception of culture did not fully liberate it from racist ideas. He saw culture in the singular, something that people had more or less of. Degree of intelligence was an important determinant of where a people fell on the hierarchy of the more and less cultured.

In a process that was largely complete early in this century, Franz Boas, the single most important figure in American anthropology, transformed the concept of culture (Stocking 1968) in ways that were to have important implications for the study of universals. For Boas, cultures were plural; each culture had its own genius and should be judged in its own terms. The notion that other peoples were more primitive and less intelligent was to some degree an artifact of judgment from our own ethnocentric perspective. The differences between peoples did not result from their differing intelligence but from their different culture histories (particularly the accidents of the diffusion of cultural traits).

It is extremely important to notice Boas's concern with racism. In the early decades of this century the eugenics movements and other trends had succeeded in, among other things, incorporating racist criteria into U.S. immigration laws. Boas and many other anthropologists took vigorous steps to employ anthropology to combat racism. Margaret Mead's master's thesis, for example, examined the environmental influences on the I.Q. test scores of Italian immigrants (Kevles 1985:134–138). This mixture of antiracist morality with cultural relativism—the view that each culture must be judged in its own terms—remains a potent force to the present.

Another aspect of the Boasian program was to shift anthropological attention away from generalizations—particularly about origins or evolutionary sequences—toward detailed studies of particular cultures. This did not, however, lead Boas to dismiss universals. He utilized the conception of the psychic unity of mankind both to dispel racism and to assert that this unity produced universals. In a section entitled "Traits common to all cultures" in his *The Mind of Primitive Man* (1963, but first published in 1911), he concurred with the German ethnologist Adolph Bastian in the "appalling monotony of the fundamental ideas[2] of mankind all over the globe."

---

[2]"Fundamental ideas" or "elementary ideas" is a translation of Adolph Bastian's *Elementargedanken*, ideas that recur again and again from society to society.

> We find not only emotion, intellect and will power of man alike
> everywhere, but also similarities in thought and action among the
> most diverse peoples. These similarities are...detailed,...far
> reaching,...vast,...and related to many subjects. (1963:154)

Boas at times lumped universals with near-universals, but he noted some
of the absolute universals.

Boas pointed out that some universals were the result of their great
antiquity. Yet he disagreed with Bastian's opinion that "elementary ideas"
could not be explained, because, Boas said, "the dynamic forces that
mould social life" are the same now as they were in the ancient past
(1963:178).

In ways that had no direct connection with elementary ideas or universals, the Boasian concept of culture came to imply an autonomy that
was made explicit by one of Boas's earliest students, A. L. Kroeber, who
is generally credited with perfecting the argument that culture is a level
of phenomena—the "superorganic"—that cannot be explained by reducing it to lower levels (1917; see also 1915). In particular, the argument goes,
one cannot explain culture traits in psychological or biological terms. This
brought to a culmination the trend initiated with Tylor's attempt to explain differences between human groups in cultural terms.

Kroeber's views warrant an extended digression and will serve to
illustrate developments among Boas's successors in American anthropology. His 1915 paper, "Eighteen Professions," drew a sharp boundary between biological science and cultural anthropology: their "differences in
aim and method," he said, were "irreconcilable" (1915:283). Cultural anthropology was a part of history, not science, and "the material studied
by history is not man, but his works" (1915:283). Kroeber's 1917 paper,
"The Superorganic," seemed to be "an antireductionist proclamation of
independence from the dominance of the biological explanation of sociocultural phenomena," as Kroeber himself noted many years later
(1952:22). Ideas expressed in Kroeber's papers, but elsewhere too, were
all too successful, and a radical opposition between biology and culture,
nature and nurture, became one of the most entrenched tenets of anthropological thought. As Kroeber put it, the contentions of his 1917 paper "passed into...[anthropology's] common body of assumptions"
(1952:22).

When one stops to think about the implications of Kroeber's statement that the subject matter of history, including cultural anthropology,
is not humanity—it was an astonishing statement. Since cultural anthropology has long been by far the greater part of all anthropology, Kroeber
was saying that anthropology—the study of humanity—was largely un-
concerned with humanity itself. Like some sort of intellectual neutron
bomb, this formulation left human artifacts intact while humans were

obliterated from anthropological purview. Trying to understand human culture and society divorced from the problem of trying to understand flesh-and-blood people could only produce a blinkered, one-armed kind of anthropology, still able to function but at a considerable handicap.[3]

Although Kroeber's antireductionist ideas are among his best known contributions, he was not in fact such an extremist. In "Eighteen Professions," the very paper that drew a sharp boundary between nature and nurture, Kroeber said that the "relation of biological and social factors" was a "special province" of anthropological study that would one day "be surveyed, fenced, and improved" (1915:283). It was not his aim at the time, however, to enter that "no-man's land," but to delimit "the scope of history from that of science" (1915:283). Several years later, in a textbook on anthropology, Kroeber (1923:3) saw "the interpretation of those phenomena into which both organic and social causes enter" as "a specific task and place in the sun for anthropology." He still expressed this view in the postwar revision of the textbook (1948:3).

As he later wrote, "The Superorganic" was not *intended* to be a declaration of independence, because Kroeber saw no signs of "oppression or threatened annexation by biologists" (1952:22). Instead, the paper was intended to point out the error of explaining sociocultural developments in racial terms. In his later commentary on the paper, Kroeber also retracted some of the reificatory language he had used in describing the superorganic nature of culture (1952:23). His later papers were decidedly reductionist, repeatedly stressing that there is no alternative to considering flesh-and-blood human beings as the efficient causes of culture (1949), while concluding that culture had only a "degree of autonomy" from the organic realm on which it rested and that history should be included in science (1960:3, 12).

There is good reason to think that Kroeber was actually some sort of psychological reductionist throughout his life. In one of his earliest papers, based on his doctoral dissertation, Kroeber spoke of the "tendencies" that "are at the root of all anthropological phenomena" (1952 [1901]:18). Some are purely "physiological" and can be studied in any individual; others, which were his main concern, are also present in the individual, but they reflect the particular society or culture of the individual. "These several tendencies" are "inherent in the mind" (1952 [1901]:18). Because these tendencies "do not exist separately" from "ethnic phenomena" (i.e., society and culture), "the whole of life...is the only profitable subject of study for anthropology" (1952 [1901]:19). In other

[3]Kroeber clearly was not alone in this. For example, another of Boas's students, Robert Lowie, said that "culture...is the *sole* and exclusive subject-matter of ethnology" (1966 [1917]:5, my italics). Not many modern anthropologists will say this in principle, but the practice is hardy.

words, anthropological study—if it is to be worthwhile—must include tendencies "inherent in the mind."

In 1935 Kroeber stated his views more clearly. He agreed with Tylor in positing the psychic unity of humanity, but said that contemporary anthropologists disagreed with Tylor by being more cautious in drawing "specific inferences from this postulate" (1935:565). As he saw it, current methods involved putting the "protean X of the mind to the rear," but this did "not abolish the X." Indeed, "The X, or its relation to the Y of culture, does remain our ultimate problem. This fact...we tend to forget; and, probably more than we know, we are bringing up our students and successors in an ultra-behavioristic attitude....If there is a human mind, it has a structure and constitution, and these must enter into its phenomenal products....[I]t is well to remember that we are making a deliberate omission for practical purposes for the time being; and above all we have not yet proved that X equals 0" (1935:565–566).

If Kroeber failed to explore "the interrelation of the organic and the cultural...the reasons were the obvious one of difficulty and the present slender promise of productive results" (1928:325). But throughout his life Kroeber emphasized cultural studies, and it is fair to say that he is much less remembered for his reductionist and interactionist views than for his view of the autonomy of culture. I think it is also fair to say that for many anthropologists a very long period of stressing cultural determinants *in practice* has made them think that biological determinants are out of the question *in principle*. They may think that Kroeber was one of those who established the principle, but this is not so.

Neither Boas nor other anthropologists at the time seem to have noticed any conflict between the view of culture as an autonomous entity and the existence of universals, which they took as fact (Boas's *The Mind of Primitive Man* was often reprinted, and the section on universals was retained when Boas revised the book in 1938). But as the Boasian view was worked out more clearly, universals were to become more problematical than they had seemed to Tylor or Boas.

In the meantime, however, Clark Wissler published an influential chapter entitled "The Universal Pattern" in his *Man and Culture* (1923). The universal pattern contained the following "cultural scheme":

   I. Speech
      Languages, writings systems, etc.
  II. Material Traits
     A Food habits
     B Shelter
     C Transportation and travel
     D Dress

    E Utensils, tools, etc.
    F Weapons
    G Occupations and industries
III. Art. Carving, painting, drawing, music, etc.
IV. Mythology and Scientific Knowledge
 V. Religious Practices
    A Ritualistic forms
    B Treatment of the sick
    C Treatment of dead
VI. Family and Social Systems
    A The forms of marriage
    B Methods of reckoning relationship
    C Inheritance
    D Social control
    E Sports and games
VII. Property
    A Real and personal
    B Standards of value and exchange
    C Trade
VIII. Government
    A Political forms
    B Judicial and legal procedures
 IX. War

This outline provided a framework for the collection and presentation of ethnographic reports because it would suit any and all societies. It was equivalent to the chapter headings and subdivisions of a standard ethnography and was therefore more a matter, he said, of "classification" than of "concrete trait-complexes." But Wissler went on to note that some universals, such as the drill, string, and certain beliefs, are quite specific, so that it is not merely the "pattern" that is the same but the "materials," too. In this context, I believe, "pattern" means "classification" or "class," and "material" means "content," so that Wissler was asserting not only the universality of abstract or broad classes of phenomena, such as government and religion, but also of some specific elements within the classes: universals of classification and of content. The distinction between these two conceptions of universals became orthodox. No less persistently orthodox was Wissler's opinion that human universals were rooted in a common human biology (1923:73–98; Sahlins 1976:8). (Even Boas was to take this position: universals that were "not carried by early man all over the world...may be interpreted as determined by human nature" [1930:109]).

Although Wissler attempted to sharpen the perspective on universals, the attempt was called into question by a much stronger trend. Per-

haps the most visible marker of this trend in anthropology was the success of Margaret Mead's *Coming of Age in Samoa* (1928), which was
examined in chapter 1. Mead's research was part of a series of investi-
gations of the relationship between race and culture that were conducted
under Boas's direction. Mead's report, and similar ones that both preceded and followed it, made culture look more autonomous than had
hitherto been thought and made ever weaker the notion that race—or
biology in general—could explain important ranges of human behavior.

In addition to the Boasian concept of culture, there were other important complements to the empirical reports of which Mead's was a striking example: the sociological dictum that social facts should be explained
by social facts, the phenomenal rise of behaviorist psychology with its
view of the human mind as a virtually blank slate, and theoretical turmoil within the biological sciences. In *The Rules of the Sociological
Method*, first published in 1895, Émile Durkheim defined social facts as
those "ways of acting, thinking, and feeling, external to the individual,
and endowed with a power of coercion, by reason of which they control
him" (1962:3). Social facts were not to be confused with or reduced to
biological or psychological phenomena; the "substratum" of social facts,
in Durkheim's view, is society or various groups within it (1962:3).
Durkheim supported his position by what seemed to him to be two clear
lines of evidence. One was that sociocultural differences could not be
explained in racial terms. The other was that the alleged innate tendencies of humans—a "religious sentiment,…sexual jealousy, filial piety, paternal love, etc."—"are often," he thought, "totally lacking" (Durkheim
1962:107). It thus seemed clear to Durkheim that psychology could not
explain social facts. This view remains very influential in sociology (and
anthropology) and is reinforced by Marxist thought in the social sciences.
Although it does not go uncontested in Marxist writings, nor even in
Marx's writings, the "official" Marxist position is that there is no universal human nature, only the various human natures determined by specific historical-material conditions (Marković 1983; see also Fromm 1961).

According to behaviorism, the human mind acquires virtually all its
content by means of general learning processes mediated by rewards and
punishments. Possessing at birth only the elementary instinctual reactions of love, fear, and rage (Birnbaum 1955:17), humans are fundamentally products of their environments. As John B. Watson, the founder of
behaviorism, put it:

> Give me a dozen healthy infants, well-formed, and my own
> specified world to bring them up in and I'll guarantee to take any
> one at random and train him to become any type of specialist I
> might select—doctor, lawyer, artist, merchant-chief, and, yes, even

beggar-man and thief, regardless of his talents, penchants, tendencies, abilities, vocations, and race of his ancestors. (Watson 1925:82)

In hindsight it is clear that this famous statement about the influence of the environment *on individual differences* is entirely compatible with the most extreme of the "faculty" or "modular" views of the human mind—in which it comprises numerous innate and highly specific mechanisms (see, e.g., Fodor 1983). But sociologists and anthropologists of the time seem to have detected no flaw in Watson's reasoning, and they drew conclusions compatible with his: people are products of their societies or cultures; change society or culture and you change people; discover the dynamics of society or culture and human affairs are brought under control. Intelligent, scientific socialization can make us whatever we want to be. These views were not merely congenial to large numbers of social scientists, they embodied an optimistic faith in egalitarianism and science that appealed to wide segments of the American public. Watson was hailed as a prophet, and his ideas promised to solve problems in the family, the work force, industry, and society at large (Birnbaum 1955; Ross 1979; Samuelson 1981).

But although Watson "presented a beautiful example of an idea" (Samuelson 1981:416), the experimental evidence that he provided to support his ideas was all but nil. The success of Mead's *Coming of Age in Samoa*, which was no less a beautiful example of an idea, needs to be seen in this context: it seemed strikingly to validate the claims of behaviorism (Freeman 1983:99).

Mead was not alone in validating the behaviorist view of the mind. Those neurologists who favored a "holistic" view of the brain (i.e., one in which specific mental functions are not localized) found support for their views in the findings of Karl Lashley (1929), a behavioral psychologist who concluded from his experiments with animals that behaviors were impaired not by the location of brain damage but simply by the amount of damage. With this support, the holists dismissed decades of neurological research and virtually halted further study of the specific functions of specific anatomical regions of the brain (Gardner 1974:25–26, 122–123).[4]

The acceptance of Mead's views, where they were long to remain entrenched in social science textbooks (Minderhout 1986), reflected the apt way in which they illustrated what were becoming the predominant

[4]If Gardner (1974) and others (e.g., Sacks 1985) are correct in their depictions of the human mind, the long period in which "localizers" (e.g., faculty psychologists) were discredited was scientifically and medically very costly. One can only speculate if the same *Zeitgeist* that brought the holists to prominence among neurologists might not have had equally costly effects in the social sciences.

views in anthropology and wider circles. The equation of an arch environmentalism (including cultural relativism) with optimism about the practical application of social science to the problems of society remains a force to the present.

Surely it is no coincidence that these developments took place at a time when the biological sciences provided relatively little clear guidance for the social sciences. Darwinian thought had been tainted by its association with social Darwinism in general and the eugenics movement in particular (Freeman 1983; Kevles 1985). Furthermore, positive developments in evolutionary theory awaited a synthesis of the contributions of Darwin and Mendel. By the time this synthesis did occur, conventionally dated to R. A. Fisher's *The Genetical Theory of Natural Selection* (1930), few social scientists were paying much attention to theoretical developments in biology.

As a consequence of the sweeping success of cultural relativism by the 1930s, anthropology in the United States was locked into a dilemma: universals existed and were likely to rest upon psychobiological factors; yet human behavior was fundamentally shaped by culture, and culture was an autonomous phenomenal realm that was not determined by psychobiological factors. From this time onward, as Hatch (1973a:236) says, "Explanations of cultural universals in terms of inborn psychological principles led almost inevitably to dead ends in American anthropology" because they "ran directly counter...to a view that the Boasians had struggled to foster within the social sciences since almost the turn of the century." This was the view that the human psyche is "almost infinitely malleable," is "largely the product of cultural conditioning," and so "cannot provide the basis for a comparative science" (Hatch 1973a:236).

George Peter Murdock's "The Science of Culture" (1932) well illustrates the difficulties that anthropological conceptions presented. On the one hand, Murdock says that culture is "independent of the laws of biology and psychology" (1932:200) and that "cultural phenomena...are in no respect hereditary but are characteristically and without exception acquired" (1932:202). Except for those who disagree—the "racists, eugenists, and instinctivists"—these points, he said, are a matter of "universal agreement" (1932:200).

On the other hand, heredity "underlies culture," equips humans with "a vast number of unorganized responses," and furnishes "the mechanism—sensory, nervous, and motor apparatus—through which all behavior, acquired as well as instinctive,...finds expression" (1932:202). Hereditary "impulses" "direct human activities into certain main channels" and "lie at the root" of the "marriage relation,...language, economic organization, religion, etc." (1932:203). In human behavior "heredity furnishes the warp and [cultural] habits form the woof, the warp remain[ing] everywhere much the same" (1932:203)

Cultural "habits...overlie the hereditary warp so thickly that it is extremely difficult to perceive the latter at all" (1932:204). Yet, as we have just seen, hereditary impulses direct human action into such highly visible institutions as marriage and the economy.

While "all analogies" between human and animal societies "are never more than superficial" (1932:208), both animals and humans have society—they differ only "by degree" in intelligence, and animals can form habits too (1932:211–212). The apes even have "fads," which fail to be cultural only because of their briefer duration (1932:213–214).

Murdock, and many of his colleagues, were sure that culture was (1) a distinct phenomenal realm that (2) could not be explained in terms of biology/psychology: "the principles of psychology are as incapable of accounting for the phenomena of culture as is gravitation to account for architectural styles" (1932:207, quoting Robert Lowie 1966 [1917]:25–26). Since many anthropologists still agree with these propositions, it is important to see precisely where they err.

There is no insurmountable problem with (1), particularly if "phenomenal" is not taken literally, so that we think of culture as an *analytically distinguishable* realm, a logical construct that we fashion from patterns of thought, feeling, action, and artifact. And if some word such as "entirely" or "satisfactorily" were inserted before "explained" in (2), many problems could have been (and now could be) avoided. But without such an insertion, (2) is false or misleading. *All* architectural styles result from an interaction between cultural patterns and the potentialities and limits set by gravity and other aspects of nature[5]; there is no reason to think that an interactionist framework would not have eliminated the contradictions in Murdock's essay. However, Murdock and others wanted, on the one hand, to deny *any* significant biopsychological determination of culture, while, on the other hand, they could not deny the obvious.[6]

Another problem with the culture concept is that if culture is genuinely autonomous, cultural universals are highly improbable: unless they occurred by sheer coincidence they could only result from having existed in the very infancy of humanity and thus having descended by uninterrupted cultural transmission to all its branches (see, e.g., the discus-

---

[5]Lowie was aware of this, because the sentence Murdock quoted was preceded by the statement that "culture cannot construct houses contrary to the laws of gravitation" (Lowie 1966 [1917]:25). While this should have led to an interactionist formulation, and Lowie comes close to saying as much, he was uncompromising in stating the autonomy of culture. "Culture is a thing *sui generis* which can be explained only in terms of itself....*Omnis cultura ex cultura*" (1966 [1917]:66).

[6]Years later Murdock (1972) recanted his earlier views. He rejected the autonomy or causal efficacy of either society or culture and argued that it would probably be better to start the social sciences again from scratch than to salvage these reified supraindividual entities. It may be relevant that Murdock was trained outside the Boasian school.

sion of universals as "cradle" traits in Benedict [1934:19]). Any other explanation would involve something other than culture causing culture and hence would deny its autonomy. In a later essay Kroeber (1949) confronted this problem by dispensing with universals in two different ways. First, he claimed that they were mere artifacts of our Western mode of classification, not of ethnographic reality (the argument was foreshadowed in Kroeber 1935). "Religion," for example, is our way of classifying certain ranges of information; the term conveys little if anything of the complex ethnographic reality it allegedly designates. Second, he argued that if a trait or complex were biologically determined, it was by definition not a *cultural* universal; consequently, such universals had no relevance to cultural anthropology. After the elimination of illusory and biologically founded universals, there would be few to perplex most of anthropology, which was—as it remains—mostly cultural anthropology. Kroeber did not explain how a trait or complex was to be identified as cultural or noncultural other than by its universality or nonuniversality. Murdock (1932) had faced the same problem and offered no guidelines either: while insisting that a scientific anthropology must focus on *behavior*, which might, he said, be either instinctive or cultural, he was silent on how to tell them apart.

These silences and contradictions can be partly explained, I think, in a fashion similar to Mary Douglas's (1966) explanation of taboos. According to Douglas, things that violate the boundaries of deeply held systems of classification are often tabooed. In terms of the folk conceptions of the anthropology of the time (and of many anthropologists today), a cultural universal confounds the traits of the cultural and the biological: it is neither fish nor fowl. This by itself may explain some of the ambivalence anthropologists have exhibited toward the study of universals. Transcending the boundaries of nature and culture, universals were difficult to even think about.[7] Lying in an anthropological limbo—Kroeber's (1915) "no-man's land"—universals were not literally or consciously tabooed, but they weren't embraced with much enthusiasm either.

The flip side of the anthropological preconceptions that effectively tabooed universals was an unwarranted willingness to accept ethnographic reports and analyses that purported to show that culture was autonomous and was the supreme determinant of human behavior. The continued willingness to accept those reports—however limited the evidence upon which they were based—leads in our time to the charges cited in chapter 1 that they had become anthropological myths.[8]

[7]In the opening chapters of The Elementary Structures of Kinship, Lévi-Strauss (1969 [1949]) used this line of reasoning to explain why social scientists had not been able to come to grips with the incest taboo.
[8]Suggs (1971) presents another astonishing example, and he urges anthropologists to consider carefully how such things come about (1971:185).

But to return to the chronological order of events, another of the most important and popular of all texts in cultural relativism, first published in 1934, was Ruth Benedict's *Patterns of Culture*. Like Kroeber, Benedict had been one of Boas's earliest students, and she was a major influence on Margaret Mead from the beginning of the latter's graduate training. Resulting in the two best-selling books in the history of anthropology, the "intellectual collaboration" of Mead and Benedict "was to have momentous consequences for the development of cultural anthropology" (Freeman 1983:58).

In *Patterns of Culture* Benedict presented colorful and sharply contrasting descriptions of the Zuni, "a ceremonious people...who value sobriety and inoffensiveness above all other virtues" (1934:59); the Dobuans, among whom life "fosters extreme forms of animosity and malignancy" (1934:172); and the Kwakiutl, whose behavior "was dominated at every point by the need to demonstrate the greatness of the individual and the inferiority of his rivals" (1934:214–215). Her aim was to illustrate the enormous and apparently arbitrary variability of cultural orientations, while arguing for a tolerance that would lead to each culture being judged in its own terms.

But as Williams (1947) pointed out when Benedict's book was published in a 25-cent version for the masses, there were two serious problems with her argument. For one, a plea for tolerance for *all* cultural orientations could make little sense to those who had just fought against or suffered at the hands of Nazi Germany. Second, it was clear in numerous passages of her book that Benedict routinely judged the cultures she described, leaving little doubt that, for example, she condemned violence, authority, and, interestingly, "asocial" usages that ran "counter to biological drives" (1934:32). Although Williams had no problems with these pragmatic judgments, he condemned Benedict's book for its untenable advocacy of a principled relativistic tolerance that would deny the validity of such judgments. This advocacy of tolerance, he said, was at "anthropology's root and core" (1947:85), and Benedict's preaching it, while practicing something quite different, was a measure of "the compulsiveness of theoretical postulates" (1947:87 n4).

I think, however, that the tolerance Benedict advocated was not based on theoretical propositions. Insofar as theory accounts for the peculiarities of *Patterns of Culture*, it was the theory that culture is autonomous and therefore essentially arbitrary, in combination with the further theory that human nature is little more than what culture determines it to be. Benedict's book expresses these theoretical conceptions very clearly, and they involved her in contradictions similar to those discussed earlier with reference to a paper by Murdock.

Consider Benedict's views on temperament. In an essay published in the same year as *Patterns of Culture*, Benedict suggested that human "temperamental types are very likely of universal occurrence" (1959 [1934]:278). Which type will be normal or idealized in a particular culture—and which types will then be culturally identified as abnormal—varies from one society to another. That is what *Patterns of Culture* illustrated. Individuals are readily socialized to manifest the ideal type because, "happily, the majority of mankind quite readily take any shape that is presented them" (1959 [1934]:278). This alleged malleability of human temperament, and the culturally arbitrary labeling of normal and abnormal, is much of what *Patterns of Culture* is remembered for. How one would reconcile these views with the commonsense judgments Benedict rendered about "biological drives" and their relationship to cultural practices was not explained. Benedict's book registered a high-water mark in the notion of the extreme variability of cultures. It may, by its very extremity, have led some anthropologists to rethink the direction of American anthropology.[9]

Not all anthropologists were swept along with the general trends in American anthropology. In an article first published in 1935 the British anthropologist Radcliffe-Brown expounded a science of society in which the concept of culture had very little part to play. He developed a framework that rested on the study of phenomena universally present. Thus

> Any social system, to survive, must conform to certain conditions.
> If we can define adequately one of these universal conditions, i.e.,
> one to which all human societies must conform, we have a
> sociological law. (Radcliffe-Brown 1952:43)

Radcliffe-Brown was one of the two principal founders of what came to be known as British social anthropology—a school that, like its prewar American counterpart, shunned interest in origins or evolution. The other founder was Bronislaw Malinowski, who formulated a framework for analyzing culture that used as its fixed points of reference certain universal givens of human life.

Malinowski's posthumously published *A Scientific Theory of Culture* (1960 [1944]) presented a "List of Universal Institutional Types," in which seven "principles of integration" informed various institutional responses (see similar conceptions in Warden 1936). The principles were

---

[9]As Goldschmidt (1960) points out, complaints were lodged very quickly about Benedict's account of the Zuni, and somewhat later about the Kwakiutl. In each case the alternative descriptions that were presented revealed people who were much less exotic than in Benedict's account. Goldschmidt's interpretation is that anthropologists tend to "put literary emphasis on the unusual" (1960:100). That is, they focus on the more exotic societies and on normative rather than actual behavior. Because it is a product of a human nature that is not entirely constrained by culture, the actual behavior of humans, according to Goldschmidt, is less variable from society to society than the norms are.

reproduction, territoriality, physiology, voluntary association, occupation and profession, rank and status, and "comprehensive" (integration of the community). The institutions informed by reproduction, for example, included the family, courtship, marriage, and extended kinship groups. Malinowski implied that each of the principles is itself a universal—each, at any rate, poses a universal problem. Furthermore, each of the kinds of groupings that the principles give rise to have the same general features, consisting of a charter, personnel, norms, material apparatus, activities, and function.

Malinowski also thought that "any theory of culture has to start with the organic needs of man" (1960 [1944]:72). These needs—in combination with the further "imperative needs" called spiritual, economic, or social—provided the framework for a scientific theory of culture. The following "basic" needs give rise to the following cultural responses:

Basic Needs	Cultural Responses
metabolism	commissariat
reproduction	kinship
bodily comforts	shelter
safety	protection
movement	activities
growth	training
health	hygiene

To take the first need as an example, in every society there must be arrangements for the supply of the physical material each person must ingest in order to live, must be allowance for the digestive processes to occur, and must be arrangements for the sanitary disposal of the end products of digestion. These necessities are met by the institutional arrangements of each society.

In addition to basic needs, which are essential elements in the definition of human nature, Malinowski also posited the above-mentioned "imperative needs" or "derived needs." They included production and reproduction of the means of production (economics); the codification and regulation of human behavior (social control); renewal of the human material of each institution (education); and an organization of authority and power (political organization). The analysis of culture consisted of showing the way the institutions peculiar to each society discharged the function of meeting each of the basic and derived needs. From Malinowski we get not so much a list of universals as a list of universal conditions for the existence of society and culture.

As a further aspect of his universalism, Malinowski's works are permeated with the idea that human impulses are everywhere much the same and that culture is rooted in "innate or natural tendencies of the human mind" (Hatch 1973b:283). But this aspect of Malinowski's thought was not followed up; it, too, "led to a dead-end in anthropology" (Hatch 1973b:289).

Back in the United States, dissatisfaction with some aspects of Boasian anthropology surfaced just before World War II. As a consequence of this dissatisfaction, a series of materialistic determinants of culture—economic, subsistence, and ecological—were soon to be studied with renewed vigor, and have become orthodox limitations on the idea of the autonomy of culture. According to Hatch (1973a), these kinds of determinants were acceptable because there were precedents for them in Boasian thought. But psychobiological determinants were something else. Thus Herskovits's (1940) suggestion that Thorstein Veblen's concept of "conspicuous consumption" might be applicable in any society was ignored because it "ran counter to some fundamental assumptions behind the Boasian...tradition" (Hatch 1973a:237). The one idea that few anthropologists could live with was the idea that there are fixed and specific features of human nature.

However, there were ways in which some kinds of explicit universalism then reemerged in anthropology. At the 1939 meetings of the American Anthropological Association, Alexander Lesser and Leslie White read papers defending the study of sociocultural evolution (Belmonte 1985; Lesser 1952). Lesser's paper discussed a series of implicational universals, referred to moral universals, and described the prevailing attitude toward the study of sociocultural evolution as a "taboo." White's paper was more explicitly anti-Boasian, and defended a more rigidly universalistic view of evolution. Only a year later, A. V. Kidder (1940:534–535) summarized evolutionary parallels in the Old and New Worlds:

> In both hemispheres man started...as a nomadic hunter, a user of stone tools, a palaeolithic savage. In both he spread over great continents and shaped his life to cope with every sort of environment. Then, in both hemispheres, wild plants were brought under cultivation; population increased; concentrations of people brought elaboration of social groupings and rapid progress in the arts. Pottery came into use, fibers and wools were woven into cloth, animals were domesticated, metal working began—first in gold and copper, then in the harder alloy, bronze. Systems of writing were evolved.
>
> Not only in material things do the parallels hold. In the New World as well as the Old, priesthoods grew and, allying themselves with temporal powers, or becoming rulers in their own right, reared to

their gods vast temples adorned with painting and sculpture. The priests and chiefs provided for themselves elaborate tombs richly stocked for the future life. In political history it is the same. In both hemispheres group joined group to form tribes; coalitions and conquests brought pre-eminence; empires grew and assumed the paraphernalia of glory.

These are astounding similarities. And if we believe, as most modern students do, that the Indians' achievement was made independently, and their progress was not stimulated from overseas, then we reach a very significant conclusion. We...must consider that civilization is an inevitable response to laws governing the growth of culture and controlling the man-culture relationship.

Kidder posited some sort of "innate urge" to develop civilization. We needn't accept the existence of this urge—nor each detail of his summary—in order to grasp the significance of the complex parallels in Old and New World cultural developments, parallels that suggest some sort of universal evolutionary pattern.

Events leading to World War II, and the war itself, probably stimulated many anthropologists to rethink extreme forms of cultural relativism—much as Williams (1947) was led to rethink the relativism espoused in Ruth Benedict's *Patterns of Culture* (1934). Carried to its logical conclusions, relativism implied a tolerance for cultural otherness that few anthropologists were anxious to apply to Nazism (Hatch 1983:103–104).

In 1945 Murdock published "The Common Denominator of Cultures." It was a comprehensive essay on universals that brought them back into the mainstream of American anthropology. It also provided a "partial list" of universals:

age-grading, athletic sports, bodily adornment, calendar, cleanliness training, community organization, cooking, cooperative labor, cosmology, courtship, dancing, decorative art, divination, division of labor, dream interpretation, education, eschatology, ethics, ethnobotany, etiquette, faith healing, family, feasting, fire making, folklore, food taboos, funeral rites, games, gestures, gift giving, government, greetings, hair styles, hospitality, housing, hygiene, incest taboos, inheritance rules, joking, kin-groups, kinship nomenclature, language, law, luck superstitions, magic, marriage, mealtimes, medicine, modesty concerning natural functions, mourning, music, mythology, numerals, obstetrics, penal sanctions, personal names, population policy, postnatal care, pregnancy usages, property rights, propitiation of supernatural beings, puberty customs, religious ritual, residence rules, sexual restrictions, soul concepts, status differentiation, surgery, tool making, trade, visiting, weaning, and weather control. (1945:124)

When the various items on the list were broken down to further uniformities, "cross-cultural similarities" were even "more far-reaching." Murdock gave the example of funeral rites, which he thought were not only universals themselves but which in turn contained further universals: expressions of grief, means of disposing of the body, and magical protection for the participants.

Murdock agreed with the opinion that the universals were of classification, not of content. He thought it "highly doubtful" that "any specific element of behavior" was a true universal. But he rejected Kroeber's (1935) argument that the classifications were "a mere artifact of classificatory ingenuity." Competent authorities of diverse theoretical viewpoints all agreed upon the classifications, which meant that the universal pattern could only find its basis in "the fundamental biological and psychological nature of man and in the universal conditions of human existence" (1945:125; this already marked a considerable revision of the views presented in his 1932 paper). Universals, thus, had an objective reality. Murdock went on to discuss humanity's common "impulses" and "drives" as ingredients—but not the sole ingredients—in the production of universals.

Long before his paper on universals was published, Murdock had been at work on a vast scheme to codify the findings of world ethnography. This resulted in the Human Relations Area Files, in which a large number of ethnographies from all major areas of the world, and representing varying levels of cultural complexity, are presented in a manner that allows one to look up information on each of them in terms of standard categories (Murdock 1971). These categories are not necessarily universals—not every society would, for example, have a "navy," which is a subheading under "armed forces," itself not likely to be a universal—but the categories are intended to cover all known major topics (a grand sort of universal pool), and some are ordinary universals.

In a 1947 paper entitled "Human Nature and the Cultural Process" the philosopher-anthropologist David Bidney reiterated his charge (1944) that it is a fallacy to reify culture as an autonomous phenomenon. He saw "superorganicism" as just the extreme opposite of the reductionist "organicism" that racism entails, and he argued that culture should best be understood "as the dynamic process and product of the self-cultivation of human nature" (1947:383, 387). It is true, he said, that "the variety of human cultures [can]not be deduced from the so-called instinctive endowment of individuals or racial groups, and...cultural development is not bound up with improvement in mental capacity," but it does not follow from this that "culture is a process *sui generis*...which...precedes the individual and determines the type of human nature he is to acquire" (1947:389–391). On the contrary, "*Omnis cultura ex natura*," for "cultural phenomena are not intelligible apart from the structure and functions of human nature" (1947:390, 391). Bidney thus agrees with Wissler, Malinowski, and Murdock in rooting universal human institutions in a universal human nature and its needs (1947:391).

Given the contingent effects of time and place in cultural development, Bidney doubted that there could ever be a predictive science of culture. But he thought that human nature was a proper subject for natural science, so that "adequate self-knowledge requires a comprehension of both nature and history" (1947:396). Bidney described his views as "humanistic," and in the sense that they restored what Kroeber's superorganicism obliterated—the human being—the term is apt. Although Bidney's critique of the reification of culture was definitive, his views did not receive much attention from anthropologists at large.

Melville Herskovits's *Man and His Works*, first published in 1947, contained a chapter entitled "The Universals of Civilization." Herskovits stressed the classificatory function of universals, pointing out that the categories Murdock provided in his *Outline of Cultural Materials* (1971, but prepared in draft in the 1930s) were in many respects simply an expanded and refined version of Wissler's "cultural scheme." Herskovits proposed his own short list and used it to order ethnographic materials. He summarized Malinowski's scheme for analyzing cultures in terms of human needs, but pointed to the scheme's difficulties—particularly the one of trying to explain religion and aesthetic elements of culture in any framework based on Malinowski's conception of biological needs. Herskovits did not propose a solution to this problem, but he added that the alternative to explanations in terms of basic needs is in terms of "historic phenomena": an origin so early that the universals in question became so by spreading *with* humanity to all parts of the world. Herskovits concluded his book with an unusual reconciliation of cultural relativism with universals: the former, in opposition to "ethnocentric absolutism," stresses universals, because tolerance rests on the recognition that justice and beauty are known in all cultures, even though their manifestations differ from one culture to another (1952:76–77, 229–240, 347–348, 575, 655). Cultural relativism is often conceived of as the opposite of universalism, but there is this sense in which they can be harmonized.

In 1948 Carleton Coon published a reader in anthropology with an appendix that gave an overview of anthropology. In the course of developing a universalistic model for the analysis of society and culture, the appendix presents a fairly extensive discussion of the physical nature of humans, along with frequent mention of specific universals (1948:563–614).

In the same year Leslie White, who, as noted earlier, had already begun to question certain aspects of the cultural relativity of American anthropology, attempted to explain the universality of the incest taboo. He defended E. B. Tylor's argument that those who failed to marry out died out. Marrying out promoted the cooperation that set human culture above animal existence. Focused attempts to explain particular universals were, however, to remain somewhat rare for another decade or so.[10]

Outside the United States there were continued signs of interest in universals—if not in their study, at least in their use. For example, in 1949 Lévi-Strauss published his *Les Structures élémentaires de la Parenté*, in which he posited innate "mental structures" to explain certain features of kinship. Lévi-Strauss was very attuned to American anthropological thought, and he was aware that he was breaking a sort of taboo (see footnote 7, above). Lévi-Strauss's views have been particularly influential in turning at least some anthropologists' thoughts toward the human mind and its relationship to human cultures.

Although I mentioned it above, it was in this period that Kroeber (1949)—somewhat out of step with the times—argued against universals on the grounds that they were either vague and ethnocentric labels or were not within the purview of cultural anthropology anyway.

Clyde Kluckhohn's "Universal Categories of Culture" (1953) considerably advanced the discussion of universals. He expressed dissatisfaction with "the tautology that culture alone begets or determines culture." He quoted A. V. Kidder's (1940) summary of the impressive similarity of developments in the Old and New Worlds as evidence for uniform forces at work in isolated locations, and from a variety of sources he pulled together materials that rested on the assumption of universals or demonstrated their reality. He found explanations for universals in human biology and psychology, and in uniformities of human social interactions and environmental situations. Recent studies of the neuroanatomy of primates and humans led him to express the opinion that some of our behaviors depended "less on sociocultural factors than had previously been thought" and to wonder if there might not be "specific biological bases for certain of our social habits" (1953:514).

Kluckhohn took issue with Kroeber's reduction of universals to noncultural status: however much they may reflect human biology, they

---

[10]Note that as much as he scorned the particularism of the Boasian school, and its notion of the arbitrariness of culture, White maintained a consistently ultraorthodox denial of any psychobiological influences on culture.

are still "socially transmitted" (without using the term, he apparently was expressing what is now called an interactionist position). And universals provide fixed points for cross-cultural comparisons that "are not ethno-centric." He retained the point of view that universals are of classifica-tion, not content: "likenesses, not identities" (quoting A. V. Kidder).

Murdock's and Kluckhohn's works have clearly ranked among the most influential statements on universals from the time they were writ-ten until now. They contain much, perhaps most, of the reasoning be-hind the study of universals that is generally familiar to anthropologists.

The following decade or so did not show a continuing rise in the number of general and explicit discussions of universals in mainstream anthropology, and in much of anthropology there was a significant re-treat. In addition to the ambivalence that many anthropologists still felt toward universals, there were two other possible reasons why the im-mediate post-war enthusiasm for them slackened. Insofar as interest in them was stimulated by the desire to have some fixed basis for dealing with the major crisis of the late thirties and forties—the rise of Nazism—it might follow that when this crisis faded so did interest in universals. Indeed, the subsequent major world crisis—the threat of World War III—led many academics to call for a renewed espousal of tolerance and the cultural relativism that supports it. Second, insofar as anthropologists were willing to accept universals, it was not very clear how they were to be explained or, perhaps more importantly, how an interest in them could be turned into research programs. Psychology was still very much ori-ented toward behaviorism and so could offer little guidance. Few anthro-pologists had any sense of what was happening in evolutionary biology or whether it could be of help—in spite of the anthropological interest in cultural evolution.[11]

An important exception was A. Irving Hallowell, whose paper "Per-sonality, Culture, and Society in Behavioral Evolution" (1963) argued that universals necessarily raise questions about human psychology and the evolution of the human mind. He criticized anthropology for paying no more than lip service to a vague concept of the psychic unity of human-ity, and he criticized both anthropology and psychology for assuming that humanity is a product of evolution and yet failing to explore humanity's psychobiological nature in an evolutionary perspective. Hallowell argued that anthropologists tended to emphasize the unique aspects of humans, thereby sidestepping important evolutionary ques-

---

[11]It is possible that the cultural evolutionists felt it was particularly important that they not be confused with evolutionists in general and so overstated their antireductionism. Or, as seems clear in some cases, they may have been particularly influenced by the strong en-vironmentalist stance of orthodox Marxist thought.

tions, and he advocated a program of comparative psychology that would link human and animal studies.

Two years later the mainstream anthropological unease about universals found expression when Clifford Geertz (1965) took a critical look at the concept of cultural universals, particularly at the idea that only universals are of primary importance in defining human nature. He argues that this is a prejudice that was carried over from the Enlightenment and given a concrete research strategy by anthropology in the middle decades of this century. In accordance with the social scientific conceptions of the time—i.e., that the biological, the psychological, the social, and the cultural are all distinct and autonomous levels of analysis—the research strategy consisted of finding cultural universals and then associating them in an intuitive manner with constancies from the biological, psychological, or social levels.

Geertz finds a number of problems with this strategy. Like Kroeber before him, Geertz sees no constant content to such universals as religion, marriage, or property, and so he finds them "fake" (1965:101). Furthermore, the alleged linkages of cultural universals with their subcultural underpinnings are, he says, either vague or improbable. Consequently, Geertz sees no good reason to seek the definition of human nature in cultural universals. On the contrary, he sees good reason to seek the essence of humanity in its variousness. To incorporate this variousness in the concept of human nature, he argues for a new research strategy that accommodates itself to a new framework for understanding humanity that had only become clear a decade or so before he wrote.

The key ingredient in this new framework involves replacing the conception of autonomous levels of analysis with one that allows theoretical analysis in terms of interaction between biology, psychology, social organization, and culture. This interactionist framework is required because we now have every reason to think not that our bodies evolved first, then our brains, and then our societies and cultures—a sequence implied by the autonomous-levels-of-analysis framework—but that they all coevolved. As a consequence of this coevolution, humans are dependent on culture—our brain and body presume culture. No humans exist without culture, and in all cases, Geertz notes, they have particular cultures, not generic culture. Humans have evolved such dependence on cultural "control mechanisms—plans, recipes, rules, instructions"—that humans are now "incomplete" without them (1965:107, 109).

Thus, at the same time that our nervous system evolved ever greater complexity, we also abandoned "the regularity and precision of detailed genetic control over our conduct for the flexibility and adaptability of a more generalized, though of course no less real, genetic control over it" (Geertz 1965:112). Our nervous system itself, according to Geertz, is now

a product of culture. Without the particularities of culture, human behavior would be "a mere chaos of pointless acts and exploding emotions"
and our experience would be "virtually shapeless" (1965:108).

Surely Geertz is correct in pointing to the difficulty of drawing a
boundary between the innate and the cultural and in noting that most
complex behaviors must be some sort of "vector outcome" of the two
(1965:113). Geertz is likewise correct in his assertions that we need to chart
human variability if we seek a true understanding of human nature, that
science finds its generalities in particulars, and that a true science of humanity may well find the "generically human" in such "cultural particularities" as Himalayan polyandry (1965:105). As Symons (1979:225–226)
argues, for example, the very rarity of polyandry and the conditions that
bring it about are telling evidence for innate panhuman sex differences.
But to imply that only the variables reveal the generically human is surely
wrong, and the assertion that humans "are, above all other things, various" (Geertz 1965:115) is at best a judgment call with numerous arguments against it.

Geertz probably overstates the importance of culture in other ways,
too: to say that humans are dependent upon *some* aspects of culture—
tools notably (Mann 1972)—is quite different from saying that humans
are dependent in general on "the guidance provided by systems of significant symbols" (1965:112). It also remains to be seen that all emotions,
say, are as chaotic as Geertz says—even though they may always be given
a culturally variable gloss.

In addition to Hallowell's paper, described above, there were a few
other exceptions—some only implicit or unintended—to the lessened anthropological interest in universals that could be seen in the late 1950s
and early 1960s. One was the universalism (of one kind or another) that
is implicit in the search for valid cross-cultural generalizations of almost
any sort (see chapter 2). These were the subject of much anthropological
research and writing from the fifties into the seventies, and I suggest that
the paucity of explicit discussion of the universals that such studies implied was yet a further indication of the ambivalence anthropologists feel
toward universals.

Another exception was the development of "componential analysis" (see, e.g., Goodenough 1956). Also called "ethnosemantics," and included under the rubric of "ethnoscience," componential analysis is an
ethnographic method in which a given lexical domain—say the set of
words for plants, or kin, or colors—is isolated so that by inquiry and observation the anthropologist may determine what underlying semantic
"components" give the domain its form. For example, in the domain of
address terms in English, comprising "Mister," "Mrs.," "Miss," and "Ms.,"
there are two semantic components: sex (male and female) and marital

status (married, unmarried, and undesignated). "Mister" is defined as "address term male," "Mrs." as "address term female married," etc. In a similar domain among Brunei Malays, by contrast, a component of rank is not only present but ubiquitous: it has four gradations that must be kept in mind to use Brunei address terms (Brown 1976:163–164). The presence or absence of a rank component distinguishes English from Malay address terms, but the common presence of sex and marital status links them. By analogy with the linguistic ideas from which this mode of analysis was derived, the raw facts that are the native's own terms are emic, while the facts derived beneath the surface, and expressed in cross-culturally valid terms, are etic (see the discussion of emic and etic in chapter 2).

The only thing explicitly universalistic about componential analysis was that it was presumed to be universally applicable; it was a universal model. What is particularly noteworthy in the method is its success in remaining faithful to emic fact—starting as it does with the very words by which another people captures its own modes of organizing thought—while routinely penetrating beneath the surface facts to the underlying semantic elements that structure cognition. In its harmonization of these two goals, componential analysis was a remarkable breakthrough in method. As time went by, this method produced evidence that beneath the bewildering variety of words by which peoples classify the world about them there were some important universal conceptions in the underlying semantic components (Bloch 1977; discussed further below and in the next chapter).

Walter Goldschmidt's *Comparative Functionalism: An Essay in Anthropological Theory* (1966) contained an explicit consideration of universals. Goldschmidt presented a universal model for the analysis of society that was apparently inspired by Malinowski's model (1960 [1944]). Goldschmidt argued that underlying the diversity of human institutions is a universal set of problems or functions that must be solved or discharged in all societies. Consequently, these functions provide a common framework for the analysis of all societies. In the course of his essay Goldschmidt drew attention to the profound influence that anthropological relativism had exerted on the moral philosophy of the modern world, and he criticized extreme forms of cultural relativism and anthropology's overemphasis on exceptional cases. He also defended reductionist explanations against the superorganicists.

But if an interest in universals had slipped somewhat in anthropology for a while, great strides in their study continued to be made in linguistics. The relationship between linguistics and cultural anthropology has been long, intimate, and productive, particularly in the United States (Hymes 1970). Language is often thought of as the epitome of culture, and forms of analysis employed in one field often apply to the other as well. Linguistic phenomena are cited for some of the clearest statements of relativity, the classification of color being a notable instance. It is a commonplace assumption, for example, that speech sounds have only an arbitrary connection with what they signify.[12] Thus there is, according to this assumption, no intrinsic connection between the sounds we make in the word "horse" and the creature it stands for. The German word *Pferd* is just as arbitrary and just as fitting as a way to signify the same creature. This apparent or actual arbitrariness has often been extended to other aspects of language and elevated to a general principle.

But although linguists had no particular reason to be looking for universals—indeed they had many reasons to expect relativity—they found them. There are two important reasons for this. One is the objectivity of their methods, whose scientific power was demonstrated already in the nineteenth century, particularly in the study of sound shifts (as formulated, for example in Grimm's laws of sound shifts in Indo-European languages),[13] which is crucial in the reconstruction of the relationships between languages. The other was the relative simplicity of the materials they treat: linguists delimit the scope of their research more than cultural anthropologists do, and in many if not most contexts pursue a strictly formal mode of analysis that ignores causation.

A pioneering but very brief essay on linguistic universals by the Aginskys (1948) was closely linked to the anthropological revival of interest in universals in the United States that began just before World War II. But the most important works appeared in the late 1950s or 1960s. The linguist Noam Chomsky's influential review of B. F. Skinner's *Verbal Behavior* was published in 1959. This review had three notable consequences. First, it was a devastating criticism of behaviorism, along with all that behaviorism stood for in the nature-nurture controversy. Second, it posited "deeper processes" of language acquisition that were innate and therefore presumably universal. This led to a search for grammatical universals (the "deep structure" of language) that remains a preoccupation in linguistics to the present. Third, by referring to work then in progress by Eric H. Lenneberg (see, e.g., 1967), Chomsky drew attention to the biological foundations of language. Chomsky was soon to write of the "speech organ," in order to draw attention to the profound sense in which language is not learned: in a natural environment of other speakers, an individual acquires language as naturally as pubic hair. Referring to the studies of ethologists, Chomsky likened speech to those instinctive behaviors

---

[12]This arbitrariness, which is one of the hallmarks of cultural relativism (Shweder and Bourne 1984:164), is greatly exaggerated (Kluckhohn 1953:897; Friedrich 1975). See the discussion of marking below and, especially, the explanation for it in the next chapter.

[13]E.g., the initial *p*- of Latin words regularly shifts to *f*- in English, as in *ped* and "foot" or *pisces* and "fish."

in lower animals that are acquired by "imprinting" during sharply delimited periods of an organism's development.[14]

Joseph Greenberg's *Language Universals*, first published in 1966, was detailed in its listing of universals and signaled a broader search for linguistic universals that also remains strong to the present. In this work Greenberg gives particular attention to the phenomenon of "marked" versus "unmarked" categories, a phenomenon found in all languages at the three major levels of linguistic analysis: phonemic, grammatical, and semantic. Marking, a universal process, generally produces implicational universals; occasionally it results in unrestricted universals. Since linguistic universals are not generally familiar, even to most anthropologists, examples will be given.

The phenomenon of marking is easily illustrated. In English *he* is unmarked, *she* marked. We use the former as a default term when sex is left ambiguous or unknown (at least we did until the recent introduction of unisex forms like "s/he"). Similarly, *author* is unmarked, *authoress* marked; *nurse* is unmarked, *male nurse* marked. Marking in these instances refers to the addition of *s-*, *-ess*, and *male* to mark one term of each pair and hence distinguish it from the other. The unmarked term is sometimes said to have "zero expression," meaning that nothing is added to it. Note that the overt marking seen in these examples is not always present. Marking is normally accompanied by a number of other characteristics (Greenberg 1987; Schwartz 1980); if enough of the other characteristics are present, even though overt marking is not, linguistic elements may still be designated as a marked and unmarked pair.

An example of marked versus unmarked phonemes is found in the German word-final *-d/-t*. Whichever phoneme occurs at the end of a word, it is pronounced as though it were *-t*. Thus *Tod* (death) is pronounced "tot." So, too, with the other final consonants in German that form a contrast set of voiced versus unvoiced. In these cases the voiced consonant is the marked phoneme, the unvoiced the unmarked. The unmarked can take the place of the marked, but not vice versa. In the event of the two phonemes ultimately merging into a single one—which is one of the major evolutionary processes of language drift—they will normally merge into the unmarked form, so that no phoneme retains as one of its necessary and distinctive features a feature that does not contrast with the absence of that feature (for example, no initial consonants must be voiced if there are not unvoiced initial consonants).

An example of the marked versus the unmarked at the level of gram-

---

[14]Ethological studies of "instinctive" behaviors had begun well before World War II, particularly in Europe, but it was not until much later that the results of these studies could make headway against behaviorism in the United States. Ethology is discussed further below and in chapter 4.

mar is provided by the contrast between singular and plural. In all languages where one is marked, as occurs in English generally with the addition of -s, it is always the plural. A further example is that the negative of a sentence is always marked, the positive usually having zero expression. For example, conceivably a sentence of the form "it goes" could be understood to mean "it goes [not]," and one would have to add something, for example, "it does go," to make it positive—just as, in theory, words could be plural unless one added something to make them singular. In spite of the equally sound logic of these two possibilities, neither occurs in any language. A partial exception that Greenberg cites is that in Vietnamese there is a form to indicate the positive, but it is not compulsory.

Straddling the boundary between grammatical and semantic universals are regularities in the expression of "good" and "bad." In all languages that have a word for "good," its opposite may be expressed in two ways: some languages contrast it with a word for "bad," some with "not good," (and some with both). No language has the words "bad" and "not bad" with no word "good," although "bad" and "not bad" are the logical equivalents of "good" and "not good" or "good" and "bad." Thus "good" is universally unmarked; it is never the marked term of a contrast set.

A similar set of contrasts involves terms such as "long" and "short," "wide" and "narrow," "deep" and "shallow," "many" and "few." In some languages "shallow" is "not deep," but no language has only "shallow" and "not shallow"; the same holds for all the other contrasting terms just mentioned. The former, unmarked term in each of these sets is the "neutral" form, the one that can stand for the other. Thus in English we normally ask "how deep," "how many," etc., not "how shallow," "how few," etc. So, too, in other languages, though nothing logically precludes their speakers from doing just the opposite.

Of particular interest to anthropologists is Greenberg's suggestion that the common tendency for peoples to call themselves by the word for "people" is not necessarily ethnocentrism—i.e., is not a claim that only they are really people (which is the standard anthropological interpretation of this usage)—but rather is just another kind of marking. Thus the people called the Maidu Indians call themselves *majdy*, which is their word for "people." But they call blacks *pibutim majdy*, whites *wolem majdy*, etc. Thus *majdy* is an unmarked term which serves at different levels in the hierarchy of labels for peoples of all sorts.

Of even more interest to anthropologists are the semantic universals in kinship terminology (some of his discussion of this topic is updated in Greenberg 1979). Greenberg points out that all languages use different terms for "father" and "mother." Each might be merged with other kin (e.g., fathers with uncles, mothers with aunts), but in no language is it obligatory to refer to one's parents with terms that merge them.

All kinship terminologies employ at least two specific semantic components in distinguishing kin: generation and sex.

In English, lineal kin terms are unmarked in contrast with the marked collateral kin terms; consanguineal kin terms are unmarked in contrast with affinal kin terms, which are marked. This appears to be a universal pattern, in that wherever these two contrasts are found the lineals in the one case and the consanguineals in the other are unmarked. Greenberg notes that a great many further universals can be found in kin terminologies.

The significance of marking lies primarily in what correlates with it and thereby suggests the underlying factors producing it. This will be discussed in the next chapter.

Anthropologists with linguistic interests, or who employed linguistic methods, were particularly sensitive to these developments in linguistics, and from their initial relativistic stances were led to universalistic conclusions. The findings of componential analysis, which were already mentioned, were specially relevant. We have also already examined one of the most famous cases of linguistics-inspired research: Berlin and Kay's (1969) discovery that basic color terms develop in a universal sequence.

One of the most important general discussions of universals after Kluckhohn's was Ward Goodenough's (1970) on the role that universals play in anthropological description and comparison. As previously noted, Goodenough was one of the founders of componential analysis, and his thought is clearly indebted to linguistic models. Goodenough's position is that there are (at least) two basic elements in anthropological description and comparison: the rights and duties of individuals or persons, and the "problems with which all societies have to deal" (1970:38). His discussion also draws attention to the anthropological usefulness of universally valid definitions.

Goodenough argues, for example, that a cross-culturally valid and universally applicable definition of marriage can be formulated (the matter was hotly debated in the fifties and sixties and simmers still; see, e.g., di Leonardo 1979; Sperber 1986). Such definitions are useful because they allow the greatest possible scope for comparison and generalization without precluding narrower analyses for particular purposes. But his definition of marriage is more than merely useful: it borders on explanation. The definition focuses on the regulation of sexual access to women eligible to bear children, and he argues that this regulation is a response to universals of human nature, including male dominance and male competitiveness for access to females (1970:11, 38).

Goodenough links the search for cross-culturally valid (etic) concepts to universals and to what he sees as the grand aim of anthropology: once we have ascertained all the etic concepts that are required to make sense of "the elementary emic units of any culture," we may then abstract from those etic concepts an empirically determined list of the "universal attributes of culture and, by inference from them, the universal attributes of men as creators and users of cultures" (1970:129-30). This for Goodenough is the foremost aim of scientific anthropology.

A year after the publication of Goodenough's book, an extensive exploration of the link between universals and human biology appeared in Lionel Tiger and Robin Fox's *The Imperial Animal* (1971), to which an important precursor had been Tiger's *Men in Groups* (1969). The latter argued that the need of males to bond with each other is a human universal that is rooted in a human biology shaped by an adaptation to hunting.

Identifying an inadequate understanding of human nature as the "most serious failing of social science" (1971:2), Tiger and Fox drew inspiration from evolutionary theory, studies of animal behavior (ethology), the fossil record, and anthropological studies to construct a human "biogrammar," consisting of "those elements of human behavior that are the lexicon of social action" (1971:7). Universals were important to their argument both to construct the biogrammar and as evidence of its existence. Tiger and Fox argued that if an experimental Adam and Eve could somehow be raised apart from human culture their descendants within a few generations would have societies and cultures that replicated the universal pattern—because the pattern is in our nature.

Both in their joint work (Tiger and Fox 1971) and in a series of his own publications, Fox (e.g., 1967, 1971, 1980, 1989) also argued that the important universals are not at the "substantive" level, where anthropologists usually seek them, but at the level of "process." Processes may be universal even though their results are highly variable. The universal process of reproduction, for example, may or may not give rise to "families" as we understand this term.

All published in the space of three years, the books of Berlin and Kay (1969), Goodenough (1970), and Tiger and Fox (1971) marked a resurgent interest in universals that persists without break to the present. But while universals most certainly were not ignored in the 1970s and 1980s, neither did they inform the bulk of anthropological writings in those years. Although no one has taken a head count, I suspect that most anthropologists—still under the influence of the suppositions that animate Mead's essay on Samoa—have been, and still are, wary of the very concept of universals.[15]

[15]This in spite of the fact that Mead herself had withdrawn from the ranks of the arch relativists. In the 1972 introduction to her *Male and Female*, she states a willingness to "lay more emphasis on man's specific biological inheritance" because recent years had seen a "vivid interaction between cultural theory and observations and experiments on other living creatures, primates, ungulates, and birds," that yielded "new insights into biologically given behavior and possible types of more specifically instinctive behavior in man."

In a lengthy discussion of the issues that universals raise, Ronald P. Rohner (1975) drew attention to this wariness on the part of social scientists in general. For many of them, he says, the issues are "slightly 'indecent'" (1975:165). Rohner surveys the developments, particularly in ethology and linguistics, that were leading some anthropologists and others to look for universals, rethink the problem of human nature, and question extreme forms of relativism. Rohner spells out a "universalist approach" (1975:1–38), which combines psychological research with the community studies and cross-cultural surveys of anthropology, and he applies this approach to the specific problem of determining uniformities in how children everywhere respond to parental acceptance and rejection.

Another important discussion of universals appeared in Maurice Bloch's (1977) Malinowski lecture, which assessed the relevance of developments in ethnosemantics. In brief, Bloch argues that universals—such as the cognition of time—are produced in practical interactions with nature, while such social factors as "instituted hierarchy" are the source of the culturally peculiar. For various reasons, he adds, anthropologists have tended to emphasize the culturally relative rather than universals. Since his lecture is primarily concerned with the explanation of universals, it will be discussed at greater length in the next chapter.

A potent factor in the currently revived interest in universals results from recent thinking in various branches of the biological sciences, notably in evolutionary theory and the study of the brain. Theoretical refinements with respect to kin selection, reciprocal altruism, and sexual selection are particularly important. These refinements stem from a small number of seminal articles, including W. D. Hamilton's "The Genetical Evolution of Social Behavior" (1964), J. Maynard Smith's "Group Selection and Kin Selection" (1964), and R. L. Trivers's "The Evolution of Reciprocal Altruism" (1971) and "Parental Investment and Sexual Selection" (1972). E. O. Wilson's *Sociobiology* (1975) gave these ideas a wide audience and suggested—very controversially—their relevance to understanding human affairs. Wilson followed up this suggestion himself with his book *On Human Nature* (1978), in which he quotes Murdock's (1945) list of universals as part of his evidence. A related development has been the deepening conviction that the locus of evolutionary processes is not the group or species but either the individual or the gene (Williams 1966; Maynard Smith 1976).

Kin selection refers to behaviors that are directed toward individuals bearing copies of one's own genes by proximate common descent, behaviors that are interpersonally altruistic yet potentially result in no reduction of one's genetic representation in the next generation. The idea that altruism makes evolutionary sense when directed toward genetic relatives (whether offspring or others), and hence is highly likely to evolve, rang bells in the minds of some anthropologists: at one stroke it offered insight into the universality of kinship and of nepotism (favoring kin over strangers, close kin over distant kin).

By offering to explain reciprocity, an exceedingly important element in anthropological thought (Gouldner 1960), the concept of reciprocal altruism also rang bells in anthropological minds. So too did sexual selection, since it seemed to bring order to numerous uniform differences between the sexes. These refinements of evolutionary biology are primarily relevant because they offer explanations for universals and so will be discussed in more detail in the next chapter.

Very much linked to these new formulations in evolutionary biology is ethology—the field study of animal behavior. Ethology offers insights into universals, in part by making careful observations among numerous animal species of behaviors that appear to have analogues among humans, in part by developing explanations and methods that students of human behavior can put to use (e.g., Tiger and Fox 1971; Eibl-Eibesfeldt 1989). Ethology has even documented the elusive universals of content. Eibl-Eibesfeldt (1979:20) presents, for example, photos (from a film strip) of a coyness display by a Himba girl. Any anthropologist looking at this sequence of photos is forcibly struck by its identity with the same kinds of display among any people he has observed. We know that much of what we do with our faces is culturally patterned, and until recently many anthropologists would have said that we do not have any good reason to think that it isn't all cultural (see the discussion of the facial display of emotion in chapter 1). But the coyness display is complex, fixed, and, for whatever reason, apparently innate. Eibl-Eibesfeldt's (1979) reports of normal smiling, laughing, and·crying among thalidomide children born without sight, hearing, and normal limbs with which to feel other faces, provide further evidence for universals of content.

Another result of the influence of recent trends in biology on the social sciences has been the development of evolutionary psychology, which attempts to understand the human psyche in evolutionary terms, and which in many ways is an alternative and rival to attempts to understand human behavior in evolutionary terms (Barkow 1973; Cosmides and Tooby 1987; Daly and Wilson 1988; Ghiselin 1973; Symons 1987a, 1989, n.d.; Tooby 1985; Tooby and Cosmides 1989c and 1989d).[16] A strongly rel-

[16]Many of what are called "sociobiological" studies by anthropologists involve a leap from quite general processes—such as maximizing reproductive success—to quite specific behaviors—such as female infanticide among particular peoples. However, natural selection does not select directly for behaviors; it selects for the psychological processes that (in conjunction with the environment) underlie behavior. Evolutionary psychology attempts to discover the innate psychological processes that constitute (or are key ingredients in) human nature, that were shaped by evolution, and that may—in our present environment—result in behavior that makes no sense at all in terms of maximizing reproductive success (Cosmides and Tooby 1987; Symons 1989, n.d.; Tooby and Cosmides 1989c).

ativistic anthropology, underpinned by behavioristic psychology, assumed that the human mind was virtually a tabula rasa: it had little wiring, and that of a very general sort. But behaviorism, or extreme versions of it, has been shown to have severe limitations. Particularly telling were the experimental findings of John Garcia and others (see especially Garcia and Koelling 1966; see also Breland and Breland 1961; and, for an anthropological perspective and summary, Konner 1982a:25–28). Garcia and Koelling (1966) found that it was easy to get rats to associate tastes with (x–ray induced) nausea and to associate lights or sound with shocks, but it was difficult to get them to associate tastes with shocks or lights and sounds with nausea. Some things were easier to "learn" than others, and this could only reflect a structuring of the brain that existed before conditioning. The brain, therefore, was not so blank as behaviorism assumed.

It seems entirely reasonable to assume that the specific structuring of the rat's brain that these experiments uncovered is a product of evolution: mechanisms that associate things eaten with nausea, for example, would have great survival value, would be strongly selected, and would result in organisms that make that association quickly. Reasonable as this seems, the difficulties Garcia and his colleagues faced in publishing and winning acceptance of their research findings are now legendary. The seminal paper described above (Garcia and Koelling 1966) was turned down by the "blue ribbon" journals of experimental psychology (Seligman and Hager 1972:8), and the findings of a later paper were dismissed as "no more likely than birdshit in a cuckoo clock" (quoted in Seligman and Hager 1972:15). These reactions are understandable: the experiments of Garcia and his collaborators undermined the whole notion that associational learning, a generalized learning process, provides a satisfactory explanation for how behavior is acquired. That notion was firmly entrenched in psychology—and elsewhere in the social sciences.

One of the key shifts in thought that has been stimulated both by ethology and by studies such as Garcia's is summarized in the distinction between "learning" and "acquisition." Because "learning" often connotes "learning theory," behavioristic associationism, and social or cultural conditioning—all of which presume only very general mental mechanisms—the more neutral term, "acquisition," has come into use to refer to actions or behaviors that develop in a manner suggesting some sort of specific genetic programming for them. Thus Chomsky says we "acquire" language, and he is critical of the notion that it is, in the frequently employed senses of the term, learned (see, e.g., 1959:57).

But learning is a word that cannot easily be discarded. Thus Gould and Marler (1987) coin the phrase "learning by instinct" to describe behaviors that are phylogenetic adaptations and yet require some practice or imprinting experience in order to develop normally. They give bird songs in certain species, and human speech, as examples. Developed more within the tradition of learning theory is the idea of "preparedness" (Seligman 1971; Seligman and Hager 1972; see also Lenneberg's [1967:373, 375] "readiness" and "resonance" in reference to age-delimited preparedness). Preparedness refers to the extent to which an organism or species is genetically prepared to learn something. If highly prepared, "one-trial" learning may suffice: humans sometimes learn to detest a food from a single experience in which it induced, or seemed to induce, illness (Seligman and Hager 1972:8). Some human phobias may result from prepared learning. All these ideas represent a substantial departure from the tabula rasa view of the mind, which holds that there is only general wiring in the brain.

Current thought—forcefully supported by data on the highly specific cognitive, emotional, or behavioral deficits that result from brain lesions in specific locations (Gardner 1974; Sacks 1985)—thus has it that the mind is wired in great detail. With respect to vision, consider the following (from Sekular and Blake 1990): At the level of brain cells, those in the visual cortex specialize in the angle of edges, the speed of motion, and the direction of motion registered in their field of vision. Others specialize in the color they detect or in the degree to which they are ocular dominant or binocular. At a higher level of organization, brain regions may be so specialized that their neurons respond, for example, only to the human face when viewed from a particular angle.

This restoration of the localizing or faculty theory of the brain, which had been swept aside by behaviorism, is further buttressed by lessons from the attempts to develop artificial intelligence and by evolutionary theory. Creating artificial intelligence has been much more complicated than was first thought, and constructing systems that duplicate the performance of even relatively simple mental tasks requires considerable preprogramming that is specific to the task and that is analogous to "innate knowledge" (Tooby 1985). In other words, the model of the human mind as comprising general-purpose "intelligence" finds no support in artificial intelligence.

The relevant theoretical consideration is that in the course of its evolution the human species did not encounter general problems, it encountered specific problems, such as recognizing faces and detecting cheaters in social exchanges (Tooby 1985; Cosmides and Tooby 1989). We should no more expect a general-purpose mental organ to evolve than we should expect general-purpose anatomical or physiological organs (Cosmides and Tooby 1987; Symons n.d.; see also Fodor 1983). Whatever the details of brain specialization may be—producing fixed responses such as the coyness display and the smile, or producing no more than aims ("look after close kin") and inclinations ("be wary around snakes") and hence resulting in numerous particular actions—anthropology has very special roles to play in their study.

First, these mental mechanisms—with very few possible exceptions—must be panhuman and must have evolved in the long period in which humans were hunters and gatherers (Cosmides and Tooby 1987; Symons n.d.; Tooby and DeVore 1987). Since anthropologists are specialists in the study of hunters and gatherers, past and present, and in the evolution of humans, there are no scholars better equipped to identify and understand the environmental conditions in which panhuman mental mechanisms evolved.

Second, anthropological documentation of universality is in itself an important part of the study of the mind. Thus indirect research into the wiring of the human brain—by showing for example that taxonomy is fundamental to cognition (Frake 1963), that male and female temperaments differ in cross-culturally consistent ways (Daly and Wilson 1982 [1978]; Symons 1979), or that the sense of time is universal (Bloch 1977)—is very much a part of the current scene in anthropology. As species-typical phenomena, human universals are specially privileged considerations in developing a cross-culturally valid conception of human nature.

If the foregoing accurately grasps the outlines of the history of the anthropological study of universals, the key elements are as follows. First, universals were long taken to be facts and were thought to rest in large measure on panhuman features of the human psyche. Accordingly, when the dichotomy of nature versus culture became entrenched, universals were largely assigned to nature. As the anthropological pendulum swung to an ever stronger emphasis on culture, universals received less attention from anthropologists. The pendulum moved away from a strong culturological position in the years adjacent to World War II and again in the last decade or so.

What distinguishes the present move toward a more neutral position of the pendulum is at least partly a growing awareness that human affairs have to be understood as an interaction between human nature and human culture. Mere awareness cannot be the whole story, however, because prominent anthropologists from Boas and Kroeber to Mead and Geertz have repeatedly (but ineffectually) reminded themselves and their colleagues that in spite of their emphasis on culture a full understanding of human behavior will necessarily be interactionist.[17] Thus what

[17]The reluctance of anthropologists and other social scientists to embrace the biological in human affairs may have folk cultural roots. Both Bidney (1947) and Kroeber (1949) trace the nature-culture dichotomy at least in part to the dichotomy of flesh and spirit. The ancient and profound exultation of the latter and denigration of the former shapes Western thought to our day.

is perhaps most important at present is the stimulating climate in biology and psychology. In the years adjacent to World War II, when anthropologists sought to give some sort of theoretical explanation for why universals were significant, or even existed at all, there was little to be inspired by in those fields. But the new and rapidly progressing understanding of the human mind and its evolution now offer real insight into human nature. Since the concept of the psychic unity of humanity is pivotal in anthropological thought, a sustained effort to discover its content—Kroeber's "X"—is long overdue and now feasible.

In the final chapter I will look in more detail at those culturological ideas that seized the high ground in anthropology early in this century. Those ideas need considerable modification, and the existence of universals is a large part of what necessitates those modifications.

4

Explaining Universals

Unlike most anthropologists, the late Joseph Shepher (1983) said it was particularly the universal that interested him. I find that some students, and others, agree—for various reasons. One reason is a curious reversal of the reason that the astonishingly relative is interesting: once one has absorbed the lesson of cultural relativity, what was initially astonishing becomes mundane or fully expectable. It poses no great problem for explanation. Indeed, any outrageously different custom or belief can get the same explanation: it's because of their culture. But when the kaleidoscope of world cultures becomes normal, then the fixed points, the universals, stand out as curiosities. And the explanation that it is because of their culture becomes meaningless. A new question emerges: given the inherent tendency for disparate peoples to develop disparate cultures, how on earth can some things be the same everywhere?

This chapter presents a number of ways in which universals have been or could be explained. These kinds, ways, or strategies of explanation are neither all of equal importance nor all mutually exclusive. On the contrary, they are often complementary and must be used in combination in order to explain any particular universal.

One of the points that emerges from an analysis of explanation is that a great many universals do require explanation, at least in part, in biological terms. Many seem to require explanation in "interactionist" frameworks—i.e., in terms of a combination of biological and cultural factors. If we want to understand universals in the context of particular societies, the necessity of an interactionist framework is all the greater. "Interaction" is a vague word (Scarr and McCartney 1983), as are "cultural" and "biological," and it is clear that anthropology does not yet have suitable concepts for combining (or replacing) the biological and cultural frameworks of analysis, which for too long have been kept separate.

The various modes of explaining universals will be presented and illustrated under the following headings: (1) explaining a universal with a universal; (2) cultural reflection or recognition of biological fact; (3) logical extension from (usually biological) givens; (4) diffusionist explanations that rest upon the great age of the trait and, usually, its great utility; (5) archoses; (6) conservation of energy; (7) the nature of the human organism, with emphasis on the brain; (8) evolutionary theory; (9) interspecific comparison; (10) ontogeny; and (11) partial explanations. There is no particular order to this list, and cross-references between them will be frequent. I will illustrate the explanatory modes with discussions of particular universals.

EXPLAINING A UNIVERSAL WITH A UNIVERSAL

The method of concomitant variation is a quintessential anthropological method. By this method two traits that are thought to be linked to each other are examined cross-culturally to see if they covary. For example, one could test hypotheses that link matrilineal descent with unstable marriages by seeing if high rates of divorce are nonrandomly associated with societies that have matrilineal descent. Even though covariation does not demonstrate any particular causal connection, a study that shows distinct traits systematically covarying with each other carries considerable weight because it suggests that some sort of causation is at work. The closer the correlation, the weightier the suggestion. In a discipline riven by fundamental disagreements over what causes what (e.g., whether matrilineal descent generates high rates of divorce, or whether the latter leads to the former), covariation comes close to being a common currency of discourse.

But universals pose a real problem for the use of the method of concomitant variation: every universal is equally a correlate of every other, so the degree of correlation between any of them ceases to be a criterion for judging arguments that posit connections between them. Consequently, the actual causal argument is particularly critical in attempts to explain a universal with a universal. Right-handedness and male dominance will provide illustrations of this first form of explanation.

All peoples are predominantly right-handed, and among almost all peoples the right hand is symbolic of good, the left is not. Because modern students of hand symbolism speak of "near-universality," I presume that in some societies there is no cultural elaboration of handedness: their members are mostly right-handed but do not associate right (or left) with positive values. The positive evaluation of the right is thus a near-universal and an implicational universal: where symbolic value is attached to the hands as a societywide norm, the right hand is always positively evaluated.[1]

There has long been evidence that handedness is linked to cerebral specialization: we are predominantly "left-brained" (control of our left and right limbs are lodged in opposite sides of the brain). Consequently, explanations of these three interconnected phenomena—handedness, brain asymmetry, and symbolic preference for the right—have often been given in terms of each other, with the direction of the causal chain being the main bone of contention. If we are predominantly right-handed because we are left-brained, then presumably the causal chain traces back to our genes; but if we are predominantly left-brained because we are right-handed, then the causal chain might go back to the symbolic preference for the right—it is the latter possibility that most concerns us here.

The classic anthropological work is Robert Hertz's "The Pre-Eminence of the Right Hand: A Study in Religious Polarity" (1960 [1909]). Hertz thought that brain asymmetry had a genetic basis and at least partially determined handedness, but he thought that brain asymmetry was too weak a determinant to result in the universal or near-universal cultural evaluation of handedness. He thought, on the contrary, that the socially determined emphasis on the right hand might be responsible for the degree of dominance of the left cerebral hemisphere (because the socially determined preference for the right hand gave the left brain more exercise).[2]

The main ingredient in Hertz's explanation was yet another universal: dualistic thought (good/evil, light/dark, high/low, right/left, etc.). Given the human propensity to think dualistically and to attach moral, religious, or ritual significance to dualisms, it was possible that the slight propensity for the hands to differ in skill and strength was magnified socially into yet another profound dualism. Why human thought is fundamentally dualistic and why the human body should so universally be caught up in dualistic thinking were large questions yet to be answered. Whatever the answer, it lay in the "collective conscious," and Hertz thought it likely that we were on the threshold of organizing societies within which we would arrive at a more "harmonious development of the organism" because we would not rank the hands (and cerebral hemispheres).

In some ways Hertz's prophecy was correct: right-handedness is less enforced in modern Western societies, and children are now taught in school to exercise their right brains. But the notion that handedness is

---

[1]Among at least one people a ritual official stands in contrast to the societywide norm; it is his left hand that is preeminent (Needham 1973).

[2]With reference to the cerebral hemispheres, "dominance" is somewhat misleading. The two halves are specialized and complementary, so that while the left side may normally be dominant for speech the right side dominates in other functions.

fundamentally or even largely a cultural phenomenon has not fared well. Although there is no full consensus on any one genetic model for the transmission of handedness, and some sort of environmental influences appear to be involved in left-handedness, these influences appear to be prenatal (Annett 1985; Boklage 1984). In populations where children are pressured to use the right hand for writing, the proportion of right-handed writers can be increased, but the same population will show the normal proportions of left-handed individuals for other activities, such as throwing balls or striking matches. Most children who are left-handed were raised by parents both of whom are right-handed; couples in which both are left-handed will raise children who are mostly right-handed (Annett 1985; see also Levy 1976).

But the genetic factors that explain handedness do not explain why the hands serve symbolic functions. No student of brain asymmetry and its evolution advances the argument that we have a specific innate propensity to feel emotionally positive about the right, negative about the left. How to explain this positive evaluation of the right will be discussed further below.

An attempt to explain the universality of male dominance provides a more recent but quite similar attempt to explain one universal in terms of others. Having concluded that, in spite of diligent searches for contrary cases, women prove everywhere to be second-class citizens in the public-political domain, Sherry Ortner (1974; see also Bamberger 1974) offers an explanation of this in terms of a universal opposition between nature and culture, a universal devaluation of nature in comparison to culture, and a universal assumption that women are closer to nature than men are.[3] Because humans everywhere use culture to overcome nature, culture everywhere is superior. Because more of a woman's body and time are devoted to reproduction, she is seen as closer to nature. Because she is closer to nature, woman is culturally conceived as inferior to man.

The evidence that women everywhere are seen as closer to nature is not entirely compelling: in the United States today, men are often derogatorily described as "like animals," and a prominent element in con-

---

[3]The universality of male dominance has been challenged on two grounds. One is that dominance is not a global or unitary phenomenon, so that even in societies seemingly dominated by men there may still be spheres—say in domestic arrangements—in which women dominate (Quinn 1977). This is surely correct, but it does not preclude the possibility that in some sort of summation men always dominate in more spheres or more of the important spheres than women do. The second challenge is that in terms of cultural ideals some peoples may see men and women as just different, perhaps complementary, but not with men ranking above women. This does not, however, preclude an etic conclusion to the contrary. Neither of these objections eliminates the universal dominance of men in the public-political arena.

servative thought is that women civilize men (hence the importance of maintaining "family values," etc.). But whatever the empirical issues, the logic of Ortner's explanation is clear, and she explicitly states (1974:71) that she will try to explain one universal in terms of one or more other universals.

CULTURAL REFLECTION OR RECOGNITION OF PHYSICAL FACT

This aspect of explanation is present in both Hertz's (1960) and Ortner's (1974) explanations for universals but is deemphasized. In Hertz's argument, dualistic thought—which he saw as an essentially social phenomenon (a matter of the collective conscious)—magnifies a trivial biological tendency. Ortner's position is similar: the physically differing reproductive roles of male and female figure in Ortner's explanation, but the real emphasis is on the ideological dualism of nature-culture. This dualism is not clearly a biological given (at least it isn't for Ortner), nor is the higher evaluation of culture, nor is the association of men with culture and women with nature. So the biological facts are presented as only minor elements in a culturally complex phenomenon. After reviewing explanations for universals of knowledge and for the universality of kinship terminologies, I will say more about the recognition of biological facts in explaining handedness.

Maurice Bloch (1977) presents an explanation of universals in which the reflection of physical fact is a key element. He argues that human cognition comprises two distinct elements: knowledge and ideology. Knowledge results from interaction with nature (i.e., from practical activities such as production and reproduction). The function of knowledge is utilitarian. Ideology results from social structure—especially "institutionalized hierarchy." Bloch's notion of institutionalized hierarchy should probably be understood to mean hereditary hierarchy (all the examples he gives are hereditary). The function of ideology is to rationalize or justify instituted inequality, a task that does not require universal validity.

Knowledge, says Bloch, contains universally valid concepts, such as the durational conception of time that ethnosemanticists have found in language after language, and which is virtually essential to the conduct of practical affairs. Knowledge reflects the world as it is. Ideology by contrast is relative, tending to be minimal where instituted hierarchy is minimal, and to be rich where instituted hierarchy is great—as in Hindu, caste-organized India. Ideology does not need to reflect the world as it is, and often obscures its realities.

Bloch's views require some qualification. For example, knowledge

93

does not always flow automatically from practical activities. To the contrary, knowledge often accumulates gradually, with many false starts along the way. Similarly, instituted hierarchy is not the only source of ideology. But as an attempt to explain major parts of the broad contrast between the universal and universally valid on the one hand, and the culturally specific on the other, Bloch's argument is both sweeping and testable. My own research (1988) on the conditions that produce history (knowledge) as opposed to myth (ideology) among literate peoples provides strong support for Bloch's argument.

Knowledge is generally thought to be cultural (and it may be that Bloch sees it this way). But there are two ways in which considerations of human biology impinge on Bloch's argument. The specific universal that Bloch dwells on is durational time (as opposed to "non-durational" cyclic or static conceptions of time). Since humans, along with myriad other species, have built-in biological clocks of various sorts, it is not at all clear that the conception of time is ever fundamentally cultural—in spite of variations in the marking of time or of the cultural elaboration of time (Young 1988). Moreover, the "production" and "reproduction" of Bloch's larger framework are intrinsically linked to noncultural aspects of human life: it is only by reference to human biology—e.g., our dietary needs—that activities can be described as practical. Thus Bloch's argument essentially says that some universals reflect biological facts, even though these universals themselves are cultural.

The universality of kinship terminologies provides a further case of cultural reflection or recognition of physical fact. A kinship terminology is that linguistic domain (discrete set of terms) found among every people, in which domain most or all terms are translatable by the terms required for sexual reproduction, or combinations of them: father, mother, son, daughter (Gellner 1957; Schneider 1972). Among many peoples the combination terms are very complex, and extrakinship factors are reflected in the kinship terminologies, too. (Marriage—which is distinct from procreation per se—so regularly impinges on kinship terminologies that it is usually counted as one of the two fundamental building blocks of kinship. Accordingly, the father and mother of an individual are normally husband and wife.)

The reasons why the relationships involved in procreation are singled out for universal recognition will have to be pursued later. For the time being it is important to note that this sort of interaction in which the human construction of cultural categories overwhelmingly or unanimously recognizes, accepts, and builds upon certain brute features of nature must certainly be included among the means of explaining universals. It is a process well attested in statistical universals too (Brown and Witkowski 1981). Consequently, we must explain an astonishingly uniform and essentially cultural phenomenon—the labeling of kin—in terms of the cognizance of brute facts of human biology.

I suggest the following. Humans everywhere have innate abilities and propensities to see the world the way it is (in addition to Bloch [1977], Sperber [1985] expresses a similar idea). This is not, of course, to say that humans see anything and everything the way it is. Brute, ubiquitous (or universal), and important features of the world are especially likely to be incorporated in language and, moreover, to serve symbolic functions, or to serve as metaphors for, and measures of, other features of the world or of imagination. In this light, consider right-handedness again. From the time of our remote ancestors to the present, our dependence on tool making and tool using must again and again have presented to the human mind the remarkable difference between the skill and strength of the two hands, and the right handers have always greatly outvoted the lefties. What metaphor for all that is wondrous and good, then, is more at hand than the right hand itself? If I read Lakoff and Johnson's *Metaphors We Live By* (1980) correctly, this is not mere speculation: metaphors with similar bases are indeed the widespread ones. So the nearly universal cultural priority of the right, as well as the universality of kinship terminologies and aspects of knowledge such as the durational conception of time, are all in one form or another reflections of human biology in human culture. The universal classification of people by sex and age are further examples (Brown 1982).

LOGICAL EXTENSION FROM (USUALLY BIOLOGICAL) GIVENS

This is yet another variant of explaining a universal with a universal and is closely related to cultural reflection. It usually consists of arguing that any particular universal is more or less entailed by one or another of the gross and unquestioned characteristics of the species, i.e., that humans are large-brained, slow-maturing, sexually reproducing, group-living, terrestrial, omnivorous, and often quarrelsome mammals with moderate sexual dimorphism and no estrus. This kind of an explanation is thought to be self-evident, so the logic is not closely examined, the causal chain is not traced in detail, and the conclusions are not subjected to empirical test against alternatives. (To the extent that logic and causation are examined more closely, and are tested, different modes of explanation are involved.)

Malinowski's (1960 [1944]) framework for the analysis of culture, as described in chapter 3, is fundamentally of this type. His list of human "needs" and "derived needs" are the givens that account for cultural institutions to be found in any society.

DIFFUSIONIST EXPLANATIONS THAT REST UPON THE GREAT AGE OF THE UNIVERSAL AND, USUALLY, ITS GREAT UTILITY

The use of fire and cooking are universal, and both are of great antiquity and utility. Fire-making is about 40,000 to 100,000 years old, while evidence for the opportunistic use of fire goes back 1,500,000 years (Clark 1986). One or two peoples known to ethnography did not know how to make fire, but all peoples used it. Its advantages include temperature control, illumination, protection from animals, purification, and aid in shaping tools.

Cooking is the most important use of fire. Besides making some food taste better, it can make food easier to chew and digest, it kills bacteria in food, and is an important aid to food preservation. Cooking greatly expanded the range of substances humans could eat. Evidence of cooking is ancient and widespread.

It is presumably because of their great antiquity and utility that fire-making and cooking have spread to all human societies (or spread with humanity—*Homo sapiens sapiens*—to all its locations). In other words, the explanation for the universality of fire and cooking is at least in part a matter of invention (or discovery) and diffusion, which are cultural processes par excellence.

Although the fascination humans have for fire might conceivably reflect something extracultural, there is little reason to think of the use of fire or cooking as anything like instincts. Both lack direct counterparts outside the hominid line. The traits show no sign of spontaneous emergence in the individual at any particular time in life. We have almost no reason to think that humans would do either if not taught to. For these and other reasons, cooking and the use of fire are prototypically cultural (Blum 1963:45).

But the assertion that fire and cooking have utility, which provides a motive for their spread and subsequent retention in the cultural repertoire of all peoples, rests upon physical features of the human organism. Fire and cooking have other uses than the ones mentioned above, but each that was mentioned has reference to human physiology: our requirements in terms of body temperature, our vulnerability to certain kinds of predators, the nature of the human digestive system, the nature of our interactions with microscopic organisms, and more. It should also be noted that not all these uses of fire, and even more so of cooking, are "obvious." It is possible that even the well-informed among us do not yet fully understand the benefits our distant ancestors realized by cooking their food (nor, for that matter, do we understand the ways in which humans may have physiologically adapted—perhaps in terms of dentition or digestive enzymes—to the use of cooking).

ARCHOSES

These form a bizarre and only hypothetical subtype of (4), in which the diffusion is with humanity (rather than from one group to another) and the utility is zero or less. Weston La Barre (1984:10) coined the term and defined archoses as beliefs that consist of "nonsense and mis-information so ancient and pervasive as to be seemingly inextricable from our thinking." Archoses may be illustrated by an alleged near-universal, the "muelos" belief as described by La Barre (1984).

La Barre's argument concerns a series of beliefs and practices that are rooted in a few interrelated misconceptions about human anatomy and physiology. These misconceptions stem from the reasonable observations that the brain is not merely the seat of consciousness but of life too, and that semen is a substance that transmits life. These two observations are linked by the notion that bone marrow and brain, which physically resemble each other and semen, are a common substance, muelos, that is the source of semen. The spinal column is a conduit from the main supply of muelos to the genital organ (this conception appears in some of Leonardo da Vinci's anatomical sketches; see frontispiece in La Barre 1984). From these erroneous conceptions flow a whole series of further beliefs—among them, for example, the belief that life can be reconstructed from one's bones—and also some practices that have worked extraordinary mischief among humans.

Headhunting is the unfortunate practice to which La Barre gives most attention. The practice was widespread in both the Old and New Worlds. Drawing particularly on Indo-European and Southeast Asian materials, La Barre shows that headhunting is widely associated with fertility. Taking heads ensures fertility of crops, animals, and people. The practice is believed to produce fertility because it is a traffic in life-substance. Scalping was a variant: because hair sprouts from the life-carrying organs—head and genitals—it is thought to carry life-giving force too.

A less malign but still unfortunate spinoff of these mistaken conceptions, according to La Barre, is the set of beliefs and practices involved in husbanding semen. Thus masturbation is thought to weaken or madden because it drains the bones and brain of their substance.

La Barre traces a variety of other widespread beliefs or practices to the muelos belief. Its connections with the religions of the world—whether great or small—are numerous.

La Barre places the origin of these beliefs in a Palaeolithic *Urkultur*. The beliefs spread so far and survived because there was no way to correct them. Perhaps it is possible that a cultural trait or complex could achieve universality in the absence of clear utility, possibly even with numerous harmful effects, so long as it had no superior competitors (and assuming that no belief at all is for some reason not a viable alternative). Until the advent of scientific anatomy and physiology, the muelos belief lacked such positive competition.

But there are various interrelated objections to La Barre's argument. One hinges on a problem of evidence: if all, or nearly all, elements of the muelos complex were widespread, the complexity of its pattern would strongly suggest a single origin. But this is not the case. Among some peoples—e.g., the ancient Indo-Europeans—we find the full complex. Among many others we find no more than disparate elements and can only assert that they are remnant parts of an earlier full complex. They could be false cognates, associations independently hit upon. Accordingly, we cannot rule out the possibility that what La Barre sees as manifestations of a single belief complex is actually a set of unrelated complexes that happen to overlap at some points.

Even if we were to concede the widespread nature of the core of the complex—the posited connection between brain, spinal column, marrow, and semen—why shouldn't we think that their resemblance *repeatedly* suggested connections between them that we now know to be false? Why shouldn't we think that the belief is an elementary idea or statistical universal rather than an archosis?

Materialists would offer further objections, especially by pointing out that beliefs underlying headhunting, for example, may be rationalizations rather than explanations. And the practices, however they may be justified or explained, may therefore benefit some people even if harmful to numerous others.

In spite of these objections, I have dwelled on this case at length because, if correct, it is one of the most culturologically pure of all explanations for universals. Granted it does have reference to biological facts, but the reference cannot easily be thought of as a reflection, recognition, or logical extension from those facts; it is more of a distortion. However, if we delve into the assumptions that La Barre seems to make, we still find some possible underlying psychobiological elements of explanation. One is that people are prone to learn and transmit traditional lore with minimal change over long periods of time. Another is that people are prone to explain the unknown. When problems present themselves to human consciousness, humans are not content with no explanation at all, which rules that out as a viable alternative to false and harmful explanations. (The propensity to explain the unknown is discussed again below.) Yet another is that people are prone to an interest in certain things more than others, and so to have theories about the things that interest them. La Barre demonstrates people's unusual interest in life force and reproduction. So even archoses yield in part to noncultural explanation.

CONSERVATION OF ENERGY

This explanation is called upon specifically to explain linguistic "marking," which was described in chapter 3. At all levels in which marking occurs there is an intuitively grasped similarity. Generally the unmarked is the more common (its text frequency is greater), it is linguistically less complex, and it can show more irregularity.

George K. Zipf's (1949) pioneering studies of word frequencies resulted in his "principle of least effort," which offers a general explanation for many marking patterns (Greenberg 1966): the more frequently used word will tend to be unmarked because this simplifies language or reduces the energy that speech consumes. The tendency to conserve speech energy in this manner is so uniform over time that it produces numerous universals or near-universals. Conservation of speech energy everywhere produces certain regularities in language, and these regularities qualify the notion that speech sounds and patterns are essentially arbitrary. There is of course much arbitrariness in language, but where the economy of energy can exert pressure without loss of communicative effectiveness, sound and sense come together (see also Friedrich 1975).

Because of the considerable scope for arbitrariness in language it is often thought of as cultural. Yet the process that shapes marking universals operates through human physiology: conservation of energy refers to the energy utilized by the human body. Marking, thus, can only be understood as an interaction between human biology and the cultural aspects of language. Moreover, economy of effort or energy is an evolutionary factor that almost certainly impinges upon more than language: "Economy and efficiency are universal characteristics of biological mechanisms" (Williams 1966:41).

THE NATURE OF THE HUMAN ORGANISM, WITH EMPHASIS ON THE BRAIN

In chapter 1 we saw that Ekman and his associates posited a neuromuscular "facial affect program" to explain universal expressions of emotions. And in this chapter we have already seen that handedness is at least partly explained in terms of the division of labor and internal structure of the human brain. These are examples of universals explained in terms of the human organism.

It is well known in anthropology that in his famous book on *The Elementary Structures of Kinship* Lévi-Strauss (1969 [1949]) explains various features of kinship in terms of three universal "mental structures": (1) the innate recognition of rules, (2) reciprocity, and (3) the bond created between givers and receivers of gifts. Since Lévi-Strauss does not link his discussion in any detailed way to the anatomy of the brain, no specialized knowledge is required to follow his argument. It rests largely on the assumption that these structures must somehow be a part of the mind if we are to make sense of uniformities in human behavior. More recent appeals to the human mind in explaining universals are often based on much more specialized knowledge of its structure and function—and hence involve knowledge that many sociocultural anthropologists lack.

For example, d'Aquili and Laughlin (1979) offer an explanation for the myths that normally or universally accompany ritual in terms of "three critical higher cortical functions: conceptualization, abstract causal thinking, and antinomous thinking" (1979:162). (The latter refers to the dualistic thought mentioned above with respect to handedness.) These functions are lodged in particular regions of the brain (the supramarginal and angular gyri and adjacent regions)—so one or more may be eliminated by trauma to those regions—and the functions appear to the authors to be adaptations (as defined below).

D'Aquili and Laughlin argue that these cortical functions not only give us the capacity to mythologize but that by virtue of what they call the "cognitive imperative" humans are *driven* to "organize unexplained external stimuli into some coherent cognitive matrix" (1979:161). Thus, except where such matters as scientific caution are engaged to temper the results of this mechanism, humans are everywhere driven to try to explain what they perceive; where these explanations are not objectively apparent, first causes in the form of supernatural entities are generated.

Given that a number of anthropologists have noted the tendency for humans everywhere to impose meaning on the world, and that curiosity is lifelong for humans (Eibl-Eibesfeldt 1989:580–583), it is clear that d'Aquili and Laughlin offer an explanation for a real problem. But few anthropologists are in a position to evaluate their evidence in terms of neurobiology. Further examples of this sort will be given below in the section on partial explanations.

EVOLUTIONARY THEORY

If we assume that society and culture are products of human action, or that society and culture (including language) are evolved characteristics of humans, and that humans themselves are products of organic evolution, then evolutionary theory offers the only explanatory framework for universals that is potentially all-inclusive. In order to assess this claim it is first necessary to outline basic elements of evolutionary biology. This task is necessary in part because there are some terms that anthropologists and evolutionary biologists use with differing meanings.

The concept of natural selection is a central element in evolutionary theory. Natural selection is the process whereby organisms that are better adapted outbreed (and hence are more "fit" than) those that are less well adapted; by virtue of this process species undergo changes in their features over time. "Better adapted" refers to appropriateness of design toward particular ends. Let me illustrate this hypothetically. A certain conformation of beak might allow a particular species of bird to break seeds better and thus confer greater fitness on the individual birds with the superior beak conformation. Insofar as the superior conformation has a heritable basis (i.e., insofar as specific genes—a *genotype*—differentiate the superior from the inferior conformation of beak—the *phenotype*), it is then transmitted in larger proportion to the next generation of the bird species in question. In the face of a continuous environmental challenge (i.e., cracking a seed of particularly nutritive value in a specific environment) over many generations, a feature of beak conformation may evolve that can be said to be an adaptation to seed cracking.

For many biologists (e.g., Williams 1966; Burian 1983), this is the only correct usage of the term "adaptation." It requires a rigorous explication of the relationship between (phenotypic) design and function in the context of a stable relationship between a species and its environment. Sometimes, however, adaptiveness is gauged or measured not in terms of the relative fitness of design with respect to function but in terms of reproductive differentials: fitness is measured not by its immediate cause (such as the superior beak conformation) but by its real or alleged immediate effect in terms of "reproductive success."[4]

Natural selection generally being a slow process occurring over many generations, it is widely assumed among biologically knowledgeable anthropologists that human nature evolved during the long Palaeolithic period in which humans were foragers: too little time has elapsed since then for substantial evolution of human nature to have taken place. Moreover, the environments of postforaging human groups have in many respects been far from uniform or stable, which further militates against any patterned evolution of human nature away from the characteristics forged in the Palaeolithic. *Homo sapiens* now lives in environments that must differ in numerous ways from the "natural" environments in which its universal features evolved. The discrepancy between the environment in which we evolved and the many novel environments in which humans

---

[4]In the long run, the sequence of appropriateness of design, reproductive success, appropriateness of design, reproductive success (and so on in alteration) forms links in a chain of causation that results in adaptations.

now live is both a research curse and a blessing. Having to reconstruct the features of the former—in order to determine which features of human nature may be adaptations in the sense described above—is clearly a complication, and yet the many novel environments in which humans now live constitute a wealth of unplanned experiments that sometimes make features of human nature stand out in bold relief (see, e.g., chapter 5 or Symons's [1979] comparison of homosexual communities to illuminate male and female differences).[5]

Since sociocultural anthropologists use the word "adaptation" in much wider contexts, and often in a much looser way, it is clear that this is a point at which they are particularly likely to misunderstand biologists and be misunderstood by them. In contexts where confusion might exist, it is helpful to refer to adaptations in the evolutionary biological sense as "phylogenetic adaptations."

Differing usages of the term "behavior" also divide the biological from the social sciences. The behaviors that ethologists classically studied and sought to explain are conceived of as "fixed action patterns," coordinated movements that are presumably underpinned by complex neuromuscular programs that are elicited by specific entities or actions that are called "releasers" (Eibl-Eibesfeldt 1979). More recent students of animal behavior are much less concerned with the fixity of the behaviors they study, but the behaviors are still *physical* patterns of action. In either case, it is relatively straightforward to specify the phenotypes that have undergone selection: features of anatomy and physiology in particular. Social scientists, by contrast, almost always use the term "behavior" in a wider sense that includes activities that have in common only their ends, not neuromuscular response patterns. Political "behavior," and many much less complex forms of human behavior, have nothing approaching the neuroanatomical fixity of animal behaviors. There are exceptions, of course, such as the infant's sucking reflex, certain facial expressions of emotion, and the coyness display—but they are few. Consequently, the phenotypes upon which selection could act to fix such behaviors as adaptations would generally have to be features of psyche: ends, goals, motives, or drives. These ends or drives might be fixed but not the actions they give rise to.

Another fruitful source of misunderstanding concerns the distinction between the *function* of an adaptation and its various *effects*. The bird whose beak has been modified in our hypothetical example may, as

[5]Nothing I have just said should be taken to indicate that evolution has ceased. Some features of human nature that were present in the Palaeolithic might conceivably have deteriorated or become less than universal. Adaptation to specific environments has gone on apace but can only account for racial or population differences, not new features of human nature.

an incidental side effect of its new beak form, engage in somewhat different aggressive acts—because its beak is wider, harder, longer, shorter, or whatever. But to confuse incidental effect with the function that was central to the selective process is a cardinal error. Because it is hardly ever possible to reconstruct in detail the evolutionary history of a species, the attempt to distinguish functions from effects requires a rigorous analysis of design—in a comparative perspective when possible—along with whatever knowledge can be achieved of the environment(s) in which the trait was fixed by natural selection.

Thus to say that one of the functions of human fingers is to type is absurd to the evolutionary biologist—because typing (indeed any form of writing) was not a part of the environment in which human fingers evolved. Not many anthropologists would make this mistake, but mistakes of a less obvious but similar nature are common enough.

Sometimes the distinction between functions and effects is not as important to the average anthropologist as it is to the evolutionary biologist. Both functions and effects are aspects of human nature, and both provide instances in which the biological impinges upon the cultural or upon human behavior. But there *are* times when evolutionary reasoning and data have practical relevance.

Consider the following example. Probably all women have the potential of orgasm. But is female orgasm an adaptation? There are two points of view. Symons (1979, 1987b) and Gould (1987) argue that female orgasm is an effect, not a function: like nipples on any male mammal, female orgasm is the nonfunctional homologue of a process that does have a function for the opposite sex. Since the clitoris is not designed to produce female orgasm, that it sometimes does so is an incidental effect (however desirable this effect may be for some individuals). Alcock (1987), by contrast, argues that female orgasm does have a function, as a "Mr. Right detector" (the term is Symons's). When a woman is with a man who is truly good for her, she will have orgasms.

These different interpretations have very different practical implications. If Alcock is right, anorgasmic women may need to change mates if they really want orgasms; if Symons and Gould are correct, much less drastic steps should suffice. Sex therapist Helen Singer Kaplan (1981) throws some light on the matter by recounting her experience as a sex counselor for anorgasmic poor women at New York's Metropolitan Hospital. She could not give them long-term treatment and had to dispense the equivalent of instructions on how to run an appliance: she showed them where the clitoris is located and explained how long it takes for arousal. To her surprise, these simple instructions helped approximately 90 percent of her patients. This success rate does not support Alcock's position.

It must also be kept in mind that adaptations may be either "obligate" or "facultative." Williams (1966) illustrates these, respectively, with the thickening of the skin on the soles of our feet that is already present at birth, and the thickening of the skin that can occur on many parts of the body when the skin is repeatedly exposed to friction (thus forming a callus). A facultative adaptation is analogous to an implicational universal, and it represents a complex sort of universal potential the manifestation of which is not universally present (genetically it is more complex to program a facultative than an obligate trait).[6]

Some particularly important adaptations result from sexual selection. Whereas natural selection reflects the fit of an organism to its environment in general, sexual selection specifically reflects fitness in obtaining mates. It has two forms: intersexual selection (often typified by female choice of males) and intrasexual selection (often typified by the male-male competition for access to females). Features that render an organism fit to attract or obtain a mate—the gaudy feathers of the male peacock, for example—may make no sense in terms of adjustment to the wider environment. Whereas natural selection usually accounts for features common to a species, sexual selection often produces differences between the sexes of the same species.

From the viewpoint of social science, one of the most troublesome features of evolutionary biological thought concerns the level at which, or the unit upon which, adaptation occurs. Clearly, genes are selected, and almost equally certainly the phenotypes of individual organisms are selected. But there is substantial agreement among evolutionary biologists that levels of organization higher than that of the individual organism—particularly the level of the group—can rarely if ever be considered as units upon which selection acts. Conservative opinion (e.g., Williams 1966; Maynard Smith 1976) has it that no adaptation should be explained at any higher level than is absolutely necessary: in effect, this means at no level higher than the individual organism. In other words, traits should be explained in terms of the way they make individuals fit, not in terms of group or species benefits. Since social scientists often attribute adaptation, as they understand the term, to the level of the group and the species, this is a point at which biological and social scientists are particularly likely to misinterpret each other—or to disagree.

Before concluding this discussion of evolutionary theory, it is essential to note the role of accident, conservatism, and compromise in ev-

---

[6]The existence of phylogenetic facultative adaptations in humans renders obsolete the notion that if something varies it must be cultural. If it varies in a regular pattern, it may well not be cultural. This is a complication for anthropological analysis that has scarcely even been recognized (Tooby and Cosmides 1989a).

olution. Traits do not necessarily develop because they are needed (even though they are more or less predictable under certain conditions). Traits develop as a result of a random process (gene mutation) that may from time to time confer greater fitness. This random process is the ultimate source of all organic change, but it has no direction. The pressure of environmental circumstances can only, so to say, pick and choose from among mutational accidents. Moreover, under certain circumstances selection may result in adaptations that have a short-term advantage but long-term costs, which further enlarges the role of accident. For a variety of reasons—ranging from molecular and mechanical considerations through those imposed on the constitution of a species by its recent evolutionary history—there are limits on the directions evolution may take. The phylogenetic constraints peculiar to our own species, for example, make it much more likely that smell might become our paramount sense of perception than that we fletch and fly. Finally, genes that confer selective advantages in one respect may have negative consequences in others, so that selection results in many traits that are compromises with each other. Because of these factors, in addition to the (side) effects of adaptations that were mentioned earlier, we cannot expect anything approaching a perfect fit between organism and environment.

There are two further considerations that must be noted in order to make the body of theory that was just presented useful. First, what has been described above concerns "ultimate" or evolutionary explanations (Mayr 1961): how we got the genetic constitution we have. The "proximate" explanations of phylogenetically determined traits often concern matters of anatomy and physiology that a sociocultural anthropologist is usually poorly equipped to study. Perhaps the most familiar example concerns hormones: whatever the ultimate causes of certain male-female differences may be, it is now generally accepted, even in the feminist literature, that an important proximate cause is the differential production of certain hormones in the two sexes. Generally, sociocultural anthropologists utilize this kind of knowledge but are not trained to produce it.

Second, there are certain clues—present in externally observable human behavior—that point toward phylogenetic traits. Clues, of course, are not infallible markers; seeing one or another clue gives us no more than a hunch, or a basis for hypothesizing that some behavioral or psychological pattern was specifically shaped by selection. Because they can serve to guide research, identifying these clues is of utmost importance. Among the most important clues to phylogenetic adaptation are the following: unusual ease (or difficulty) in acquiring specific skills or knowledge, a "critical period" for their acquisition, emotionally motivated actions that run counter to consciously held ideals, unusually intense preoccupation with certain topics, similar behavior among animals, and universality itself, including implicational universality (see Buss 1984 and Boehm 1989 for related clues). Some of these clues have already been discussed and illustrated; others will be illustrated below. We may now turn to specific applications of evolutionary theory.

Kinship

Earlier I suggested that kinship terminologies are universal because kinship is universally important. But what is kinship, and why is it important? Along with mate selection or marriage, the essence of kinship comprises those sentimental attachments that distinguish kin from nonkin and close kin from distant kin. Such nepotistic sentiments are thoroughly familiar features in world ethnography, and careful analyses of adoption (Silk 1980) or domestic homicide (Daly and Wilson 1988) document them with some precision.

One of the striking clues to the biological foundation of nepotism is indicated by Meyer Fortes's (1969) concept of "complementary filiation." This term was coined to refer to a phenomenon found repeatedly in societies that ideologically reckon kinship either matrilineally or patrilineally. In either case, in spite of the prevailing ideology of descent, an individual typically has strong sentimental ties to those (usually close) genetic kin who are not ideologically reckoned as kin, i.e., some close genetic relatives through the mother in a patrilineal society, through the father in a matrilineal society. By virtue of this phenomenon, the sentimental ties between kin are always to some degree effectively bilateral.

The genetic foundation of nepotism finds its explanation in recent developments in "kin selection" theory (Hamilton 1964; Maynard Smith 1964), which provides one of the solutions to the evolutionary puzzle of how altruism could evolve. In particular, how could altruistic behaviors be adaptations if they are detrimental, or seemingly detrimental, to the survival of one's own genes? One answer is to point out that behaviors that are directed toward individuals bearing copies of one's own genes by proximate common descent would be interpersonally altruistic yet potentially result in no reduction of one's genetic representation in the next generation.

This line of reasoning was worked out particularly to explain the sterile castes of certain insects (bees, ants, and wasps, for example). Among these insects, group livers *par excellence*, members of the sterile castes seemed to toil and lay down their lives for their fellows without any reproductive benefits for themselves. The realization that the sterile castes served very close kin (all or nearly all having the same mother) made good evolutionary sense of the altruism: if it didn't benefit themselves individually it did nonetheless benefit carriers of their own genes. The reasoning is no less applicable to humans. For example, the behavior of a man risking his life defending his sister against an abusive husband or by coming to the aid of a brother in a blood feud becomes evolutionarily intelligible if the average result is that, even though the altruist chances to lose his life, his siblings and the offspring of his siblings—all of whom share his genes to a high degree—thereby have an increased chance to survive and reproduce at a rate that results in greater replication of his genes in subsequent generations than if the man left his siblings to fend for themselves.

Precisely how to apply kin selection theory to the elucidation of human affairs has occasioned much debate. A number of anthropologists have operated under the assumption that the human mind is, in effect, a fitness calculator: consciously or unconsciously it weighs the effects of various actions on various degrees of kin and then tends to choose those actions that promote fitness. Consequently, individual actions, and often the customs that presumably have their origin and reality in such actions, make sense as fitness-promoting strategies. Ethnographic materials analyzed in this way have generally not been universals, although the analyses of them rest on the assumption at a high level of generalization that promoting inclusive fitness is universal (e.g., various essays in Chagnon and Irons 1979).

These kinds of analyses have been criticized (Barkow 1984; Cosmides and Tooby 1987; Kitcher 1985; Symons 1989; Tooby and Cosmides 1989c), primarily on the grounds that there is little reason to think that the human mind is a general fitness calculator—even if, in some cases, people act as though they had calculated fitness. That the human mind—or any other mind, for that matter—would evolve such a capacity is one of those features of evolution that one might think ought to occur but probably never has (in principle, according to Cosmides and Tooby [1987], such a mind could not evolve). In the course of their evolution, humans (and other species) did not face generalized problems, they faced specific problems. Consequently, what has evolved (disregarding effects, compromises, accidents, and the like) is a *disparate collection of adaptations* each separately selected because it contributed to fitness.

This is easily illustrated by an example that will momentarily take us away from nepotism. Symons (1979) argues that the human male is adapted to prefer sex with relatively young women, and in the plural when that is feasible. Under natural conditions, the human male who acted on such impulses—the emotional power of which is universally attested— did much to promote his reproductive success, whether he calculated its reproductive consequences or not. However, in present-day conditions, where effective contraceptive measures are readily available, men are much more content to forgo reproduction than sex. This strongly suggests that the phenotypic mental mechanism(s), upon which selective forces acted, was not the calculation of fitness (too often a matter of indifference to men), but such traits as a propensity to sexual arousal at the sight of nubile women.

Another problem in the application of kin selection theory to anthropological problems concerns the distance at which kinship ties are calculated. It is not at all clear that humans (or any other species) are adapted to distinguish between degrees of distant kin—even though this can be done with genealogical charts and other more scientific procedures that surely were absent in the alaeolithic. Thus attempts to explain ethnic or racial sentiments as an extension of kin selection (e.g., van den Berghe 1981) have been rightly criticized (Smith 1983).[7]

What the evidence suggests, therefore, is that those kinship sentiments constituted by phylogenetic adaptation generally work within a narrow range of kin. Three of the most important series of studies of these narrow-based sentiments concern incest avoidance, which will be taken up in chapter 5; male sexual jealousy, which is a mechanism to avoid a man's investing in offspring other than his own (Daly, Wilson, and Weghorst 1982); and the mother-infant bond, which is probably a complex of adaptations both in mothers and in infants (Freeman 1974; Konner 1982; Stern 1977). Without denying that cultural conceptions of kinship always or often include more than the matters just discussed, kinship has its universal core in these highly specific mechanisms. And although it goes beyond kinship, the subject of the next section, reciprocity, is an aspect of phylogenetic adaptation that also lies near the core of kinship.

Reciprocity

Another solution to the puzzle entailed by the evolution of altruism is the idea of "reciprocal altruism" (Trivers 1971). An altruistic behavior that is reciprocated has its cost canceled and hence does not pose a serious evolutionary dilemma. But in order for this kind of behavior to prevail— to be more than neutral in its consequences—it must have some benefit for its practitioners. Insofar as reciprocated behaviors create coalitions of reciprocators, who may by virtue of their coalition prevail over those who do not reciprocate, then reciprocity should be selected. As is true of kin selection, the idea of reciprocal altruism rings bells in the minds of at

---

[7]On the other hand, "stranger recognition" mechanisms, which are probably triggered not only by personal unfamiliarity but by such cultural differences as language, accent, and body adornment, do seem to be very much involved in ethnocentrism (Boyd and Richerson 1985; Reynolds, Falger, and Vine 1987). In the environments in which humans evolved, a dichotomous distinction between the familiar and friendly on the one hand and the stranger on the other would, on average, correlate with degree of kinship.

least some anthropologists, since reciprocity has long been recognized as a universal cornerstone of morality, rational action, and group life—and has therefore been central to some of the most famous studies in the whole of anthropology (most are reviewed in Gouldner 1960). The strong moral feeling attached to reciprocity, and the assiduousness with which reciprocal action and reaction are watched also suggest some degree of innateness. The solidarity of kinsmen typically rests on both nepotism and reciprocity.

Sex Differences in Sexuality, Aggressiveness, and Dominance

In the understanding of sex differences great strides have been made in the last decade or two. Some of the differences quite clearly are themselves adaptations brought about by sexual selection. A key element in the modern understanding of sexual selection is "parental investment" (Trivers 1972): the total energy or other resources a parent invests in an offspring (which limits what can be contributed to other offspring). Parental investment is related to sexual selection by the observation that whichever sex typically invests the most in its offspring will be a limited resource from the viewpoint of the sex investing less. For example, in a species in which the female devotes considerable time to rearing offspring, and the male no time beyond that required to inseminate the female, from the viewpoint of reproduction there is in effect no shortage of males (the reproductive demands on their time being so minimal)[8] while females (tied up as they are by lengthy gestation and offspring care) are in relatively short supply. A female who wanted to maximize her reproduction would gain little by having more males to inseminate her, but a male with the same aim would benefit by trying to monopolize access to females.

The sex that invests more in offspring is a "limiting" resource; it is the sexual resource that limits reproductive rates. The sex with the lesser investment tends to be larger and/or more colorful, to compete more actively with its fellows for access to the limiting sex, and to seek monopoly of multiple mates. The sex with the greater parental investment tends to rely more on choosiness (rather than active competition) in mate selection. Other factors being equal, the greater the sex difference in parental investment, the greater the other differences between the sexes, i.e., the greater the sexual dimorphism.

In mammals it is almost always the male that invests less, is larger, is more actively competitive, and is more prone to seek multiple mates. This pattern presumably results, in the long evolutionary perspective, from the typical difference in reproductive cells—the ovum is vastly more costly

[8]There may of course be a shortage of "good" males.

to the female than a sperm is to a male. This initial difference in parental investment biases the sexes of numerous species toward different reproductive strategies. Moreover, the mammalian pattern of internal gestation and postpartum lactation further enhances the female investment in offspring.[9]

These insights into the dynamics of sexual selection are directly applicable to humans. Humans are mildly dimorphic, their mating patterns are mildly polygynous, and the parental investments of humans seem to differ in the expected direction. The minimal investments (gestation and lactation versus insemination) are grossly different, but precisely what the *typical* investments may be is a matter of current research interest. Data from Aka Pygmies, who make a near approach to egalitarianism sexually and otherwise, show that mothers make a considerably larger direct investment in child care than do fathers—even though Aka males make unusually large parental investments (Hewlett 1988).

Starting from assumptions generated by an evolutionary perspective, Symons (1979) and Daly and Wilson (1983 [1978]) explain and document a complex of universal or near-universal differences between the sexes. Among them are the following: Sex is seen as a service given by females to males (females being the limiting resource); male sexual jealousy is more violent (confidence of paternity being a problem without a female counterpart); men are more quickly aroused, and more by visual stimuli (females being more choosy, and the signs of reproductive potential being more visibly discernible in the female); and the average husband is older than his wife (because a male's reproductive potential—linked as it is to his ability to invest in child care—typically peaks later than a female's).[10]

The greater aggressiveness of males is at least partly a result of sex-

[9]Eberhard (1985) argues that the typically protruding genitals of males rather than females is yet another consequence of the initial sexual difference in parental investment, for protruding genitals allow a more aggressive strategy of mating and are found on females only in species with substantial male parental investment. In these atypical species—the seahorses and pipefish—females possess an intromittent organ with which they insert their eggs in males who then fertilize and brood them; in those species of seahorses and pipefish for which courtship information is available, it is females who are promiscuous and aggressive, males who are choosy. See also Williams (1966).

[10]Female reproductive potential is more delimited by the ability to *produce* children, which is maximal shortly after puberty and declines until it reaches zero at menopause. The male ability to produce children shows no such precipitous decline with age and may persist until death. Consequently, male reproductive potential is more delimited by the ability to *support* children, and their mother(s). It is this male ability to support children that typically peaks later than the female ability to produce children—and that accounts for males typically remaining attractive to women later in life than women to men. On the other hand, it is the stringent and predictable delimitation by age of a female's reproductive potential that accounts for the universal or near-universal sexual attractiveness of women who are postpubescent but still youthful.

ual selection, aggression being an effective male strategy in the competition for females. Male aggressiveness is, thus, the behavioral and motivational counterpart of the greater physical stature of males. Hormonal factors, among others, underpin both the morphological and temperamental differences between the sexes—some of which are apparent from earliest infancy (Stern 1977).

The universal dominance of men—particularly in the public sphere, as discussed earlier—may well result from the more fundamental human sex differences: above all, the difference in size (Handwerker and Crosbie 1982), in propensity to violence, and in the minimal handicaps entailed for each sex by reproduction (gestation and lactation are considerably greater handicaps to political action than is insemination).

Presumed Evolutionary Theory

Not every explanation of a universal in terms of adaptation is based on sophisticated use of theory. In some cases explanation merely presumes that the human organism has an evolutionary history that determined some feature of human nature that in turn serves to explain some universal. Two explanations for religious phenomena will serve to illustrate.

George Steiner, an authority on the translation of verse, provides an interesting example in his *After Babel* (1975), which tackles the question of why humans have many languages rather than just one (or even just a few). A major part of his answer turns round his idea of humanity's constructions of "alternities": conceptions of the way the world isn't, whether these be conceptions of past worlds, future worlds, hypothetical worlds, or counterfactual worlds. Steiner argues that, once humans could think sufficiently abstractly about themselves that they could grasp their condition, it was a *sine qua non* of their further existence that they be able to imagine other conditions. Without articulated visions of conditions other than "the treadmill of organic decay and death,...the individual and the species would have withered" (1975:227, 235). In this view, religion is a product of an adaptation for the generation of alternities (so that languages, whose functions may be as much to create alternities as to grasp realities, therefore proliferate).

Dan Sperber (1985) suggests another explanation for religious phenomena that is equally evolutionist but makes no more than a casual reference to evolutionary theory. In his plea for a more psychologically slanted anthropology, Sperber notes that although we may safely assume that humans have genetically determined cognitive abilities that were shaped by natural selection, this does not indicate that all the effects of these abilities promote fitness. He thus draws a distinction between mental "dispositions" and "susceptibilities." The former "have been positively selected in the process of biological evolution"; the latter "are side-effects" of the former (1985:80). Most susceptibilities have only "marginal effects" on our well-being and hence do not come under much selective pressure. It is not always easy to distinguish dispositions from susceptibilities, and sometimes one may become the other, as when our disposition to eat sweets gave way to a susceptibility to overconsume sugar. Sperber's (1985:85) conclusion: "Unlike everyday empirical knowledge, religious beliefs develop not because of a disposition, but because of susceptibility." In other words, religion is not an adaptation—a biologically advantageous or necessary alternity, as Steiner would have it, but is a side effect of other adaptations.

Evaluating explanations of this sort requires that they be rethought in order to take account of what they omit: a theoretically informed analysis of the possibility and probability that they might be correct and useful explanations. Sperber's explanation requires less effort of this sort because, for example, some of his terms readily translate into the concepts of evolutionary biology (e.g., dispositions and susceptibilities are adaptations and effects). Furthermore, there is some support for Sperber's position. D'Aquili and Laughlin (1979), reviewed earlier, argue that divining causes is an adaptation, but they imply that divining first causes that go beyond the evidence is an effect; studies reviewed below in the section on partial explanations also involve effects rather than adaptations.

INTERSPECIFIC COMPARISON

This mode of explanation is more or less entailed by evolutionary explanations but sometimes makes sense on its own. For example, Franz De Waal's *Chimpanzee Politics* (1982) provides evidence among chimpanzees for what the author calls "triangular awareness," the ability of an individual A to calculate the interdependence of the three separate relationships composed by his relationships with individuals B and C and the relationship between B and C themselves. This sort of ability among our nearest relatives in the animal world suggests that the same ability in us has phylogenetically deep roots and is therefore innate.

Richard Alexander's (1979) ultimate explanation of why humans are a group-living species rests on a very broad cross-specific comparison. A great many species, of course, do not live in groups, for it has some real costs (such as considerably enhanced transmission of diseases). Alexander finds only three general factors that, singly or in combination, appear to underlie group living as an adaptation: protection from predators (own species or others), more effective utilization of food resources, and highly localized resources. The evidence suggests to Alexander that it is the first factor that primarily accounts for group living in primates, including humans. Alexander contrasts his mode of explanation with the common assumption that group living needs no explanation, that its advantages are obvious, or that humans are just naturally cooperative and social.

ONTOGENY

This mode of explanation is fundamental both to evolutionary and cultural explanations, since in either case the precise steps by which universal traits emerge in individuals must be traced in any thorough explanation of the traits' universality (even nonuniversals require this kind of explanation).

An anthropological example is Spiro's explanation for the apparent universality of the Oedipus complex, described in chapter 1. At a specific stage in a little boy's life a specific configuration in his environment induces the complex in him. Were that configuration to be absent at the critical period, the complex would not develop. It is the universality of the critical environing conditions at the critical period that, according to Spiro, account for the universality of the Oedipus complex.

Further examples are provided by studies of the mother-infant bond, which I mentioned earlier while stressing their importance for understanding kinship, and studies of incest avoidance, which will be the subject of the next chapter.

The ontogeny of facial recognition has received much attention, generally in Western settings. In spite of the Western settings, the subject is directly relevant to anthropology. Kinship requires the ability to recognize kin, which entails the ability to recognize individuals, an ability possessed by many species. Recognition by face is the commonest means employed by humans. Daphne Maurer (1985) prefaces a study that reviews a considerable literature on the ontogeny of facial recognition with the comment that humans have a remarkable ability to recognize the human face in greatly decomposed or blurred images of it, and, moreover, to recognize very large numbers of individual faces. While it might be a mere coincidence, a newborn infant can only focus on objects about eight inches from its eyes, which is the distance between the infant's eyes and those of its nursing mother; in this position the two typically spend long periods gazing into each other's faces (Stern 1977; for an apparent or partial exception see Ochs and Schieffelin 1984). Studies of primates raised without ever seeing another conspecific's face show that at a certain age they recognize it and some of its expressions innately (Sackett 1966). In humans, facial recognition apparently develops in complex interaction between the infant's developing nervous system and the give and take between the infant and its care givers.

Stern (1985) cites an infant experiment by Meltzoff and Borton (1979) in order to speculate on the ontogeny of our ability to create and understand metaphors. The experiment shows that human neonates at 29 days of age can distinguish by sight the shape of the specific pacifier nipple that has been in their mouth, even though they only feel, not see, its shape. This inbuilt capacity to transfer information from one sensory mode to another not only is crucial to maintaining a unified conception of the world but may be part of the mental mechanism that generates and interprets metaphors.

One of the most important areas of study in which the ontogeny of a universal is central is linguistics. Eric Lenneberg (1967) and Noam Chomsky (1959; 1980; see also Piatelli-Palmarini, ed., 1980)—citing the ease or difficulty with which children acquire particular grammatical forms, which implies an innate "deep structure" of language—argue that we should think of language as analogous to an organ, little different in principle from the other organs of our body, in the sense that they come into being as the result of interaction between genes and environmental cues rather than as the result of simple "learning." Humans normally "learn" their first language with such extraordinary ease that there is reason to suspect some kind of wiring in the brain for language acquisition: at the right time of life (a "critical period") it is brought into activity by quite minimal environmental stimuli. At other times—as many of us know from experience—language acquisition is a much more difficult and less successful matter. The regular forms in which deaf children spontaneously construct a communication system (in the absence of models) provides additional evidence of inbuilt wiring for language acquisition (Goldin-Meadow and Feldman 1977). Although the "deep structure" of language remains in many respects elusive and controversial, the age-delimited ontogeny of language is rarely if ever contested nowadays (a fact that was very much involved in the demise of associationist learning theory and the tabula rasa model of the brain that accompanied it; see chapter 2).

Since they are compatible with both cultural or biological explanations for universals, ontogenetic explanations are numerous. Since they can be crucial in determining the precise mix of nature and culture in shaping behavior, they deserve to be even more numerous.

PARTIAL EXPLANATIONS

Many universals seem to lack a unitary explanation. Religion and aesthetics are examples. Both are perennial puzzles for anthropology because of the absence or uncertainty of their utility or practical value. This makes it difficult to explain them as adaptations in any usual sense of the term (though attempts like Steiner's are made; for art, see Dissanayake 1988).

In spite of the difficulties presented by an overall explanation, quite a few attempts have been made to explain *some aspects* of religion/ritual and aesthetics/pleasure in evolutionary or biological terms.[11] Some of them, as I indicated earlier, support Sperber's views about religious phenomena resulting from susceptibilities. Consider the following:

Partial Explanations of Religious Phenomena

There is a long history of explaining a wide range of religious experiences in terms of specific brain dysfunctions—such as epilepsy—or in terms of those features of ritual settings—such as sleep deprivation and prolonged rhythmic activities—that may in various degrees induce or mimic those dysfunctions (see, e.g., Beyerstein 1988). Closely related explanations do not necessarily involve dysfunction but nonetheless involve a channeling of brain function into paths that are, at least, outside the humdrum routine of everyday life.

Rodney Needham (1967), for example, notes the widespread use of percussion to mark transitions in ritual, and he offers an explanation in terms of the nature of the human brain. It is somehow affected by percussive sounds in a way that makes percussion peculiarly appropriate to ritual activities. Later (1978) he linked percussion to a wider discussion of what he called "primary factors" (akin to Bastian's "elementary ideas"), many of which are recurrent elements in world ethnography because they somehow reflect the way the brain is.

Noting the frequent use in religious activities of swings and other means of achieving vertigo, Alfred Gell (1980) proposes a "vestibular" theory of trance induction. By means of an "assault on the equilibrium sense," swinging induces an altered state of consciousness, which is interpreted by religious practitioners as a form of religious experience. Techniques such as those employed by whirling dervishes are no doubt similar.

Donald Tuzin (1984) draws attention to the frequent use in religious practices around the world of certain deep-noted instruments, particularly the bull roarer and large drums (large flutes could probably be added). These instruments are believed to produce the sound of the spirits, and Tuzin explains this in terms of the physiological effects on the human

[11]Universals that seem to lack a unitary explanation are apparently what Geertz (1965:102), citing Kroeber, has in mind when he speaks of "fake" universals. Whether some unifying factors will be found still to underlie such universals, and thus to validate their broad rubrics after their various parts are separately explained, remains to be determined.

brain of the sounds the instruments make. More precisely, it is the infrasonic waves they produce while they are sounding, for these infrasonic waves produce an uncanny feeling which is particularly apt for mystical settings.

The extraordinary number of mind-altering drugs employed to induce trance or other mystical states has received considerable attention from anthropologists (Weil 1972; La Barre 1980). The discovery of endorphins—naturally produced pain-killing substances in the brain— may throw light on a wide variety of hitherto inexplicable ritual practices.

A detailed study of a connection between religion and the character of our psyche is presented by Mundkur (1983), who argues that the widespread presence of the serpent in religious thought and iconography rests upon our innate wariness of snakes, a trait we share with other primates (Hebb 1946). Animal counterparts, the extreme ease with which the fear is acquired and the difficulty with which it is suppressed, the essentially emotional rather than rational basis for the fear, and the sensibleness of the fear in humanity's natural environments all conspire to render the innateness of this fear intelligible. Death by snakebite has long been a real danger in many of humanity's environments. Even peoples with traditions of reverence for snakes still show wariness if not fear toward them (Russell 1983).

Note that in most if not all of these cases there is no argument that the specific practices are phylogenetic adaptations, but there is an argument that it is the nature of the human brain to react in specific ways to the practices. Each of these ways of reacting accounts for some part of widespread religious phenomena.

Partial Explanations of Aesthetics/Pleasure

One of the fundamental assumptions of evolutionary psychology is that matters closely related to our survival and reproduction have a likelihood of engaging our emotions. Thus, although there might be little evidence of a general adaptation for an aesthetic sense (but cf. the argument of Dissanayake described below), a disparate collection of emotion-producing activities and entities may structure what we consider aesthetic. Surely the most notable of all examples of pleasure in the service of our reproductive interests is the sexual drive, particularly male orgasm. The imagery of reproduction—ranging from genitals and breasts through nude bodies and the infinite themes of love—is too pervasive to require documentation.

Orians (1980) has examined such matters as the emotional reactions of explorers to different natural settings, the landscaping and planting of parks, and the criteria that make particular pieces of real estate especially valuable, to show that humans seem to have an innate preference for settings that would have been optimal habitats for our Pleistocene foraging ancestors. We like "lakes, rivers, cliffs, and savannahs," settings in which food, water, and protection (as in caves) were in optimal combination. Key elements in Orians's argument are the emotional nature of the human preferences, and comparisons with habitat selection in other species, where its innate component is less questionable. Here the argument is that we have an innate tendency to prefer, seek out, and construct certain kinds of settings because we feel good in them.

Mundkur's (1983) analysis of the snake in religion is simultaneously an explanation of why it figures so widely in visual representations: we are wired to react to it; it is an inherently potent symbol. Here the argument is not that we find the image good but that it evokes a response that can be put to some use. Gell's (1980) hypothesis about the relationship between the vestibule and trance is no less an explanation for a number of very familiar pleasures: teeter-totters, merry-go-rounds, horseback riding, children's whirling games, and so on (Caillois 1961). Turner and Pöppel (1983) provide a remarkable analysis of certain universal features of poetry—particularly its tendency to have lines of about 3 seconds in duration—in terms of various information processing features of the human brain.

If there is anything that comes close to a generic aesthetic sense it might be an appreciation for skill. Given our long dependence on manual skill to make tools, a sense of pleasure in seeing the products of skill—and in producing them—is not an unexpectable trait. Given the utility of verbal skills, the widespread appreciation of them is no less expectable.

Although it argues that art results from an adaptive "human proclivity" for "making special," which involves "apprehending [and creating] an order different from the everyday," a very recent book, *What Is Art For?*, also argues that art results from the intertwining of a collection of traits of human nature (Dissanayake 1988:126–128). The collection includes symbolization, classification, ordering, tool making, emotionality, and sociality. Each of these traits, which are closely allied to traits that underlie ritual and play (Dissanayake 1988:127), provides a partial explanation of art or aesthetics.

Now to put some order into these explanatory modes. First note that some are essentially formal or methodological, i.e., derivative of the logic or method of explanation alone. This is particularly true of the eleventh (partial explanations) but also of the first (explaining a universal with a universal), ninth (interspecific comparison), and tenth (ontogeny). Because of their formality, they are compatible with or complementary to most if not all the other modes of explanation. But also note that if the eleventh is correct, it prevents the first from being a necessary mode of explanation: universals would, then, only sometimes require explanation in terms of other universals.

Three of the explanatory modes—the second (cultural reflection), fourth (diffusion), and fifth (archoses)—have substantial culturological components. And yet none is devoid of biological considerations. The fifth may be the most culturological, but it is not clear that there are any universals that really do find their explanation in its terms. Accordingly, it must be concluded that probably all explanations of particular universals must be biological or interactionist.

The third (logical extension) and sixth through ninth (conservation of energy, nature of the organism, evolutionary theory, and interspecific comparison) all give substantial recognition to biological causation. In the case of the third, this is only a matter of practice, since the "givens" are only normally biological. To the extent that they are not necessarily biological, then the third mode would be strictly formal like the first and eleventh. Since the third mode does not involve tracing the causal chain between the given starting point and the universal to be explained, it is an inherently weak or limited mode of explanation.

Explanatory modes six through ten are closely interrelated: the conservation of energy is a universal feature of the evolutionary process; the nature of the human organism is a result of evolution; interspecific comparisons derive their rationale from evolution and are conducted to illuminate that process; while ontogenetic studies are not inherently biological, they are normally employed to determine the proximate means by which evolutionarily shaped traits emerge in individual organisms. It follows that number eight, evolutionary theory, is the superordinate explanatory mode among them: only it gives order to the others, only it offers ultimate explanations for universals characteristic of the human organism.

From the viewpoint of theory, there are only two or three distinct alternatives to evolutionary theory. Diffusion is one alternative, and if archoses exist and are to be distinguished from diffusion, they comprise another. Cultural reflection or recognition of biological fact is the only remaining alternative that is not simply logical or methodological. Given the importance that explanation has in the development of any sort of anthropological theory, the matters explored in this chapter deserve more attention than they have so far received.

5

Incest Avoidance

The apparent universality, or near-universality, of the incest taboo perennially fascinates anthropologists and has given rise to numerous speculations about its origin and function. The principal point of agreement is probably that incest is in some way harmful, so that avoiding it confers some benefit. What the harm, what the benefit, and how the taboo or avoidance comes about are points of contention.

Progress in understanding the whole issue has been retarded by several false starts and misconceptions (summarized in Fox 1980, Arens 1986). For example, there has been a tendency to conflate marriage rules with sexual regulations. While these concerns may impinge on one another—and might very well be equated in the folk categories of a given people[1]—there is no necessary connection between them: incest fundamentally concerns sex, only coincidentally may it concern marriage.

There was also an assumption that animals—unlike humans—do mate incestuously, so that the human prohibition of incest was a distinctively cultural marker of humanity's separation from the animal world. It is now known that incest is rare among animals in the wild (domestic animals, whose breeding patterns have been altered by human interference, are another matter). Between human incest avoidance and the patterns of behavior among other animals there may thus be a continuity that was previously denied.

As a corollary of the assumption that the incest taboo was a distinctively cultural invention—that would leave no obvious material re-

---

[1]Following up the leads suggested by folk classifications might lead to an analysis of incest along with bestiality, irreverence, and sundry other topics. Whether to follow the leads suggested by folk classifications is a complication I will not treat here. But I should note that some anthropologists have recently explored incest from the viewpoint of child abuse, the category under which some forms of incest are classified in the West today (see especially Willner [1983] but also La Fontaine [1988]).

mains in the archeological record—the actual origins of the taboo, being lost in antiquity, were not subject to empirical research. Indeed, most discussion of the incest taboo was little more than a sideline to other issues.

Another assumption now known to be wrong was that the incest taboo was universal. But in a number of societies royalty were enjoined to commit incest (or, at any rate, to marry very close kin).[2] And in some societies there are no obvious incest taboos in the sense of rules (and sanctioned rules especially) against it, only a notion that no one would commit incest anyway.

Finally, the various relationships in which incest might occur—e.g., between brother and sister, or between father and daughter—tended to be all run together.

The present chapter is primarily about brother-sister incest, and a recent line of research conducted primarily by anthropologists to test an idea formulated in the last century—but long ignored—that it is human nature for brothers and sisters to avoid incest. This line of research moved an old anthropological subject out of the realm of speculation into the realm of concrete and comparative studies.

One of the leading controversies has turned fundamentally around an issue of human psychology: is incest tabooed because we naturally tend to commit it but shouldn't, or is it tabooed, somewhat paradoxically, because most humans don't want to do it? The former position was championed by Freud and others, who could see no reason why a taboo should exist for something we didn't want to do anyway. The latter position was expounded late in the nineteenth century by a Finnish anthropologist, Edward Westermarck, who argued that there is "a remarkable lack of erotic feeling between persons who have been living closely together from childhood" (1922:192). Such persons, he noted, would typically be relatives. Incest avoidance, thus, was a natural tendency that resulted from childhood association. Westermarck's reply to the objection Freud raised was that incest was tabooed for the same reason bestiality and parricide are tabooed: not because we have a general tendency to commit them but because some individuals go awry in ways that shock general sentiments. The rules are for them.

Unlike most (if not all other) anthropologists, Westermarck was centrally concerned with the incest taboo and its implications, and he wrote

[2]Marriages of royal brothers and sisters are well attested in the his.orical record, but evidence that this led to actual incest (i.e., reproduction) is extremely limited (Bixler 1982a, 1982b). Arens (1986:116) suggests that the motive of royal brother-sister marriages was not reproductive at all: such marriages merely took royal sisters out of the marriage market and thereby prevented them from bearing offspring who might rival the king. With their sisters safely married to themselves, nothing compelled kings to actually mate with them.

voluminously on the matter over decades. He took a straightforward Darwinian view, that inbreeding was directly harmful. The avoidance that resulted from childhood association was an evolved human instinct. In spite of the extraordinary effort Westermarck put into understanding the incest taboo, his views were largely eclipsed by anthropology's opposition to biological reductionism in the period through World War II, because they "violat[ed]...every canon" of anthropology (Murdock 1932:209). But in the 1950s J. R. [Robin] Fox (1962) realized that social experiments conducted in Israel provided remarkable evidence bearing on the matter of incest avoidance between siblings. The ensuing revival of Westermarck's ideas led to most of the studies summarized below.

In Israeli *kibbutzim*, communal villages first founded early in this century, there was a deliberate attempt to break down the nuclear family. Boys and girls who were close in age to one another were raised together in peer groups (*kvutza*) of six to eight children; they shared common living quarters from a time shortly after they were born through adolescence. Under the tutelage of nurses and teachers rather than parents, the children shared an intimate association and underwent a socialization and education common to all. As small children they showed a typical sexual interest in each other, but as they matured this disappeared. Although they were free to marry one another, provided they were not in fact siblings, Spiro (1958) found not a single case of this happening nor even of sexual intercourse between children who had been raised together from childhood in the same peer group.

Fox (1962) saw that the *kibbutz* data supported Westermarck, but he thought that Freud was at least partly right too. In Fox's reformulation, the close and literally physical intimacy of children who are socialized together renders them sexually uninterested in each other after puberty. Among Freud's patients, however, most siblings were not raised with the physical intimacy that was common in the *kibbutz*, and so they grew up harboring sexual desires for each other.

According to Fox, societies that are *kibbutz*-like in their child-rearing patterns are likely to be relatively indifferent to incest; they disapprove but generally do not stringently punish it, and do not need to, because for most of the members it has no great interest. Societies with child-rearing patterns more similar to those of Freud's patients are more likely to have the taboo, and it is more likely to be stringent, because their members need the taboo to overcome real desires to commit incest. Fox's summary of the pattern is that "the intensity of heterosexual attraction between cosocialized children after puberty is inversely proportionate to the intensity of heterosexual activity between them before puberty" (1962:147). As illustrations, he shows that the Tallensi of Ghana, the Pondo of Southeast Africa, the Mountain Arapesh of New Guinea, the Tikopia, and a Chinese situation described below fit the *kibbutz* pattern, while the Chiracahua Apache and the Trobriand Islanders fit the pattern described by Freud.

A study based on three further Israeli communes indicated that the Westermarck effect, as Fox called it, was not confined to the commune Spiro had studied (Talmon 1964). Whether on the basis of Israeli or other data, most studies of incest avoidance from the mid-1960s onward have focused specifically on Westermarck's position, and Fox's defense of a modified Freudian position has received little attention (but see Willner 1983 and Spain 1987).

A Chinese practice, described by Arthur Wolf (1966, 1968, 1970) and Wolf and Huang (1980), provided yet another natural experiment that supports Westermarck. In many areas of China there were until recently two forms of marriage, called "major" and "minor." In the minor form a young girl was adopted into the family of her future husband. The motivation for this kind of marriage came of course from parents. In Wolf's analysis, the strain between daughters-in-law and mothers-in-law was so serious among Chinese that it made viable the strategy of bringing the future daughter-in-law in as a very young child so that long before she became a bride she could adjust, and more readily subordinate herself, to her mother-in-law. The future husband and wife were unrelated—so there was no breaking of the incest taboo. But the boy and his future bride were raised under the conditions typical of brothers and sisters—in the intimacy of the family.

Wolf found, contrary to Freud and others who argue that familial intimacy is the breeding ground of sexual interests that must be thwarted by the incest taboo, and in support of Westermarck, that minor marriages were about 30 percent less fertile and were unhappier. Men in such marriages resorted to prostitutes, took mistresses, or sought extramarital affairs more frequently; their wives engaged in extramarital affairs more frequently; and such marriages more frequently resulted in separation or divorce. These objective indices buttressed Chinese statements to the effect that husband and wife in minor marriages found each other less romantically or erotically attractive. When various economic developments eroded parental ability to enforce minor-marriage arrangements, the couples who were to marry in this manner made other arrangements, spontaneously avoiding the minor marriages.

Wolf also drew attention to a study of sibling incest in Chicago (Weinberg 1963). It found that the only offenders who had contemplated marriage with each other were those who had been raised apart.

Wolf's conclusions have been criticized, generally by offering alternative interpretations of the same data. For example, it has been suggested that because the minor marriage is less prestigious, the bride in such a marriage will be treated poorly and hence make a poor wife, or the couple in such a marriage will be chagrined by the stigma of it and thus make a poor marriage. But Wolf and Huang (1980:173–175) point out that regular (major-marriage) brides are more mistreated when they move into their in-laws' household, and they show that couples brought together in a marriage that is clearly less prestigious than minor marriage— one in which the groom goes to live with the bride's family—have more fertile and more stable marriages than the minor marriages (1980:169, 185). Interestingly, Wolf and Huang (1980:285) report that their Chinese informants seemed unaware of the lesser fertility of minor marriages.

Further support for the Westermarck hypothesis comes from the Near East. Students of Arab societies have long been aware of a preference often found among those peoples for a man to marry his father's brother's daughter who, given the patrilineal nature of their kinship system, is a rather close relative by any sense of the term. Marriages that conform to this ideal are not in fact very common, though more common than in other parts of the world. Since brothers typically live in close social and spatial contact with each other in Arab societies, it follows that their children are likely to be close too and, hence, that the preference for them to marry appears to run counter to the Westermarck hypothesis. However, Justine McCabe (1983), who studied an Arab village in Lebanon, found that the evidence supports Westermarck.

In the village McCabe studied, "first cousins grew up in an association as close as that of siblings" (1983:58). She found that the relationship between a boy and his father's brother's daughter was essentially the same as between a boy and his sister: it rested on a constant and intimate interaction from birth (including sexual exploration when very young), and was characterized by "informality, candor, teasing, tattling, quarreling, laughing, joking" and the exchange of confidences (1983:59).

But marriages between patrilateral parallel cousins produced 23 percent fewer children during the first 25 years of marriage and were four times more likely to end in divorce than all other marriages. McCabe (1983:61) cites other scholars who, from early in this century, had noted signs of greater "sexual apathy" or "coolness" in patrilateral cousin marriages. As in the Chinese case, McCabe argues, it is parents or others, not the ones who actually marry, who prefer patrilateral parallel cousin marriages.

If the Westermarck effect is real, an important issue is the age limits within which it is created. Wolf and Huang (1980:185) offered some insight into the matter by noting that minor marriages in which the children were brought together before age 4 were two times more likely to end in divorce than minor marriages in which the children became acquainted at age 8 or later. Joseph Shepher (1983) has looked at the matter more closely. Born and raised in an Israeli commune himself, Shepher conducted the most thorough study of marriage in Israeli communes, getting data on 2769 married couples in 211 *kibbutzim*. Among them he found only 20 marriages between members of the same commune and only 14 that allegedly took place between persons who had been in the same peer group. But on contacting these 14 couples he found that all cases dissolved: there was not a single case of marriage between a boy and girl who had spent the first 6 years of their lives in the same peer group. In the one commune (his own) in which he could get reliable data on premarital sex he also found that none had occurred between persons raised from infancy in the same peer group. Boys and girls brought into the group at later ages sometimes did have an intense attraction to one of their group mates.

There was no attempt in the communes to stop the sexual experimentation of young children. There was no attempt to keep adolescents and young adults from dating or marrying their commune mates, though they were supposed to refrain from sex in general during high school. There was in fact some encouragement of intracommunal marriage.

Examining the pattern of entry and exit from peer groups, and the resulting pattern of attraction or sexual interest or uninterest among the relevant parties, Shepher concludes that a form of imprinting (or negative imprinting) occurred, that it was complete by the age of 6, and that it took about 4 years. He argues that this imprinting is a phylogenetic adaptation to reduce the harmful effects of inbreeding.

Certain lines of research conducted largely outside of anthropology also have a close bearing on the Westermarck hypothesis. They include studies of the physical or medical consequences of inbreeding among humans (as well as other animals), studies of evolved inbreeding avoidance mechanisms in nonhuman species, and studies of the social consequences of human incest.

Reviewing the scanty literature on the empirical consequences of inbreeding among humans, Shepher (1983) finds that full-sibling or parent-child incest results in about 17 percent child mortality and 25 percent child disability, for a combined result of about 42 percent nonviable offspring. The negative consequences decline rapidly for more distant inbreeding. If the figures Shepher cites are even approximately correct, mechanisms to avoid the costs of incest between close kin are quite expectable.[3]

---

[3]Arens (1986:17–23; see also May 1979) summarizes the same or similar materials, with similar results (but cf. Bittles 1983). Arens wonders how, if the consequences of inbreeding are "not controversial or debatable," it is then possible for some anthropologists to consider inbreeding costs irrelevant to understanding incest avoidance (1986:21). The answers are that by taking populations (not individuals) as units of analysis, some anthropologists have (1) noted that populations would not necessarily suffer from inbreeding, while others (2) observe that sustained inbreeding would, over the generations, actually eliminate harmful genes from the gene pool. Each of these lines of thought ignores "the immediate disadvantages for those most immediately involved" (Arens 1986:23).

A study of 38 captive mammalian species found a cross-species average of around 33 percent offspring mortality resulting from closely incestuous matings (the range of nonviability—measured rather conservatively in terms of "juvenile survival"—was all the way from 0 to nearly 100 percent) (Ralls, Ballou, and Templeton 1988). As the apparent consequence of this widespread phenomenon, equally widespread mechanisms have evolved that enable animals to avoid incest. These mechanisms operate in three distinguishable ways: by prohibition (only among humans, of course), by prevention, and by inhibition (Shepher 1983). In the case of prevention, incest simply cannot occur (because, for example, parents die before their offspring become fertile, or siblings are so widely dispersed that there is minuscule likelihood of their mating).

Inhibition, apparently brought about by imprinting or related processes, occurs when closely related and fertile individuals are in proximity but avoid mating with each other. Wolf, McCabe, and Shepher all provide evidence for some kind of negative imprinting that would, in the normal course of events, inhibit brother-sister incest among humans. Although the evidence he presents is minimal, Shepher (1983:108–110) argues that mother-son incest is also inhibited by imprinting (see also Fox 1980, Arens 1986). The opportunity for their imprinting is of course excellent, due to the prolonged and intimate contact of mother and child. In a great many societies the opportunities for developing aversion between father and child are the least.

Incest avoidance, via mechanisms of prevention or inhibition, is widely reported among many animal species (Bischof 1972), so that parent-offspring or sibling incest among animals in the wild is "apparently rather rare" (Lewin 1989:482). Consequently, the assumption that human incest avoidance is fundamentally a cultural phenomenon now rests on the inelegant assumption of a double discontinuity with the animal kingdom: unlike other species we lack innate avoidance mechanisms; unlike other species we therefore avoid incest via cultural prohibition (Arens 1986:94).

A third line of research, conducted mostly by psychologists and sociologists, and mostly in recent decades, concerns actual cases of human incest—a topic curiously neglected during most of the period in which the incest taboo has exercised the anthropological imagination. One of the most important consequences of these studies is their dismissal of the sociological or functionalist explanation of the incest taboo. In a line of thought that Arens (1986:29) traces back as far as Jeremy Bentham—but in more recent times through many distinguished anthropologists—it has often been argued that incestuous relations would confound the organization of the family, rendering it inefficient and thereby rendering society inefficient. As persuasive as this line of reasoning has been—in the absence of empirical tests—it now appears to be incorrect.

Bagley (1969; summarized in Arens 1986) analyzed 425 published cases of incest, finding 93 instances in which incest was the means that allowed the family to *maintain* its functional integrity. Typically, a father-daughter relationship replaced the father-mother relationship when the mother was either unable or unwilling to fulfill her role. Bagley (1969) describes this as "functional incest." Whatever the psychological costs may be to individuals, the study of actual cases of incest gives no obvious support to the assumption that society, or even the family, is necessarily threatened by incest (Arens 1986; see also Willner 1983 and La Fontaine 1988).

A recent study (Parker and Parker 1986) of incestuous relationships has a more direct bearing on the Westermarck hypothesis. Although the actual frequencies of the various forms of nuclear family incest—brother-sister, mother-son, and father-daughter—is a matter of uncertainty, there is substantial agreement that father-daughter incest is much commoner than mother-son incest. Furthermore, the variant of stepfather-stepdaughter incest seems to be disproportionately common. There are a number of explanations for this, not all of them mutually exclusive. One of them has to do with imprinting: if some form of imprinting results in the inhibition of incestuous desires, on the average it would, as noted earlier, probably work best between mother and son, not so well between father and daughter, and even less well between stepfather and stepdaughter.

Parker and Parker (1986) tested this line of thought by comparing sexually abusive and nonabusive fathers with comparable backgrounds. Comparing fathers who had been present in the household during the first three years of their daughters' lives, the Parkers found that abusers had been "much less frequently involved in caring and nurturing activities" (1986:540). They also found that in general stepfathers or adoptive fathers were more likely to be abusive, apparently because such fathers were less likely to have an effective bonding (imprinting) experience. When biological fathers were compared to step- or adoptive fathers with similar degrees of early childhood contacts with their daughters, no significant differences in abuse were found (1986:541). These findings support the Westermarck hypothesis and extend it beyond the brother-sister relationship that has been the principal focus of recent anthropological studies.

But in spite of the mounting evidence that supports the Westermarck hypothesis, and fails to support its rivals, such as the functionalist hypothesis, the dust has not settled on all the issues involved. Ancient Egyptian materials, for example, pose a problem precisely where the evidence for the Westermarck effect seems strongest: inhibition of brother-sister incest. Keith Hopkins (1980) provides evidence that brother-sister marriages were actually common for a period in Egypt and, hence, that incest avoidance in general, not merely the taboo, may not in fact be universal.

About 44 years after Alexander the Great conquered Egypt in 332 B.C., a Greek king of Egypt divorced his wife and married his full sister (who was about 10 years older than he). While there may have been some Greek precedent for his action—half-sibling marriages were alleged to be possible in certain ancient Greek communities—he was also following an ancient Egyptian custom. Whatever the case, 7 of the next 11 Greek kings in Egypt married their sisters. There is some vague evidence that the custom was penetrating other parts of the populace. Egypt subsequently passed to Roman rule.

Beginning in A.D. 19–20 and lasting until 257–258, the Roman administrators of Egypt conducted periodic censuses of the Egyptian population. Some 270 actual household returns survive; 172 returns, listing 880 persons, are in good enough condition to be used. While not in any sense a random sample, they report households widely spread in time, space, and social class. Seventeen of the 113 marriages ongoing at the time of the censuses were definitely between brother and sister, another 6 may have been. Thus some 15 to 21 percent of the ongoing marriages reported in these returns were brother-sister marriages. Eleven or 12 marriages were between full siblings, 8 between half siblings; in 3 the kind of sibling relationship is uncertain. Given the probable demographic structure of the family under the conditions of the time, there was only about a 40 percent likelihood of any family having a brother and sister of marriageable age. Thus a third or more of those who could marry their sisters did so. This is a very high proportion and, if correct, it provides the only known case in which brother-sister marriages were common throughout a populace.

Other forms of documentation—such as wedding invitations, letters, and marriage contracts—routinely mention brother-sister marriage, which indicates not only that it occurred but that it was considered normal. Some letters indicate real affection between the sibling couples, although this line of evidence is weakened by the Egyptian use of the term "sister" as a euphemism or term of endearment for women who were not actually one's sister (Arens 1986:111–112).

The marriages were fertile, and no source indicates an awareness of harmful genetic consequences. But Hopkins does not indicate *how* fertile they were, and perhaps it should be asked whether the high rates of infant mortality in preindustrial societies might not tend to mask any mortality brought about by inbreeding (recall also that the Chinese seemed unaware of the lesser fertility of their minor marriages).

Hopkins is unable to find any reason peculiar to the Egyptian condition that may have induced parents to foist this kind of marriage on their children (though the late average age of first marriages—in their mid-twenties—does suggest parental involvement). Hopkins cites marriage contracts between brothers and sisters that specify dowry and/or separate property and hence suggest that sibling marriage was not a device to avoid marriage expenses or the division of family property.

Addressing the problem of how else to explain brother-sister marriage, Hopkins presents what can only be called a classically cultural explanation. He draws attention to the importance in Egyptian religion of Isis and Osiris, who were brother and sister, husband and wife[4]; a romantic tradition of idealizing brother-sister love in story and poetry; and the evidence that the status of women was high and that they therefore exercised some autonomy in marriage and divorce. That love was a basis for marriage, and its cessation a basis for divorce, is well attested. Hence, Hopkins is left with the possibility that brothers and sisters married because they wanted to.

In A.D. 212–213 the Egyptians were made Roman citizens, for whom marriage with near-kin was prohibited. Sibling marriage disappeared.

Given the spottiness of the Egyptian data it is difficult to decide how much credence to give them. But a few points should be noted. Hopkins gives the ages of five sibling couples; they were separated in age by 7, 8, 4, 8, and 20 years. With one exception, then, these are not necessarily couples who were raised together as children or, at any rate, who were raised together in the manner that produces the Westermarck effect. It would be of interest to know more about child-rearing practices among Roman Egyptians.

Shepher's (1983) response to the Egyptian case was to dismiss it on the grounds that the data were few and that a single exception can carry little weight (he thereby reversed, by the way, the de facto opinion of many anthropologists that a single exception is all it takes to dismiss claims of universality). In this context, Shepher argued that unrestricted universals were not very likely to occur anyway—since nature operates by probability—so that a near-universal was the most to be expected.

Spiro (1982) summarizes other criticisms of the Westermarck hypothesis and adds his own. He notes, for example, an alternative interpretation of the *kibbutz* case. Spiro says it is not the child rearing but rather the adolescent repression of sexuality that produces the strong tendency for boys and girls to go outside their peer group and *kibbutz* to find mates. In adolescence, children were still living together, but their childhood exploration of sexuality was to stop. They were strongly urged to forgo sex until education was complete. In Spiro's view, this adolescent frus-

---

[4]Isis was the most extensively worshiped Egyptian deity and, perhaps ironically, was particularly associated with fertility.

tration resulted in peer group members' lack of interest in one another—they responded, in effect, to a consciously stated taboo.

To support his argument, Spiro cites Kaffman (1977), a psychiatrist employed by the *kibbutz* movement, who says that liaisons between children raised in the same peer group do in fact now occur. Since infant socialization has not changed, but adolescent controls have been relaxed, it is adolescent conditions that are critical. Unfortunately, Kaffman gives no data. Shepher (1983) dismisses Kaffman's argument and notes that marriages between those who had been adolescent (but not childhood) peers did occur before; hence, adolescent repression of sexuality could not have been the crucial factor. (But note that such marriages weren't at all common. A defect in Shepher's contribution is that by narrowing imprinting to a 4-year period that must occur in the first 6 years of life he has made this a small part of what must be various controls on incest, since even individuals who were not reared in the same peer group but who were resident in the same commune seem to marry rather infrequently. The low rate of intra-*kibbutz* marriage in general must find some of its explanation in some other factors.)

Spiro also draws attention to two further considerations. One is the smallness of the peer groups, which makes finding a mate outside them statistically expectable. The other is that the boys and girls in the peer groups were the same age; since young girls tend to be interested in older boys, and older boys in younger girls, they therefore tend to seek mates outside the peer group.

What lessons, in conclusion, may be derived from the recent efforts to understand the incest taboo/avoidance? One is the sobering reflection that an alleged universal that has exercised the anthropological imagination for over 100 years is still not explained to everyone's satisfaction. It is not even certain that the phenomenon is a universal. The incest taboo clearly is not universal, though it surely is a statistical universal and might be a near-universal. On the other hand, incest avoidance may be universal.

Even more sobering has been the impact of biological considerations that for decades were all but banned from mainstream anthropological thought. The ethological discovery that humans are far from unique in avoiding incest has entirely reoriented the problem. The resuscitation of the Westermarck hypothesis has provided a successfully tested explanation for part of the phenomenon. In eliminating possible hypotheses, and in accumulating relevant data, then, there has been progress. This experience suggests that anthropologists might do well to look into other lines of thought that may have been neglected for no good reason (a lesson no less applicable to sociology; see Scheff 1985).

Also important to notice in the incest-avoidance example is the clear attempt to explain the phenomenon by clarifying the ultimate (evolutionary) conditions that generate the mechanisms and by specifying the proximate mechanisms that generate the universal—infant (negative) imprinting, resulting in specified psychological states in the individual. Equally important has been the exploitation of natural experiments and the role that quantitative testing or analysis has played.

In the long run it may be that the Westermarck hypothesis will not stand up; certainly it is only a partial explanation that does not preclude other, complementary explanations. But the mode of explaining—involving ethological and evolutionary perspectives, a detailed specification of mechanisms and of individual motivation, a diligent search for natural experiments, and quantitative tests when possible—deserves emulation with other universals.

6

The Universal People

What do all people, all societies, all cultures, and all languages have in common? In the following pages I attempt to provide answers, in the form of a description of what I will call the Universal People (UP). Theirs is a description of every people or of people in general. Bear in mind the tentative nature of this chapter: as surely as it leaves out some universals it includes some that will prove in the long run not to be universal, and even more surely it divides up traits and complexes in ways that in time will give way to more accurate or meaningful divisions. At the end of the chapter I will discuss how it was put together and the ways in which it will change in the future.

Although humans are not unique in their possession of culture—patterns of doing and thinking that are passed on within and between generations by learning—they certainly are unique in the extent to which their thought and action are shaped by such patterns. The UP are aware of this uniqueness and posit a difference between their way—culture—and the way of nature.

A very significant portion of UP culture is embodied in their language, a system of communication without which their culture would necessarily be very much simpler. With language the UP think about and discuss both their internal states and the world external to each individual (this is not to deny that they also think without language—surely they do). With language, the UP organize, respond to, and manipulate the behavior of their fellows. UP language is of strategic importance for those who wish to study the UP. This is so because their language is, if not precisely a mirror of, then at least a window into, their culture and into their minds and actions. Their language is not a perfect mirror or window, for there are often discrepancies between what the UP say, think, and do. But we would be very hard pressed to understand many aspects of the UP without access to their thinking through their language. Because their language is not a simple reflex of the way the world is, we need to distinguish their (emic) conceptualization of it from objective (etic) conceptualizations of the world.

The UP's language allows them to think and speak in abstractions, and about things or processes not physically present. If one of them is proficient in the use of language—particularly if it is a male—it gains him prestige, in part because good speech allows him to more effectively manipulate, for better or worse, the behavior of his fellows. An important means of verbal manipulation among the UP is gossip.

In their conversations the UP manage in many ways to express more than their mere words indicate. For example, shifts in tone, timing, and other features of speech indicate that one person is or is not ready for another to take a turn at speaking. UP speech is used to misinform as well as inform. Even if an individual among the UP does not tell lies, he understands the concept and watches for it in others. For some UP do lie, and they dissimulate and mislead in other ways too. UP use of language includes ways to be funny and ways to insult.

UP speech is highly symbolic. Let me explain how this is different from animal communication. Many bird species vocalize a danger warning. The vocalization is substantially the same for the species from one location to another. Indeed, it is somewhat similar from one species to another. Humans have cries of fright and warning that are in some ways analogous to these bird calls, but between many, many members of our species our routine vocalizations are meaningless. This is so because speech sounds and the things they signify have very little intrinsic connection. Sound and sense, as a rule, are only arbitrarily associated. Equally arbitrary is the way units of speech that are equivalent to our words get strung together to make sentences. But in spite of this arbitrariness there are features of language at all basic levels—phonemic, grammatical, and semantic—that are found in all languages.

Thus UP phonemes—their basic speech sounds—include a contrast between vocalics (sounds produced in or channeled through the oral cavity) and nonvocalics (e.g., nasals). UP language has contrasts between vowels and contrasts between stops and nonstops (a stop, e.g., English *p* or *b*, stops the flow of air during speech). The phonemes of UP speech form a system of contrasts, and the number of their phonemes goes neither above 70 nor below 10.

In time, their language undergoes change. So it follows that the UP do not speak the language of their more remote ancestors, though it may be quite similar.

However much grammar varies from language to language, some things are always present. For example, UP language includes a series of contrasting terms that theoretically could be phrased in three different ways, but that are only phrased two ways. To illustrate, they could talk about the "good" and the "bad" (two contrasting terms, neither with a marker added to express negation); or they could talk about the "good" and the "not good" (i.e., not having the word "bad" at all but expressing its meaning with a marked version of its opposite, the marking in this case to negate), or they could talk about the "bad" and the "not bad" (i.e., not having the word "good," etc.). Logically, these alternatives are identical: each arrangement conveys the same information. Similar possibilities exist for "deep" and "shallow," "wide" and "narrow," etc. But in each case the third possibility never occurs as the obligatory or common way of talking. So the UP are never forced to express, for lack of an alternative, the ideas of "good," "wide," "deep," and so on as negated versions of their opposites.

By virtue of its grammar UP language conveys some information redundantly. In English, for example, both subject and verb indicate number, while in Spanish both noun and adjective indicate gender.

Two final points about UP grammar are that it contains nouns and verbs, and the possessive. The latter is used both for what have been called the "intimate" or "inalienable" possessions, i.e., to talk about their fingers, your hands, and her thoughts, and for "loose" or "alienable" possessions too, e.g., my axe.

The UP have special forms of speech for special occasions. Thus they have poetic or rhetorical standards deemed appropriate to speech in particular settings. They use narrative to explain how things came to be and to tell stories. Their language includes figurative speech: metaphor is particularly prominent, and metonymy (the use of a word for that with which it is associated, e.g., crown for king) is always included too. The UP can speak onomatopoeically (using words that imitate sound, like "bowwow"), and from time to time they do. They have poetry in which lines, demarcated by pauses, are about 3 seconds in duration. The poetic lines are characterized by the repetition of some structural, semantic, or auditory elements but by free variation too.

Most of the specific elementary units of meaning in UP language—units that are sometimes but not always equivalent to words—are not found in all the rest of the languages of the world. This does not prevent us from translating much of the UP speech into our own or any other particular language: centimeters and inches are not the same entities, but we can translate one to another quite precisely; people who lack a word for "chin" and thus call it the "end of the jaw" still make sense.

A few words or meanings cut across all cultural boundaries and hence form a part of UP language. I am not saying, of course, that the UP make the same speech sounds as we English speakers do for these words, but rather that the meanings for these terms are expressed by the UP in their terms. For example, the UP have terms for black and white (equivalent to dark and light when no other basic colors are encoded) and for face, hand, and so on.

Certain semantic components are found in UP language, even if the terms in which they are employed are not. For example, UP kin terminology includes terms that distinguish male from female (and thus indicate the semantic component of sex) and some generations from others. If not explicit, durational time is semantically implicit in their language, and they have units of time—such as days, months, seasons, and years. In various ways there is a temporal cyclicity or rhythmicity to UP lives. The UP can distinguish past, present, and future.

UP language also classifies parts of the body, inner states (such as emotions, sensations, or thoughts), behavioral propensities, flora, fauna, weather conditions, tools, space (by which they give directions), and many other definite topics, though each of them does not necessarily constitute an emically distinct lexical domain. The UP language refers to such semantic categories as motion, speed, location, dimension, and other physical properties; to giving (including analogous actions, such as lending); and to affecting things or people.

As is implied in their use of metaphor and metonymy, UP words (or word equivalents) are sometimes polysemous, having more than one meaning. Their antonyms and synonyms are numerous. The words or word equivalents that the UP use more frequently are generally shorter, while those they use less frequently are longer.

UP language contains both proper names and pronouns. The latter include at least three persons and two categories of number. Their language contains numerals, though they may be as few as "one, two, and many."

The UP have separate terms for kin categories that include mother and father. That is, whereas some peoples include father and father's brothers in a single kin category, and lump mother with her sisters—so that it is obligatory or normal to refer to each of one's parents with terms that lump them with others—it is not obligatory among the UP to refer to their actual parents in ways that lump mother with father.

UP kinship terms are partially or wholly translatable by reference to the relationships inherent in procreation: mother, father, son, daughter. The UP have an age terminology that includes age grades in a linear sequence similar to the sequence child, adolescent, adult, etc. Our first reflex is to think that it could not be otherwise, but it could: an elderly person can be "like a child"; an age classification that had a term indicating "dependent age" could break from the normal pattern of linearity.

The UP have a sex terminology that is fundamentally dualistic, even when it comprises three or four categories. When there are three, one is a combination of the two basic sexes (e.g., a hermaphrodite), or one is a crossover sex (e.g., a man acting as a woman). When there are four there are then two normal sexes and two crossover sexes.

Naming and taxonomy are fundamental to UP cognition. Prominent elements in UP taxonomy and other aspects of their speech and thought are binary discriminations, forming contrasting terms or semantic components (a number of which have already been mentioned—black and white, nature and culture, male and female, good and bad, etc.). But the UP also can order continua, so they can indicate not only contrasts but polar extremes with gradations between them. Thus there are middles between their opposites, or ranked orders in their classifications. The UP are able to express the measure of things and distances, though not necessarily with uniform units.

The UP employ such elementary logical notions as "not," "and," "same," "equivalent," and "opposite." They distinguish the general from the particular and parts from wholes. Unfortunately, the UP overestimate the objectivity of their mode of thought (it is particularly unobjective when they compare their in-group with out-groups).

The UP use what has been called "conjectural" reasoning to, for example, deduce from minute clues the identification, presence, and behavior of animals, or from miscellaneous symptoms the presence of a particular disease that cannot in itself be observed and is a wholly abstract conception.

Language is not the only means of symbolic communication employed by the UP. They employ gestures too, especially with their hands and arms. Some of their nonverbal communication is somewhat one-sided, in that the message is received consciously but may be sent more or less spontaneously. For example, the squeals of children, cries of fright, and the like all send messages that UP watch closely or listen to carefully, even though the sender did not consciously intend them to communicate. The UP do not merely listen and watch what is on the surface, they interpret external behavior to grasp interior intention.

Communication with their faces is particularly complex among the UP, and some of their facial expressions are recognized everywhere. Thus UP faces show happiness, sadness, anger, fear, surprise, disgust, and contempt, in a manner entirely familiar from one society to another. When they smile while greeting persons it signifies friendly intentions. UP cry when they feel unhappiness or pain. A young woman acting coy or flirting with her eyes does it in a way you would recognize quite clearly. Although some facial communication is spontaneous, as noted earlier, the UP can mask, modify, and mimic otherwise spontaneous expressions. Whether by face, words, gesture, or otherwise, the UP can show affection as well as feel it.

The UP have a concept of the person in the psychological sense. They distinguish self from others, and they can see the self both as subject and object. They do not see the person as a wholly passive recipient of external action, nor do they see the self as wholly autonomous. To some degree, they see the person as responsible for his or her actions. They distinguish actions that are under control from those that are not. They understand the concept of intention. They know that people have a private inner life, have memories, make plans, choose between alternatives, and otherwise make decisions (not without ambivalent feeling sometimes). They know that people can feel pain and other emotions. They distinguish normal from abnormal mental states. The UP personality theory allows them to think of individuals departing from the pattern of behavior associated with whatever status(es) they occupy, and they can explain these departures in terms of the individual's character. The UP are spontaneously and intuitively able to, so to say, get in the minds of others to imagine how they are thinking and feeling.

In addition to the emotions that have already been mentioned, the UP are moved by sexual attraction; sometimes they are deeply disturbed by sexual jealousy. They also have childhood fears, including fear of loud noises and—particularly toward the end of the first year of life—of strangers (this is the apparent counterpart of a strong attachment to their caretaker at this time). The UP react emotionally—generally with fear—to snakes. With effort, the UP can overcome some of their fears. Because there is normally a man present to make a claim on a boy's mother, the Oedipus complex—in the sense of a little boy's possessiveness toward his mother and coolness toward her consort—is a part of male UP psychology.

The UP recognize individuals by their faces, and in this sense they most certainly have an implicit concept of the individual (however little they may explicitly conceptualize the individual apart from social statuses). They recognize individuals in other ways too.

The UP are quintessential tool makers: not simply because they make tools—some other animals do too—but because they make so many, so many different kinds of them, and are so dependent upon them. Unlike the other animals, the UP use tools to make tools. They make cutters that improve upon what they can do with their teeth or by tearing with their hands. They make pounders that improve upon what they can do with their teeth, fists, feet, knees, shoulders, elbows, and head. They make containers that allow them to hold more things at one time, to hold them more comfortably or continuously, and to hold them when they otherwise couldn't, as over a fire. Whether it be string, cord, sinew, vine, wire, or whatever, the UP have something to use to tie things together and make interlaced materials. They know and use the lever. Some of their tools are weapons, including the spear. The UP make many of their tools with such permanence that they can use them over and over again. They also make some of their tools in uniform patterns that are more or less arbitrary—thus we can often tell one people's tools from another's. Such patterns persist beyond any one person's lifetime. Since tools are so closely related to human hands, we might note in passing that most people among the UP are right-handed.

The UP may not know how to make fire, but they know how to use it. They use fire to cook food but for other purposes too. Tools and fire do much to make them more comfortable and secure. The UP have other ways to make themselves feel better (or different). These include substances they can take to alter their moods or feelings: stimulants, narcotics, or intoxicants. These are in addition to what they take for mere sustenance.

The UP always have some form of shelter from the elements. Further ways in which they attend to their material needs will be discussed later.

The UP have distinct patterns of preparation for birth, for giving birth, and for postnatal care. They also have a more or less standard pattern and time for weaning infants.

The UP are not solitary dwellers. They live part of their lives, if not the whole of them, in groups. One of their most important groups is the family, but it is not the only group among them. One or more of the UP groups maintains a unity even though the members are dispersed.

The UP have groups defined by locality or claiming a certain territory, even if they happen to live almost their entire lives as wanderers upon the sea. They are materially, cognitively, and emotionally adjusted to the environment in which they normally live (particularly with respect to some of its flora and fauna). A sense of being a distinct people characterizes the UP, and they judge other people in their own terms.

The core of a normal UP family is composed of a mother and children. The biological mother is usually expected to be the social mother and usually is. On a more or less permanent basis there is usually a man (or men) involved, too, and he (or they) serve minimally to give the children a status in the community and/or to be a consort to the mother. Marriage, in the sense of a "person" having a publicly recognized right of sexual access to a woman deemed eligible for childbearing, is institutionalized among the UP. While the person is almost always a male, it need not necessarily be a single individual, nor even a male.[1]

The UP have a pattern of socialization: children aren't just left to grow up on their own. Senior kin are expected to contribute substan-

---

[1] Among some peoples, for example, a woman *A* may assume the status of a man, take a woman *B* as wife, and then arrange for the wife *B* to bear children to which *A* will be the social father.

tially to socialization. One of the ways children learn among the UP is by watching elders and copying them. The socialization of UP children includes toilet training. Through practice, children and adults perfect what they learn. The UP learn some things by trial and error.

One's own children and other close kin are distinguished from more distant relatives or nonrelatives among the UP, and the UP favor their close kin in various contexts.

UP families and the relationships of their family members to each other and to outsiders are affected by their sexual regulations, which sharply delimit, if not eliminate, mating between the genetically close kin. Mating between mother and son, in particular, is unthinkable or taboo. Sex is a topic of great interest to the UP, though there may be contexts in which they will not discuss it.

Some groups among the UP achieve some of their order by division into socially significant categories or subgroups on the basis of kinship, sex, and age. Since the UP have kinship, sex, and age statuses, it follows, of course, that they have statuses and roles and hence a social structure. But they have statuses beyond those of sex, age, and kinship categories. And while these are largely ascribed statuses, they have achieved statuses too. There are rules of succession to some of their statuses.

Although it may be only another way of saying that they have statuses and roles, the UP recognize social personhood: social identities, including collective identities, that are distinguishable from the individuals who bear them. The distinction between persons and individuals involves the entification of the former; i.e., the UP speak of statuses as though they were entities that can act and be acted upon, such as we do when we say, for example, that "the legislature" (a social entity) "punished the university" (another social entity).

Prestige is differentially distributed among the UP, and the members of UP society are not all economically equal. They acknowledge inequalities of various sorts, but we cannot specify whether they approve or disapprove.

The UP have a division of labor, minimally based on the sex and age statuses already mentioned. For example, their women have more direct child-care duties than do their men. Children are not expected to, and typically do not, engage in the same activities in the same way that adults do. Related to this division of labor, men and women and adults and children are seen by the UP as having different natures. Their men are in fact on the average more physically aggressive than women and are more likely to commit lethal violence than women are.

In the public political sphere men form the dominant element among the UP. Women and children are correspondingly submissive or acquiescent, particularly, again, in the public political sphere.

In addition to their division of labor, whereby different kinds of people do different things, the UP have customs of cooperative labor, in which people jointly undertake essentially similar tasks. They use reciprocal exchanges, whether of labor, or goods, or services, in a variety of settings. Reciprocity—including its negative or retaliatory forms—is an important element in the conduct of their lives. The UP also engage in trade, that is, in nonreciprocal exchanges of goods and services (i.e., one kind of good or service for another). Whether reciprocally or not, they give gifts to one another too. In certain contexts they share food.

Whether in the conduct of family life, of subsistence activities, or other matters, the UP attempt to predict and plan for the future. Some of their plans involve the maintenance or manipulation of social relations. In this context it is important to note that the UP possess "triangular awareness," the ability to think not only of their own relationships to others but of the relationships between others in relation to themselves. Without such an ability they would be unable to form their ubiquitous coalitions.

The UP have government, in the sense that they have public affairs and these affairs are regulated, and in the sense that decisions binding on a collectivity are made. Some of the regulation takes place in a framework of corporate statuses (statuses with orderly procedures for perpetuating membership in them).

The UP have leaders, though they may be ephemeral or situational. The UP admire, or profess to admire, generosity, and this is particularly desired in a leader. No leader of the UP ever has complete power lodged in himself alone. UP leaders go beyond the limits of UP reason and morality. Since the UP never have complete democracy, and never have complete autocracy, they always have a de facto oligarchy.

The UP have law, at least in the sense of rules of membership in perpetual social units and in the sense of rights and obligations attached to persons or other statuses. Among the UP's laws are those that in certain situations proscribe violence and rape. Their laws also proscribe murder—unjustified taking of human life (though they may justify taking lives in some contexts). They have sanctions for infractions, and these sanctions include removal of offenders from the social unit—whether by expulsion, incarceration, ostracism, or execution. They punish (or otherwise censure or condemn) certain acts that threaten the group or are alleged to do so.

Conflict is more familiar to the UP than they wish it were, and they have customary, though far from perfect, ways of dealing with it (their proscription of rape and other forms of violence, for example, does not eliminate them). They understand that wronged parties may seek redress. They employ consultation and mediation in some conflict cases.

Important conflicts are structured around in-group–out-group antagonisms that characterize the UP. These antagonisms both divide the UP as an ethnic group as well as set them off from other ethnic groups.

An ethical dualism distinguishes the in-group from the out-group, so that, for example, cooperation is more expectable in the former than with the latter.

The UP distinguish right from wrong, and at least implicitly, as noted earlier, recognize responsibility and intentionality. They recognize and employ promises. Reciprocity, also mentioned earlier, is a key element in their morality. So, too, is their ability to empathize. Envy is ubiquitous among the UP, and they have symbolic means for coping with its unfortunate consequences.

Etiquette and hospitality are among UP ideals. They have customary greetings and customs of visiting kin or others who dwell elsewhere. They have standardized, preferred, or typical times of day to eat, and they have occasions on which to feast. In other ways, too, they have normal daily routines of activities and are fundamentally diurnal.

They have standards of sexual modesty—even though they might customarily go about naked. People, adults in particular, do not normally copulate in public, nor do they relieve themselves without some attempt to do it modestly. Among their other taboos are taboos on certain utterances and certain kinds of food. On the other hand, there are some kinds of food—sweets in particular—that they relish.

The UP have religious or supernatural beliefs in that they believe in something beyond the visible and palpable. They anthropomorphize and (some if not all of them) believe things that are demonstrably false. They also practice magic, and their magic is designed to do such things as to sustain and increase life and to win the attention of the opposite sex. They have theories of fortune and misfortune. They have ideas about how to explain disease and death. They see a connection between sickness and death. They try to heal the sick and have medicines for this purpose. The UP practice divination. And they try to control the weather.

The UP have rituals, and these include rites of passage that demarcate the transfer of an individual from one status to another. They mourn their dead.

Their ideas include a worldview—an understanding or conception of the world about them and their place in it. In some ways their worldview is structured by features of their minds. For example, from early infancy they have the ability to identify items that they know by one sense with the same items perceived in another sense, and so they see the world as a unity, not as different worlds imposed by our different sense modalities. Their worldview is a part of their supernatural and mythological beliefs. They have folklore too. The UP dream and attempt to interpret their dreams.

However spiritual they may be, the UP are materialists also. As indicated by their language having the possessive for use on "loose property," the UP have concepts of property, distinguishing what belongs—

minimal though it may be—to the individual, or group, from what belongs to others. They also have rules for the inheritance of property.

In addition to their use of speech in poetic or polished ways, the UP have further aesthetic standards. However little clothing they wear, they nonetheless adorn their bodies in one way or another, including a distinctive way of maintaining or shaping their hair. They have standards of sexual attractiveness (including, for example, signs of good health and a clear male preference for the signs of early nubility rather than those of the postmenopausal state). Their decorative art is not confined to the body alone, for the UP apply it to their artifacts too. In addition to their patterns of grooming for essentially aesthetic reasons, they also have patterns of hygienic care.

The UP know how to dance and have music. At least some of their dance (and at least some of their religious activity) is accompanied by music. They include melody, rhythm, repetition, redundancy, and variation in their music, which is always seen as an art, a creation. Their music includes vocals, and the vocals include words—i.e., a conjunction of music and poetry. The UP have children's music.

The UP, particularly their youngsters, play and playfight. Their play, besides being fun, provides training in skills that will be useful in adulthood.

The materials presented in this chapter—essentially a list of absolute universals—draws heavily from Murdock (1945), Tiger and Fox (1971) and Hockett (1973) and also from many other sources that are cited in the bibliography. In some cases I have added items to the list because my own experience or that of a colleague or student has convinced me that the items ought to be there even though appropriate references could not be found. In a few cases I have counted something as a universal even though that required setting aside ethnographic testimony. There are, for example, some reports of societies in which getting into other people's minds (empathizing, divining intent or inner feeling, and the like) is not done or even conceived as possible. My assumption is that these reports may be emically correct but not etically. For example, Selby (1974:106–107, 109) reports that the Zapotec, at least in some situations, do not think they can get into other people's minds, but he gives a clear case of this happening (1974:56). Similarly, to the Kaluli belief that "one cannot know what another thinks or feels," Ochs and Schieffelin (1984:290) comment that the Kaluli "obviously" do "interpret and assess one another's...internal states."

In an equally few cases I omitted items from this chapter that nevertheless do appear in the bibliography—because I was not sufficiently convinced by the references. For example, after surveying ethnographic literature on abortion, Devereux (1967:98) felt the evidence was so strong for universality that he dismissed some reports of its absence. He may be correct, but his argument did not quite convince me and I decided to err on the side of caution and to count abortion as a near-universal. Similarly, Otterbein (1987) states in various places that the absolute universality of capital punishment is one of the major finds of his survey. But in other places in the same work he speaks more cautiously of the possibility that it is only a near-universal. I decided to accept the cautious judgment.

More important than uncertainties about the boundaries between universals and near-universals is the issue of adequate conceptualization or definition of particular universals. For example, the conceptualizations of marriage and the family that I presented are those that currently seem the most convincing to me; they have been differently conceived or defined in the past and may undergo further revision in the future.

There are also some general problems of conceptualization which, were they properly addressed, would have led to a different presentation than the one above. As was discussed in chapter 2, some scholars distinguish between the surface (or substantive) universals and those that lie at some deeper level. This chapter has been more concerned with the former. A more serious pursuit of universals at the deeper level of process or innate mechanism may presumably unearth universals that are at present wholly unknown and almost certainly would produce hierarchical orders among some sets of universals, orders that distinguish the fundamental processes from their more superficial consequences.

Setting aside the issue of hierarchy, there are other problems with how the list of universals is ordered: which to start with, which to put in a set with which. Murdock (1945) took the easy way out and ordered his list alphabetically. While it seemed appropriate to me to begin with culture itself, and then to explore language, the order in which the remaining sets or clusters of items is presented is arbitrary. There is arbitrariness in each cluster, too, partly because I wanted to minimize repetitions. Repetitions do occur, and a fuller and truer account would include more repetitions or perhaps would show the interconnections between items by means of a diagram. For example, empathy (phrased in different ways but with the meaning of understanding another person's inner states) occurs in the description of the UP in the context of communication, morality, and psychological personhood—and is implicit elsewhere.

In sum, a fuller and truer account of the UP would in various ways show the relationships between the universals. But then a fuller and truer account of the UP would list their conditional universals (and *their* interrelationships and hierarchies) and would also offer explanations of the universals and their interrelationships. Anthropology has scarcely begun to illuminate the architecture of human universals. It is time to get on with the task.

7

Universals, Human Nature, and Anthropology

Universals help delineate the nature of the human species as such. To do this...has been the principal scientific aim of anthropology.
Goodenough 1970:130

[There is an] uninvited guest which has been seated...beside us and which is the human mind.
Lévi-Strauss 1953:4

The present essay is for me one of the most difficult I have ever attempted. This is because I am having to submit to question some of the axioms anthropologists of my generation—and several subsequent generations—were taught to hallow. These axioms express the belief that all human behavior is the result of social conditioning.
Turner 1983:221

Universals exist, they are numerous, and they engage matters unquestionably of anthropological concern. Universals can be explained, and their ramified effects on human affairs can be traced. But universals comprise a heterogenous set—cultural, social, linguistic, individual, unrestricted, implicational, etc.—a set that may defy any single overarching explanation. If, however, a single source for universals had to be sought, human nature would be the place to look. Human nature is not, however, something that we can always ascertain directly. Thus by the same token that we may seek the explanations for universals in human nature, we may use universals, as Goodenough says, as guides in the search for human nature.

Within human nature, surely it is the big and complex human mind that deserves our greatest attention. Lévi-Strauss understated the case by noting the presence of the human mind in the symposium of linguists and anthropologists that elicited his comment above: the human mind has always been with them, and crucially so, as I tried to illustrate in the first chapter.

Laying a foundation for understanding human nature and, hence, the human mind is the single most important unfinished piece of business in the social sciences today. Undertaking this task, in which the study of universals has an important part to play, will not be easy—for reasons that Turner neatly expresses.

There is no *good* reason for this state of affairs: as described in chapter 3, it is an accident of the way the social sciences developed. In the early decades of this century evolutionary theory was in disarray, so that Darwinism was as much used to defend racism as to illuminate human nature; behaviorism, with its assumption that the mind comprises little more than generalized learning mechanisms, was sidetracking psychology; studies such as Margaret Mead's on Samoan adolescence seemed to confirm the freedom of cultural traditions from significant channeling by human nature; there was an ethnographically diverse world to be studied before it disappeared, and this task seemed more urgent than did speculation on the remote evolutionary past in which humans evolved.

Anthropologists entertained the notion that culture was a level of phenomena free of causation from lower levels, such as the psychobiological. Culture was thus separated from nature; "learned" behavior was posed against animal "instincts." "Reducing" the former to the latter was bad science. Culture came to be considered the most important of all determinants of human action, and the study of culture effectively more important than the study of humans. What was human and not cultural was merely animal.

Analysis was centered on cultures or societies and their characteristics rather than on the humans thought to be shaped like clay by their social and cultural contexts. The uniqueness of each culture seemed obvious, the variety of cultures very great, and the similarities only limited. In this context, universals seemed anomalous—unlikely to be real or significant.

There were, however, some stated reservations about all this. Kroeber, as influential as anyone in separating culture from nature, acknowledged a "no-man's land" between them that would one day have to be explored. Benedict, as influential as anyone in arguing for the variety of cultural orientations, thought that the variety resulted from one or another emphasis on what was given by human nature. Since no one denied that humans *had* evolved, and human societies and cultures *did* have a past, there would, it was thought, come a time when it would be appropriate to use the results of scientific ethnography to reconstruct the human past.

There was an important unstated problem too. Whereas some things were "obviously" natural, and some were just as "obviously" cultural, there was no method for separating the cultural from the biological in cases where they might be mixed.

In time, the notion that culture is a phenomenal entity *sui generis*, uncaused by lower phenomenal levels, came under sustained attack and for most anthropologists has long since given way to the obvious truth that material factors of environment and economy, at least, are potent determinants of cultural development. Others have posited the human mind as a shaper of culture, yet on this point there has been serious resistance. To "reduce" culture to psychobiology remains for many social scientists a sort of taboo.

Whatever the motive may be for resisting the idea that there is a human nature whose features shape culture and society, its intellectual foundations have all but collapsed. Evolutionary theory today—after the synthesis of Darwinian evolution with Mendelian genetics, the virtual dismissal of group selection, and the various contributions of ethology and sociobiology—provides a framework for the whole of biology. Adapting this framework to the needs of anthropology poses special problems, but there is no reason to think that any part of the framework is inherently inimical to anthropology.

Behaviorism and the tabula rasa view of the mind are dead in the water. Chomsky's analysis of how language is acquired, studies of the consequences of brain trauma, the discovery of brain cell specialization, the implications of attempts to construct artificial intelligence (Tooby 1985), and other lines of evidence all point to a human brain that is a very complex combination of specialized mechanisms.

Margaret Mead's influential demonstrations that adolescence is stress-free in Samoa and that sex temperaments are reversed among the Chambri—which had supported the tabula rasa view of the mind and the apparent supremacy of culture over biology in human affairs—have been cast out. So, too, Whorf's seeming demonstration of timelessness among the Hopi. Due to these and similar developments, universals— along with their implications for a human nature that underlies them and shapes human affairs—assume the renewed significance in the anthropological enterprise that is the subject of this book.

The scientifically collected ethnographic reports that were all too few at the beginning of the century now strain the shelves, and it has long since been recognized that theory must give order to the collection of data: ethnographies are not just out there to be collected (but what passes for theory in anthropology too often suffers from the assumptions made early in this century). With the present wealth of ethnography, reconstructing the human past is much less the speculative matter that it was early in this century and is, therefore, a much more respectable activity.

The ambivalence that anthropologists have shown toward universals, and the resistance many anthropologists still show toward the concept of a fixed human nature and psychobiological reductionism, are not reflections of what is known about the human condition. They are reflections of erroneous assumptions that for the most part lie at rather high, though not the highest, levels of the hierarchy of propositions that inform the anthropological enterprise. A close examination of these propositions, showing where they err, is a necessary step in the reintegration of universals, and what they entail, into the anthropological enterprise.

At the most fundamental levels of the anthropological enterprise there are a series of relatively noncontroversial assumptions that define the boundaries of anthropology roughly as follows. Anthropology is concerned with what humans are and what humans do, along with the problems of how humans got to be the way they are and came to do what they do. Phrased differently, anthropology is concerned with such broad topics as the human condition, human affairs, and (more controversially) human nature. The distinctively anthropological contribution to these concerns is its comparative perspective: anthropology pursues its subject matters among all peoples in all times and places, and even across species. When a comparative perspective is neither employed nor necessary, other disciplines step in.[1] On the other hand, anthropology freely calls upon those other disciplines to solve its problems. I will call the propositions in this paragraph first-level propositions.

At a second level lie several propositions that are still relatively noncontroversial and that constitute basic answers to some of the questions posed at the first level. Thus, anthropologists assume (or find) that humans are an evolved species with a distinct nature. As with other organisms, everything that humans do is a product of their nature (which at root is a matter of genes) in interaction with the environments in which humans live. The human species evolved over a very long period of time and shows only minor racial variation. The human mind is one of the most distinctive and important features of human nature, and (barring sex and age differences) it is fundamentally the same in all human populations. Humans live socially, and their societal arrangements show considerable variation. Humans have rich cultural traditions that also show considerable variation. Social and cultural arrangements, which are themselves ultimately products of human activity, are significant parts of the environments in which humans live.

Beneath the very basic assumptions and findings just outlined, and that establish the *raison d'être* and scientific credentials of anthropol-

---

[1]This is not to deny that some aspects of anthropological method—such as the holistic approach, participant-observation, or the analysis of symbols—might legitimately be applied in our own society with only implicit comparison at best.

ogy, are middle-level propositions, mostly connected with the concept of culture, that have an important bearing on how anthropologists have viewed universals. These propositions have a significance that transcends their level in the hierarchy of propositions informing anthropology. These propositions are now controversial, and well they should be, for almost all are false or misleading:

1. Nature and culture are two distinct phenomenal realms.
2. Nature manifests itself in instincts (which are fixed action patterns) and culture manifests itself in learned behavior.
3. Because human nature is the same everywhere, it is culture that explains differences between human populations.
4. Human universals are likely to reflect human nature.
5. Except for its extraordinary capacity to absorb culture, the human mind is a largely blank slate.
6. Culture (because of 3 and 5) is the most important determinant of human affairs.
7. Explaining what people do in biological terms (i.e., in terms of nature instead of culture) is a reductionist fallacy (in extreme forms, explaining human affairs in *any* terms other than culture itself is reductionist fallacy).
8. Being autonomous, culture has an arbitrary and highly variable character.
9. Universals (because of 5 and 8) are few (and unimportant?).

The suspicion that proposition 9 might be false, and that this had ramifications for more fundamental elements in the anthropological enterprise, was one of the principal reasons for writing this book. And the logic that underpinned the suspicion can now be spelled out.

One of the most important consequences of the middle-level propositions—summed up in the sixth—is to leave certain propositions at the two highest levels formally correct yet nearly devoid of significance. The reference to human nature at the first level is rendered nugatory by the proposition that human nature consists essentially of the capacity for culture. At the second level, half of the equation that explains human affairs (the genes in genes + environment) is similarly affected because the environment, and above all one element within it, culture, is seen as the source of almost all variation. As a consequence of the middle-level propositions, nature does little more than set a stage for culture. But if proposition 9 and others are false, the role of human nature in the anthropological enterprise surely needs reassessment. Let us examine each proposition:

1. In its worst form, the proposition that nature and culture are two distinct phenomenal realms assumes a rigid dichotomy between nature and culture: a given trait, behavior, or institution is either cultural or it is natural, there is nothing in between. In any form, this proposition ignores the obvious truth that, whatever the validity of analytically distinguishing nature from culture, the latter must come from the former. Folk beliefs notwithstanding, there is no alternative to this materialist tenet. Moreover, there is every reason to think that any number of very interesting and important questions about humans and their affairs can only be fully answered in terms of quite specific interactions between nature and culture, often in dialectical, feedback relationships. But these interactions can only be properly explored if there are ways to distinguish nature from culture, and I submit that there is little if anything in the way of an established and valid method in anthropology[2] for doing this (see also Sperber 1986). Typically, anthropologists simply do not concern themselves with this problem, because they *assume* (in accordance with other propositions) that what humans do, unless it is "obviously" natural, is essentially cultural.

2. The proposition that nature is manifest in instincts (fixed action patterns) and culture is manifest in learned behavior presumes the validity of the first proposition and falsely caricatures the relationship between genetic and environmental determinants of the characteristics of any animal species. It ignores the vast array of animal behaviors, including some human behaviors, in which instincts blend with learning to result in entirely natural behaviors (speaking and smiling, for example, among humans). It ignores the Chomskyian critique of learning and such concepts as "preparedness" or "one-trial learning." While it may be true that humans show relatively few fixed action patterns, this in no way indicates that the remaining human behaviors are learned in some manner that involves no genes specifically selected to facilitate that learning.

3. The proposition that it is culture that explains differences between human populations, because human nature is the same everywhere, falsely assumes that because differences must in some way be involved in explaining differences, similarities are therefore irrelevant to

---

[2]Things are a bit different in psychology where behavior genetics employs statistical analytic comparisons of such populations as fraternal and identical twins to partition genetic from environmental influences that underlie individual differences in behavior. However, behavior genetic methods have two important limitations. First, genes that do not normally vary from individual to individual—and presumably the genes that produce all traits that are stable adaptations are of this sort (Tooby and Cosmides 1989b)—are not detected by these methods. Second, the use of these methods cross-culturally—or even between subcultures—can pose serious problems (Gould 1981).

explaining them—as though fluid mechanics were irrelevant in explaining streambeds, because streambeds manifestly differ from each other. Proposition 3 also falsely presumes that features of human nature only manifest themselves in invariant forms—i.e., that there are, for example, no mental mechanisms that specify different responses to different inputs (Tooby and Cosmides 1989b). Different cultural traditions *do* explain many differences between populations, but there is no reason to think that culture explains them all or even most of them.[3]

4. By itself, the proposition that human universals are likely to reflect human nature is correct. It is misleading only when it is coupled with the previous proposition.

5. As outlined above, the evidence suggests that the proposition that the human mind is a largely blank slate is simply false.

6. When compared with other animal species it is correct to say that culture is particularly important in shaping human affairs. But given the invalidity of propositions 3 and 5, not to mention 1, there is no good reason to think that culture is more important than, say, genes, except when explaining certain quite particular aspects of behavior. Besides, anthropology utterly lacks a method for quantifying the cultural contribution to human affairs.

7. The general meaning of reductionism is to explain complex phenomena in terms of (overly) simple phenomena. But since the human mind is not simple—physically, the human brain is the most complex entity in the known universe—there is no reason to think that explaining human affairs in terms of psychological mechanisms is necessarily reductionist. Furthermore, reductionist explanations are routine in science (see, e.g., Williams 1985). There is, thus, no reason to assume the fallacy of reductionist explanations.

8. The proposition that culture has an arbitrary and highly variable character is a logical inference from propositions 1, 3, 6, and 7. But their invalidity renders this proposition suspect. The *potential* for arbitrariness and variability is, I think, a hallmark of the cultural. But there is much in human affairs that is presumed to be cultural that is far from arbitrary and much less variable than is logically possible (see, e.g.,

---

[3]To illustrate, among some few peoples when children playfight they do not actually strike each other, while among other peoples the children do strike. Because in all cases children playfight, any innate bases of playfighting should figure in the explanation of each case, despite the differences. Furthermore, it is entirely possible that being peaceable reflects a phylogenetic adaptation that specifies "act tough when you can get away with it, but when you can't get away with it, act mild." Peoples who, through force of circumstance, are peaceable (i.e., act mild) may curb their children's playfighting to the point that hitting disappears. But the resulting manifest difference (children who do not hit) is still an indirect consequence of human nature.

Friedrich 1975). The vast gap between the character of human affairs as they are and what would be possible if they really were arbitrary is to my mind striking evidence that fundamentally they are not arbitrary.

9. The proposition that universals are few (and maybe unimportant) is untenable, as the evidence presented in previous chapters shows. Given the invalidity of 5 and 8, this is to be expected.

The nine propositions just discussed are central to what has long been the dominant paradigm of American anthropology. And yet the deliberate or acknowledged erosion of the validity of those propositions has gone on for decades (recall, from chapter 3, the reservations about cultural autonomy expressed by Kroeber, Bidney, Kluckhohn, Mead, Murdock, and others). It only remains to admit their invalidity and to integrate some sort of an interactionist framework into anthropology. In important respects, this is no more than a matter of adjusting the balance between background and foreground: in the first chapter I showed that universals, with their unstated implications for a complex human nature, are already in the background of even the most culturologically oriented anthropological studies. Accommodating the implications in terms of method and theory is more complicated, but the necessary adjustments are well under way. Until these adjustments are made, the relationships between particulars and universals, or between nature and nurture, will continue to be obscured by the myths and contradictions that bedevil anthropology today.

Bringing universals, and the human nature within which they make sense, out of the shadows of the anthropological endeavor and into the full light in which our inquiries should be conducted has more implications than can properly be dealt with here. But I must say something about the two principal directions of research and thought that spring from the links between universals, human nature, and anthropology. One looks toward the fields of psychology and biology and is particularly concerned with explaining universals. The other traces the causal chain in the opposite direction, is concerned with using an understanding of universals and human nature to make sense of human affairs, and engages anthropology, the other social sciences, and the humanities.

Many anthropologists, pondering the thought that universals often rest on the nature of the mind, which in turn is a matter of neurology, biochemistry, and evolutionary processes that took place in a very remote past, will certainly think that universals are, then, matters for psychologists, biologists, and maybe physical anthropologists to explain. This is true, of course, but it does not mean that social or cultural anthropologists have nothing to contribute. To begin with, anthropologists are the ones to determine that something *is* a universal and whether it is unrestricted, implicational, or statistical. In the event that it is implicational or statistical, anthropologists are still the ones to determine the conditions that appear to give rise to the phenomenon—and anthropologists have a long history of doing just that. Furthermore, even what appear to be unrestricted universals may very well be illuminated by comparative study—which is just what has happened with the incest taboo, now seen as incest avoidance.

It is true that a full explanation of any universal that appears to rest on the nature of the human mind involves specialized knowledge that very few anthropologists now possess. But a full explanation also involves evolutionary theory, and here anthropologists are in a strong position: anthropologists are specialists in the evolution of the human species, and ethnographic as well as archaeological studies of foraging societies are indispensable in reconstructing the conditions in which humans evolved. Thus however much psychology or other disciplines may be involved, anthropologists have a secure place in the task of understanding the human mind (see, e.g., Gardner 1985:223–259).

To give but a single example, it is certainly my hope that the list of universals given in the previous chapter may inspire brain scientists to watch for signs of specific mechanisms that may underpin some of them. As I read through *The Shattered Mind* (Gardner 1974) and *The Man Who Mistook His Wife for a Hat* (Sacks 1985), I could not help but wonder if brain-damaged individuals might exhibit specific deficits that are directly related to universals—failing, for example, to grasp the notion of reciprocity while other mental functions are unimpaired. But unless one is specifically looking for such deficits, they might not be noticed.

Be that as it may, it remains true that relatively few anthropologists are at present well prepared to undertake the task of explaining universals. But many more anthropologists, and within the limits of the training they presently get, can, as they long have, contribute to the task of tracing the manifold consequences of universals and human nature throughout human cultures, languages, and societies. The scope of this task ranges from the numerous anthropological studies of such general topics as kinship, gender, and age, through the somewhat more specific studies of reciprocity, binary discriminations, and metaphor, and then beyond anthropology to studies of the relationship between poetic line length and brain information processing (Turner and Pöppel 1983; cf. Chafe 1987) or of the relationship between the universal mental capacity for "conjectural" reasoning that evolved with hunting and such modern preoccupations as detective work, art identification, medicine, and science (Ginzburg 1980). And this is only with reference to unrestricted universals.

The vast field of implicational and statistical universals is already extensively explored by anthropologists and others—but usually without the recognition of what this says about human nature and of what an extensive role human nature therefore plays in human society, culture, and affairs. Let me give an example from my own experience.

In the course of my study of the Brunei Malays I was struck by the paucity and impersonal nature of their (reliable) historical materials. As an early attempt to explain this, and bearing in mind the extreme rank-consciousness of the Bruneis that I mentioned in the introduction, I suggested that the exalted status of Malay sultans inhibited candid remarks about them, and thus prevented would-be historians from saying much about the very persons who were the principal actors in Malay history (Brown 1971). Although I did not think through the implications at the time, my suggestion could only make sense in terms of some universalist assumptions (as Hempel 1942 has shown). Some of the assumptions involved human nature.

For example, I was apparently assuming that people in general don't like to be reminded of their faults (and maybe the faults of persons near to them), that people in power have a special reason to worry about this (it could result in their loss of legitimacy, office, or life), that people in power—in places like old Brunei—can punish those who remind them of their faults, but that people in power probably like flattery. On the other hand, I assumed that would-be historians—for whatever reasons might motivate them to even think about writing history—would bear in mind these traits of persons in power and thus would not devote much effort to the kind of personalized, praise-*and-blame* history that is largely taken for granted in the West.

Although I started with an assumption of cultural difference—the great concern for rank in Brunei—it is clear that the rest of the assumptions are about human psychology: what people in general are prone to do (enjoy praise, dislike blame), and what people under specified conditions do. Respectively, I had assumed unrestricted and implicational universals. I didn't examine these assumptions carefully for the same reason Geertz didn't examine the behaviors he described in order to explain how he obtained rapport with Balinese villagers (see introduction): because I had no realization of anything that needed explanation. That this said something about the scope and content of human nature—and about the limits of cultural relativity—never crossed my mind, as perhaps it rarely crosses any anthropologist's mind.

But I was not entirely satisfied with my first attempt to explain the relative ahistoricity of Brunei Malays, and I did think that an explanation that worked for them ought to have a general applicability. So I conducted a general, comparative study of historical-mindedness (1988). In order to make sense of why certain literate civilizations, such as China's, were fanatically historically minded while others, such as Hindu India's, were equally prone to presenting their past in a flagrantly mythological manner, I hypothesized a contingent relationship between rank and historical mindedness. When social rank is idealized as hereditary, myth will be the predominant mode of presenting the past; when social rank is idealized as achievable, history will be the predominant mode. This formulation in turn rested on certain assumptions about human nature, one of which is that hereditary rulers have a strong preference that their ancestors be flattered rather than criticized (another is that practically no one has ancestors for whom only praise is due). Cross-cultural evidence supported the hypothesis.

Moreover, I found that the same set of ideas is hit upon everywhere to "explain" or justify hereditary stratification: most notably, the notion that humanity is not a single species, because the rulers (at least) are superhuman, quasidivine, or divine entities with inherently different character from lower humans. Accordingly, hereditary rulers are visually depicted with special attention to the regalia that sets them off (rather than to the actual appearances that could only reveal their humanity), and accounts of their lives are hagiographies rather than biographies. The opposed notion, that all people (barring sex and age differences) are basically the same but responsive to their environments, regularly accompanies conditions in which individuals are expected to rise and fall in the social hierarchy in accordance with their individual merits. And with the notion that people are basically all the same, biography and realistic portraiture tend to develop—motivated apparently by a desire to understand the fate of the individual when birth does not determine it.

Thus, just as hereditary rulers (or those who wrote on their behalf) were greatly concerned with rank (in order to explain why the rulers ranked above others), the historians of societies in which rank was achievable seem never to tire of the subject either. But for the latter it is rises and falls, and it is the patterns of social mobility that catch their attention—almost certainly because this is a subject that repays the careful attention given to it. In short, I found an apparently universal concern with rank or inequality, taking different forms in different conditions.

At the same time that I had to posit features of human nature to make sense of *differences* between cultural traditions, I also noted the different ways human nature was envisaged in those traditions. For the caste-organized societies, human nature was multiple in forms, there was no psychic unity of humanity (the result is a kind of racism or pseudospeciation). In the societies with open stratification, by contrast, the notion of the psychic unity of humanity was regularly hit upon. This complex interplay between, on the one hand, the way the world is (the human psyche *is* basically the same everywhere) and our ability to perceive it as such, in contrast to, on the other hand, the ways in which the world can be misconstrued (e.g., by positing racial conceptions of human nature) and why humans may misconstrue it, raises important questions about the relationships between culture, universals, and human nature. As discussed in earlier chapters, Bloch (1977) answered some of the questions with his formulation of the differing determinants of ideology and knowledge: hereditary stratification is particularly productive of ideology—of which, mythology (as opposed to history), hagiography (as opposed to biography), iconography (as opposed to realistic portraiture), and racist conceptions of human differences are all manifestations.

In sum, my attempt to explain variations in historical mindedness led to an exploration of the interplay between universals, human nature, the perception of human nature, and many facets of society and expressive culture.[4] That experience is also part of what motivated this book.

To show that I am not alone in seeing important connections between universals, human nature, and the subject matter of the humanities, let me quote the poet and English professor Frederick Turner's comments on Murdock's list of human universals (to which Turner added a few items himself):

> [I]t would be tempting to propose that a work of literary art can be
> fairly accurately gauged for greatness of quality by the number of
> these items it contains, embodies, and thematizes. They are all in
> the *Iliad, The Divine Comedy, King Lear,* and *War and Peace*; and
> most of them can be found in relatively short works of major
> literature, such as Wordsworth's *Intimations* ode, or Milton's
> *Nativity* ode, or even—very compressed—in Yeats' *Among School
> Children.* These topics virtually exhaust the content of the oral
> tradition; taken together they constitute a sort of deep syntax and
> deep lexicon of human culture. (1985:26)

Turner may have overstated the case—and as the list of universals grows this may be even more true—but the point is clear. Technical or arcane as it may be to explain universals, their intrusion into human affairs is too pervasive for the true humanist to ignore.

To conclude, I will turn to a question of professional responsibility that stems from the special role of anthropology. To anthropologists almost exclusively has been given the task of going into the far corners of the world to examine the way humans are in the wide range of conditions in which they live and have lived. Anthropologists have claimed and received this task because they have shown that representatives of the modern world do not and cannot tell the whole story about humanity. If

---

[4]Among the further findings were that social science, secularism, and omenry are more likely to flourish in societies with open stratification.

we want to know what even *we* are really like, we must compare ourselves with others—and all those others with each other. It is a difficult
job, and one with very special rewards and responsibilities. For it is not
merely funding agencies who rely on what anthropologists have to say,
nor even the public at large, nor Western civilization. Anthropological ideas
are relevant to the whole of humanity: not merely in the sense that they
refer to the whole of humanity but in the sense that they may well *affect*
the whole of humanity. Because they have a near-monopoly on studying
humanity as a whole, anthropologists serve—more than anyone else—as
intellectual brokers between all its peoples. What anthropologists have
to say about humanity has incalculable consequences for the peoples
they study and for the public they report to. As Goldschmidt (1966:ix)
puts it, the influence of anthropology "on the moral philosophy of our
time [has been] out of all proportion to the numerical and fiscal strength
of the discipline." Consequently, innumerable aspects of public policy
are shaped by the view of humanity that anthropology helps to create.

Discharging their task, anthropologists have enriched humanity's understanding of itself and so have probably repaid Western civilization,
the public, and the agencies that fund anthropologists. But has anthropology done as much as it could have? The answer is no.

Although they were sent into the field with the charge of getting
the whole picture, so that they could come back relieved of parochial
views and thus tell the world what people are really like, anthropologists
have failed to give a true report of their findings. They have dwelt on the
differences between peoples while saying too little about the similarities
(similarities that they rely upon at every turn in order to do their work).
At the same time, anthropologists have exaggerated the importance of
social and cultural conditioning, and have, in effect, projected an image
of humanity marked by little more than empty but programmable minds.
These are distortions that not only affect the way we look at and treat
the rest of the world's peoples but also profoundly affect our thoughts
about ourselves and the conduct of our own affairs. These distortions
pervade the "whole secular social ideology" (Fox 1990:24) of our era.

Anthropologists are not entirely responsible for the distortions I have
described—particularly for the tabula rasa conception of the mind—but
their professional motives for exaggerating sociocultural differences and
determination are not easily dismissed. The more those differences can
be shown to exist, and the more they can be thought to reflect purely
social and cultural dynamics, the more sociocultural anthropologists (or
sociologists) can justify their role in the world of intellect and practical
human affairs and thus get their salaries paid, their lectures attended,
their research funded, and their essays read. Part of the responsibility
does fall directly on the shoulder of anthropologists: they are the ones
who reported stress-free adolescence among Samoans, sex-role reversals

among the Chambri, and timelessness among Hopi—or who accepted these reports and wove them into a mythology of boundless human plasticity. This more than anything else lent the weight of empirical science to those extreme forms of relativism that hold or lead to the position that there are virtually no pancultural regularities or objective standards.

Some anthropologists have fretted for a long time about their colleagues' penchant for the exotic, their tendency to overstate sociocultural determinism, their denials that there is any human nature beyond what society and culture dictates—and in time the fretting has given way to soul-searching, anguish, and even alarm. Chapter 1 expressed some of the complaints; Kluckhohn, Kroeber, Bidney, Mead, Murdock, Hallowell, Goldschmidt, and others registered further complaints that were noted in chapter 3; Victor Turner's anguish was quoted at the beginning of this chapter. Kroeber also grumbled about the "cleverness in novelty" that anthropologists valued at the expense of wider generalization (1960:14). Bloch accuses anthropologists, "fascinated as usual by the exotic," of paying more attention to those systems of thought designed to obscure the world (as in ritual) than to those systems of thought by which people *know* the world (1977:290). Fox (1973:13) worries that we could not plead against inhuman tyrannies if we didn't know what it is to be human,[5] and Bagish elaborates this theme in his *Confessions of a Former Cultural Relativist* (1981). Spiro (1986), Spaulding (1988), and O'Meara (1989) register their dismay with the recent mushrooming of approaches to anthropology so relativistic and impressionistic that they would seem to deny the possibility of a science of humanity (or any science at all). Keesing (1989:459–460) charges anthropologists with "misreading" other cultures due to a "quest for the exotic" that is rooted in the "reward structures, criteria of publishability, and theoretical premises of [the] discipline." Outside of anthropology, the psychologists Daly and Wilson (1988:154) identify "biophobia" as a malady that infects the social sciences in general, and the philosopher Allen Bloom (1988) criticizes the inroads that an unchecked relativism has made in wider circles.

These complaints have not stemmed the strong currents in the mainstream of anthropology, where business is conducted as usual and where signs of even stronger relativism are, as I said, mushrooming. America's

[5]If peoples of different cultures lived in fundamentally "distinct worlds" (Sapir 1929:209)—which is the clear implication of any strong version of the Sapir-Whorf hypothesis described in chapter 1—there would indeed be no basis for distinguishing human from inhuman beyond surface appearances. Surely one of the nightmares of our time is the fear that animated George Orwell's *1984*, the fear that people are so programmable that they could be reduced to social automatons. Chomsky counters this fear by arguing (in Piatelli-Palmarini 1980) that our richly detailed innate mental endowment is a defense against totalitarianism. Part of Bloch's (1977) argument is that universals provide criteria by which any particular sociocultural system may be judged.

most prominent anthropologist dismisses the kinds of concerns listed above with an exhortation to anthropologists to continue to be "merchants of astonishment" who "hawk the anomalous, peddle the strange" (Geertz 1984:275).

Geertz's reasoning is that if we want to know what is generically human, there is no reason to go into the field: "if we wanted only home truths, we should have stayed at home" (1984:276). But this presumes that universals, or features of human nature, are right on the surface of behavior, so readily perceived in New York City, say, that it would be foolish to go abroad to seek or study them. Sometimes that may be true, but we can only be sure by going abroad. At other times we only discover the universal when comparison of variations reveals underlying universal mechanisms or processes.

It is wrong to think that there is some sort of zero-sum game—or even worse, a winner-takes-all game—between universals and the culturally particular or between biological and sociocultural approaches to anthropological problems. The notion that it is such a game has been a major contributor to producing a blinkered and shackled anthropology, an anthropology unable or unwilling to see the relevance of human nature, and thus severely handicapped in solving anthropological problems. The time is upon anthropologists to take off those blinkers; to rise above the self-serving motives and honest mistakes that put the blinkers on in the first place; to search for, see, study, and analyze what is universal as well as what is unique; to think long and hard about how universals and particulars relate to each other; to convert the psychic unity of humanity from a doctrine that eliminates research on the human psyche to one that stimulates it; to put the special skills and indispensable knowledge of anthropology to work in understanding the human psyche; to look again at problems that were dismissed more than half a century ago; to rewrite our textbooks; and to balance the image of humanity that we present, the latter not because symmetry has some aesthetic value but because humanity really is marked by similarities as well as differences. The point is neither trivial nor relevant to anthropologists alone. The questions that universals raise, above all the question of human nature, will find their answers and their implications in thought and study that cross the boundaries of biology, the social sciences, and the humanities. Seeking answers to these questions will lead to a truer account of what humanity is and who we are. It will be irresponsible to continue shunting these questions to the side, fraud to deny that they exist.

Bibliography

Items with an asterisk are directly pertinent to the study of universals. Many sources that attempt to explain a universal, without addressing the issue of whether it is or isn't a universal, have not been included. Annotations are provided for specific universals if not mentioned in the titles, and for works that have not been discussed in the text.

ABERLE, D. F. ET AL.

*1950 The Functional Prerequisites of Society. *Ethics* 60:100–111.
   [All societies change through time, are adjusted to the environment, regulate sex, have a system of statuses and roles, have higher and lower statuses, have a division of labor by sex and age, provide for socialization of children and others, have a shared cognitive organization, regulate the expression of affect, and control disruptive behaviors.]

ACEVES, JOSEPH B., AND H. GILL KING

1978 *Cultural Anthropology.* Morristown, New Jersey: General Learning Press.

AGINSKY, BURT W., AND ETHEL G. AGINSKY

*1948 The Importance of Language Universals. *Word* 4:168–172.
   [The spear, lever, distinctions between general and particular, thinking, dreaming, time, space, number, and other universals of psychobiology and environmental conditions.]

ALCOCK, JOHN

1987 Ardent Adaptationism. *Natural History* 4:4.

ALEXANDER, RICHARD

*1979 *Darwinism and Human Affairs.* Seattle and London: University of Washington Press.

ALLAND, ALEXANDER, JR.

*1983 *Playing with Form: Children Draw in Six Cultures.* New York: Columbia University Press.
   [Argues that certain aesthetic principles, "good form," are innate and universal.]

ALTMAN, IRWIN

*1977 Privacy Regulation: Culturally Universal or Culturally Specific? *Journal of Social Issues* 33 (3):66–84.
   [Privacy (being inaccessible to others) is universal, though the means of regulating access to oneself are variable.]

ANNETT, MARIAN

*1985 *Left, Right, Hand and Brain: The Right Shift Theory.* London: Erlbaum.

157

APPELL, G. N.

*1973   The Distinction between Ethnography and Ethnology and Other Issues in Cognitive Structuralism. *Bijdragen tot de Taal-, Land-, en Volkenkunde* 129:1–56.

*1976   The Rungus: Social Structure in a Cognatic Society and Its Ritual Symbolization. In *The Societies of Borneo: Explorations in the Theory of Cognatic Social Structure*, edited by G. N. Appell, pp. 66–86, Washington, D.C.: American Anthropological Association.
        [Entification, property, universal model.]

ARENS, W.

*1986   *The Original Sin: Incest and Its Meaning.* New York: Oxford University Press.

ARNHEIM, RUDOLF

*1988   Universals in the Arts. *Journal of Social and Biological Structures* 11:60–65.
        [Art and artistic activities are universal. Within all art there is compositional equilibrium and a tendency to simplify. The archetypical themes of love and hostility, birth and death, success and failure, and beauty and ugliness are also universal.]

BAGISH, HENRY H.

*1981   *Confessions of a Former Cultural Relativist.* Santa Barbara, California: Santa Barbara City College Publications.
        [Ethnocentrism, pragmatic choices.]

BAILEY, F. G.

*1988   *Humbuggery and Manipulation: The Art of Leadership.* Ithaca, New York: Cornell University Press.
        [Good and bad conduct are distinguished everywhere, and effective leaders everywhere must engage in some of the bad. Apathetic, regimented, "mature," and autarkic are four universal dispositions of followers.]

BAMBERGER, JOAN

*1974   The Myth of Matriarchy: Why Men Rule in Primitive Society. In *Woman, Culture, and Society*, edited by Michelle Zimbalist Rosaldo and Louise Lamphere, pp. 263–280, Stanford, California: Stanford University Press.
        [Myths that posit an early period in which women ruled men are widespread but are always myth. Women have never ruled.]

BARKOW, JEROME H.

1973   Darwinian Psychological Anthropology: A Biosocial Approach. *Current Anthropology* 14:373–387.

1984   The Distance between Genes and Culture. *Journal of Anthropological Research* 40:367–379.

BARNOUW, VICTOR

1975   *An Introduction to Anthropology.* Vol. 2: *Ethnology.* Homewood, Illinois: Dorsey Press.

1978   *An Introduction to Anthropology,* Vol. 2, 3d ed. Homewood, Illinois: Dorsey Press.

BEALS, ALAN R.

1979   *Culture in Process.* New York: Holt, Rinehart & Winston.

BELMONTE, THOMAS

*1985   Alexander Lesser (1902–1982). *American Anthropologist* 87:637–644.

BENDERLEY, BERYL LIEFF, MARY F. GALLAGHER, AND JOHN M. YOUNG

1977   *Discovering Culture: An Introduction to Anthropology.* New York: Van Nostrand.

BENEDICT, RUTH

*1934   *Patterns of Culture.* Boston: Houghton Mifflin.
[Briefly discusses universals as "cradle" traits. (p. 19).]

*1938   Religion. In Boas, ed., pp. 627–665.
[Concept of supernatural is universal. Implies the universality of animism, personification, and moralism in constructing worldviews.]

*1959   Anthropology and the Abnormal. In *An Anthropologist at Work: Writings of Ruth Benedict,* edited by Margaret Mead, pp. 262–283, Boston: Houghton Mifflin. (First published in 1934.)
[Suggests a universal range of human temperaments.]

BERLIN, BRENT

*1970   A Universalist-Evolutionary Approach in Ethnographic Semantics. In *Current Directions in Anthropology,* edited by A. Fisher, pp. 31–38, *Bulletin of the American Anthropological Association* 3.3, part 2.

BERLIN, BRENT, AND PAUL KAY

*1969   *Basic Color Terms: Their Universality and Evolution.* Berkeley and Los Angeles: University of California Press.

BERREMAN, GERALD D.

*1981   Social Inequality: A Cross-Cultural Analysis. In *Social Inequality: Comparative and Developmental Approaches,* edited by Gerald D. Berreman, pp. 3–40, New York: Academic Press.
[Some degree of inequality and dominance is universal. Empathy also universal.]

BEYERSTEIN, BARRY L.

1988   Neuropathology and the Legacy of Spiritual Possession: Three Brain Syndromes—Epilepsy, Tourette's Syndrome, and Migraine—Probably Fomented Ancient Notions of Possession and Transcendence. *The Skeptical Inquirer* 12:248–262.

BIDNEY, DAVID

1944 The Concept of Culture and Some Cultural Fallacies. *American Anthropologist* 46:30–44.

1947 Human Nature and the Cultural Process. *American Anthropologist* 49:375–399.

BIRDWHISTELL, RAY L.

1963 The Kinesic Level in the Investigation of the Emotions. In *Expression of the Emotions in Man,* edited by Peter H. Knapp, pp. 123–139. New York: International Universities Press.

*1970 *Kinesics and Context: Essays on Body Motion Communication.* Philadelphia: University of Pennsylvania Press.

BIRNBAUM, LUCILLE C.

1955 Behaviorism in the 1920's. *American Quarterly* 7:15–30.

BISCHOF, NORBERT

*1972 The Biological Foundations of the Incest Taboo. *Social Science Information* 11 (6):7–36.

BITTLES, A. H.

*1983 The Intensity of Inbreeding Depression. *Behavioral and Brain Sciences* 6:103–104.

BIXLER, RAY H.

1982a Sibling Incest in the Royal Families of Egypt, Peru, and Hawaii. *Journal of Sex Research* 18:264–281.

1982b Comment on the Incidence and Purpose of Royal Sibling Incest. *American Ethnologist* 9:580–582.

BLOCH, MAURICE

*1977 The Past and the Present in the Present. *Man* 12:278–292.

BLOOM, ALLAN

1988 *The Closing of the American Mind.* New York: Simon & Schuster.

BLUM, HAROLD F.

1963 On the Origin and Evolution of Human Culture. *American Scientist* 51:32–47.

BOAS, FRANZ

*1963 [1911] *The Mind of Primitive Man.* New York: Collier Books.

1928 Foreword. In Mead 1928, pp. xiii–xv.

*1930   Anthropology. In *Encyclopedia of the Social Sciences.* New York: Macmillan, 2:73–110.

*1938a Mythology and Folklore. In Boas, ed., pp. 609–626.
        [The play of imagination is universal and, in conjunction with situations and experiences common to all societies, gives rise to many cultural similarities. Metaphor is universal, and the word meanings that stimulate metaphors undergo constant change. Implies the universality or near-universality of statements like "if I were," "if I could," "if this had not happened"; of visits to the skyland; of personification; and of precedent.]

*1938b Methods of Research. In Boas, ed., pp. 666–686.
        [Universal social tendencies include solitary groups antagonistic to outsiders, coordination and subordination, imitation and resistance of outside influences, individual and group competition, a division of labor, and amalgamation and segregation. Also universal are attitudes to the supernatural, fear, hope, love, hate, valuation of good and bad and beautiful and ugly, and perhaps murder, theft, lying, and rape.

BOAS, FRANZ, ED.

*1938   *General Anthropology.* Boston: Heath.

BOEHM, CHRISTOPHER

*1979   Some Problems with Altruism in the Search for Moral Universals. *Behavioral Science* 24:15–24.

*1989   Ambivalence and Compromise in Human Nature. *American Anthropologist* 91:921–939.
        ["Universally occurring psychological ambivalences [are]...manifestations of competing tendencies in human nature."]

BOHANNAN, PAUL

1963   *Social Anthropology.* New York: Holt, Rinehart & Winston.

BOKLAGE, CHARLES E.

1984   Twinning, Handedness, and the Biology of Symmetry. In *Cerebral Dominance: The Biological Foundations,* edited by Norman Geschwind and Albert M. Galaburda, pp. 195–210. Cambridge: Harvard University Press.

BOLTON, RALPH

1978   Black, White, and Red All Over: The Riddle of Color Term Salience. *Ethnology* 17:287–311.

BOUSFIELD, JOHN, AND JOHN DAVIS

*1989   What If Sophistry Is Universal? *Current Anthropology* 30:517–518.

BOYD, ROBERT, AND PETER J. RICHERSON

1985   *Culture and the Evolutionary Process.* Chicago: University of Chicago Press.

BOYNTON, ROBERT M., AND CONRAD X. OLSON

1987   Locating Basic Colors in OSA Space. *Color Research and Application* 12:94–105.

BRELAND, KELLER, AND MARIAN BRELAND

1961   The Misbehavior of Organisms. *American Psychologist* 16:681–684.

BROWN, CECIL H.

*1977a Lexical Universals and the Human Language Faculty. In *Linguistics and Anthropology*, edited by Muriel Saville-Troike, pp. 75–91. Washington, D.C.: Georgetown University Press.

*1977b Folk Botanical Life-Forms: Their Universality and Growth. *American Anthropologist* 79:317–342.

*1979   Folk Zoological Life-Forms: Their Universality and Growth. *American Anthropologist* 81:791–817.

BROWN, CECIL H., AND STANLEY R. WITKOWSKI

*1981   Figurative Language in a Universalist Perspective. *American Ethnologist* 8:596–615.

BROWN, DONALD E.

1971   The Coronation of Sultan Muhammad Jamalul Alam, 1918. *Brunei Museum Journal* 2:74–80.

1976   *Principles of Social Structure: Southeast Asia.* London: Duckworth.

*1982   Social Organization and Biology. *Man* 17:551–554.
       [Classification by sex, age, and kinship.]

1988   *Hierarchy, History, and Human Nature: The Social Origins of Historical Consciousness.* Tucson: University of Arizona Press.

BROWN, PENELOPE, AND STEPHEN C. LEVINSON

*1987   Politeness: Some Universals in Language Usage. Cambridge: Cambridge University Press. (First published in 1978 as part of *Questions and Politeness*, edited by Esther N. Goody. Cambridge Papers in Social Anthropology No. 8.)

BUNZEL, RUTH

*1938   Art. In Boas, ed., pp. 535–588.
       [Decorative art, literary art, tale-telling, song, and dance are all universal.]

BURIAN, RICHARD M.

1983   Adaptation. In *Dimensions of Darwinism*, edited by Marjorie Greene, pp. 287–314. New York: Cambridge University Press.

BURLING, ROBBINS

*1970   *Man's Many Voices: Language in Its Cultural Context.* New York: Holt, Rinehart & Winston.

[The evidence suggests that a genealogical core to kinship reckoning is universal. Beats and lines in verse appear to be universal. All languages change through time.]

BUSS, DAVID M.

*1984   Evolutionary Biology and Personality Psychology: Toward a Conception of Human Nature and Individual Differences. *American Psychologist* 39:1135–1147.
[Universals as part of the definition of human nature.]

BUTTERWORTH, BRIAN, BERNARD COMRIE, AND ÖSTEN DAHL, EDS.

*1984   *Explanations for Language Universals.* Berlin: Mouton.

CAILLOIS, ROGER

1961   *Man, Play, and Games.* Translated by Meyer Barash. New York: Free Press of Glencoe.

CAMPBELL, D. T., AND R. A. LEVINE

*1972   *Ethnocentrism: Theories of Conflict, Ethnic Attitudes and Group Behavior.* New York: Wiley.

CARROLL, JOHN B., ED.

1956   *Language, Thought, and Reality: Selected Writings of Benjamin Lee Whorf.* Boston: Technology Press of MIT.

CATON, HIRAM, ED.

1990   *The Samoa Reader: Anthropologists Take Stock.* Lanham, Maryland: University Press of America.

CHAFE, WALLACE

*1987   Cognitive Constraints on Information Flow. In *Coherence and Grounding in Discourse,* edited by Russell S. Tomlin, pp. 21–51. Amsterdam: Benjamins. [Suggests that natural speech is universally broken into segments ("intonation units") of approximately 2-seconds duration, each segment usually preceded by a pause. This presumably reflects what the human mind can focus on at a single time (perhaps within the limit of short-term memory).]

CHAGNON, NAPOLEON A.

1979   Anthropology and the Nature of Things. In Chagnon and Irons 1979, pp. 522–526.

CHAGNON, NAPOLEON A., AND WILLIAM IRONS, EDS.

1979   *Evolutionary Biology and Human Social Behavior: An Anthropological Perspective.* North Scituate, Massachusetts: Duxbury Press.

CHOMSKY, NOAM

1959   Review of B. F. Skinner's Verbal Behavior. *Language* 35:26–58.

*1965 *Aspects of the Theory of Syntax.* Cambridge: MIT Press.
[Substantive and formal linguistic universals.]

*1980 *Rules and Representations.* New York: Columbia University Press.

*1988 *Language and Problems of Knowledge: The Managua Lectures.* Cambridge: MIT Press.
[Outlines his concept of a universal grammar.]

CHOMSKY, NOAM, AND MORRIS HALLE

*1968 *The Sound Pattern of English.* New York: Harper & Row.
[Linguistic universals.]

CHOMSKY, NOAM, AND STUART HAMPSHIRE

*1968 Noam Chomsky and Stuart Hampshire Discuss the Study of Language. *Listener* 79 (2044):687–688, 690–691.
[Brief explication of Chomsky's conception of a universal grammar that must reflect an innate language faculty. No language forms questions by simply reversing the word order of any declarative sentence. All rules for forming a sentence are structure dependent rather than content dependent.]

CLARK, J. DESMOND

1986 The Origins of Fire: A Basic Human Invention. Lecture delivered at the Institute of Human Origins, Berkeley.

COLLIER, JANE F., AND MICHELLE Z. ROSALDO

*1981 Politics and Gender in Simple Societies. In *Sexual Meanings: The Cultural Construction of Gender and Sexuality,* edited by Sherry B. Ortner and Harriet Whitehead, pp. 275–329. Cambridge: Cambridge University Press.
[Sex and age universals.]

COMRIE, BERNARD

*1981 *Language Universals and Linguistic Typology: Syntax and Morphology.* Chicago: University of Chicago Press.
[Defends the cross-language study of universals (a procedure generally associated with Joseph Greenberg) as opposed to the in-depth search within a single language for the universal deep structure that must underlie its surface particularities (a procedure generally associated with Noam Chomsky). Discusses formal and substantive universals, negative universals, implicational and nonimplicational universals, and absolute universals and tendencies. Discusses three basic means of explaining linguistic universals: monogenesis (cradle traits), innateness (and other psychological explanations), and explanations in terms of the functional or other pragmatic requirements of language. Among the specific universals mentioned: first- and second-person pronouns.]

CONKLIN, HAROLD C.

1955 Hanunóo Color Categories. *Southwestern Journal of Anthropology* 11:339–344.

CONNOLLY, BOB, AND ROBIN ANDERSON
1987 *First Contact.* New York: Viking Penguin.

COON, CARLETON S.
*1946 The Universality of Natural Groupings in Human Societies. *Journal of Educational Sociology* 20:163–168.
*1948 *A Reader in General Anthropology.* New York: Holt and Company.
[Besides presenting a universal framework for the study of anthropology, an appendix gives a number of universals. They include daily routines; the distinctions between self and others, people and the rest of the world; symbols; recognition of signs; sociality; marriage or the conjugal relationship; using hands to fight; tools; division of labor by age and sex; interpersonal grooming; early socialization by parents (particularly mothers) and other close kin; problem solving by trial-and-error, insight, and reasoning; rules and leadership to govern the allocation of important resources; games; artistic expression; joking; losing one's temper; procuring and processing raw materials; more time and care spent on ritual or symbolic objects than on (similar?) utilitarian objects; use of fire; tool making; containers; trade and transport of goods; activities conducted by dyads and groups; supervision or leadership; adjusting joint activities to personalities; statuses and roles; right and wrong ways to do things (rules and regulations); sexual regulations; group regulation of individual action; family; and kinship terms.]

COSMIDES, LEDA, AND JOHN TOOBY
1987 From Evolution to Behavior: Evolutionary Psychology as the Missing Link. In *The Latest on the Best: Essays on Evolution and Optimality*, edited by John Dupré, pp. 277–306. Cambridge: MIT Press.
1989 Evolutionary Psychology and the Generation of Culture, Part II. Case Study: A Computational Theory of Social Exchange. *Ethology and Sociobiology* 10:51–97.

CRICK, MALCOLM R.
*1982 Anthropology of Knowledge. *Annual Review of Anthropology* 11:287–313.
[See section entitled "Categories and Universals."]

DALY, MARTIN, AND MARGO WILSON
1983 *Sex, Evolution, and Behavior.* 2d ed. Boston: Willard Grant Press. (First published in 1978.)
*1988 Homicide. New York: Aldine de Gruyter.
[Nepotism, sex differences in homicide, the regulation of sex, revenge, lethal retribution, morality, responsibility, the senses of duty and indebtedness, the concept of provocation, resentment, and empathic understanding. This is a major exposition and application of evolutionary psychology.]

DALY, MARTIN, MARGO WILSON, AND SUZANNE J. WEGHORST
*1982 Male Sexual Jealousy. *Ethology and Sociobiology* 3:11–27.

D'AQUILI, EUGENE G., AND CHARLES D. LAUGHLIN, JR.

*1979   The Neurobiology of Myth and Ritual. In *The Spectrum of Ritual: A Bio-genetic Structural Analysis*, by Eugene G. d'Aquili, et al., pp. 152–182. New York: Columbia University Press.
[Conceptualization, causal thinking, and binary distinctions produce myth.]

DARWIN, CHARLES

1872   *The Expression of Emotion in Man and Animals*. London: Murray.

DASEN, P. R.

*1977   Are Cognitive Processes Universal? A Contribution to Cross-Cultural Piagetian Psychology. In *Studies in Cross-Cultural Psychology*, vol. 1, ed-ited by Neil Warren, pp.155–201. London: Academic Press.

DASEN, PIERRE, AND A. HERON

*1981   Cross-Cultural Tests of Piaget's Theory. *Handbook of Cross-Cultural Psy-chology*. Vol. 4, *Developmental Psychology*, edited by H. C. Triandis and A. Heron, pp. 295–335. Boston: Allyn and Bacon.
[Available studies suggest universal stages of cognitive development.]

DAVENPORT, WILLIAM H.

*1987   The Cultural Anthropology of Sex: Description (Ethnography) and Com-parison (Ethnology). In *Theories of Human Sexuality*, edited by James H. Geer and William T. O'Donohue, pp. 197–236. New York: Plenum.
[The regulation of sexuality; privacy with respect to some aspects of sex-uality; an implicit or explicit conception of reproduction; objects, actions, symbols, signals, and sayings that convey erotic, reproductive, and gen-der meanings; sexual modesty (always in some way related to the geni-tals); and personal adornment.]

DEVEREUX, GEORGE

*1967   A Typological Study of Abortion in 350 Primitive, Ancient, and Pre-Industrial Societies. In *Abortion in America: Medical, Psychiatric, Legal, Anthropo-logical, and Religious Considerations*, edited by Harold Rosen, pp. 97–152. Boston: Beacon Press. (First published in 1954.)

DE WAAL, FRANS

*1982   *Chimpanzee Politics: Power and Sex among Apes*. New York: Harper.
[Discusses various universals, among them the ability to think about so-cial relations between other individuals: triangular awareness.]

DI LEONARDO, MICAELA

*1979   Methodology and the Misinterpretation of Women's Status in Kinship Stud-ies: A Case Study of Goodenough and the Definition of Marriage. *Ameri-can Ethnologist* 6:627–637.

DISSANAYAKE, ELLEN

*1988   *What Is Art For?* Seattle: University of Washington Press.

[Body decoration, play, games, rules, the association of art with ritual, etiquette, symbol, metaphor, the concept of "specialness" or of "making special," tool making, the need to impose order, classification, consciousness of birth and death, worldview, sociality, need for novelty.]

DIXON, R. M. W.
*1977   Where Have All the Adjectives Gone? *Studies in Language* 1:19–80.
[Says that the grammatical classes verb and noun are found in all languages. Proposes a number of "universal semantic types," for which all languages have at least some items in their lexicon: *motion* (e.g., items like "go"), *giving* ("give," "donate," "lend," etc.), *corporeal* ("laugh," "sneeze"), *objects* ("stone," "tree"), *kin* ("uncle," "son"), *dimension* ("large," "deep"), *color* ("black," "white"), *value* ("good," "bad"), *human propensity* ("jealous," "clever"), *physical property* ("sweet," "solid"), *speed* ("fast," "slow"), etc.]

DOUGLAS, MARY
1966   *Purity and Danger: An Analysis of Concepts of Pollution and Taboo.* New York: Praeger.

DUMONT, LOUIS
*1980   *Homo Hierachicus: The Caste System and Its Implications.* Rev. English ed. Chicago: University of Chicago Press.
[Universality of hierarchy.]

DURDEN-SMITH, JO, AND DIANE DESIMONE
*1983   *Sex and the Brain.* New York: Arbor House.

DURKHEIM, ÉMILE
1962   *The Rules of the Sociological Method.* 8th ed., translated by Sarah A. Solovay and John H. Mueller and edited by George E. G. Catlin. Glencoe: Free Press of Glencoe.

EBERHARD, WILLIAM G.
1985   *Sexual Selection and Animal Genitalia.* Cambridge: Harvard University Press.

EIBL-EIBESFELDT, IRENÄUS
*1979   Human Ethology: Concepts and Implications for the Sciences. *Behavioral and Brain Sciences* 2:1–57.
[Includes discussions of various alleged universals, e.g., approach-avoidance ambivalence.]
*1989   *Human Ethology.* New York: Aldine de Gruyter.
[The relaxed open-mouth play face, mothers raising tonal frequency when speaking to children, sexual modesty, the eyebrow flash, the expression of surprise, naming objects, curiosity, and other possible universals.]

EKMAN, PAUL

*1972   Universals and Cultural Differences in Facial Expressions of Emotion. In *Nebraska Symposium on Motivation 1971*, edited by James K. Cole, pp. 207–283. Lincoln: University of Nebraska Press.

*1973   Cross-Cultural Studies of Facial Expression. In *Darwin and Facial Expression: A Century of Research in Review*, edited by Paul Ekman, pp. 169–222. New York: Academic Press.

*1975   The Universal Smile: Face Muscles Talk Every Language. *Psychology Today* (September):35–39.

EKMAN, PAUL, AND WALLACE V. FRIESEN

*1986   A New Pan-Cultural Facial Expression of Emotion. *Motivation and Emotion* 10:159–168.
[The facial expression of contempt is universal. Cf. Izard and Haynes 1987.]

EKMAN, PAUL, E. R. SORENSON, AND W. V. FRIESEN

*1969   Pan-Cultural Elements in Facial Displays of Emotion. *Science* 164:86–88.

ELLEN, ROY

*1988   Fetishism. *Man* 23:213–235.
[Concretisation, anthropomorphisation, and conflation of signifier with signified are universal thought processes.]

EMBER, CAROL R., AND MELVIN EMBER

1973   *Cultural Anthropology*. New York: Appleton-Century-Crofts.

ERASMUS, CHARLES

1961   Review of *The Evolution of Man*, edited by Sol Tax. *American Anthropologist* 63:383–389.

ETHNOMUSICOLOGY

*1971   [Vol. 15, no. 3 publishes four papers on the possibility of universals in music.]

FAGEN, ROBERT

*1981   *Animal Play Behavior*. New York: Oxford University Press.
[Includes data and analyses of human play.]

FARR, ROBERT M.

*1981   On the Nature of Human Nature and the Science of Behaviour. In Heelas and Lock, pp. 303–317.
[Interpreting rather than merely observing human behavior is universal.]

FIELD, TIFFANY M., AND NATHAN A. FOX, EDS.

1985   *Social Perception in Infants*. Norwood, New Jersey: Ablex.

FINKELHOR, DAVID

1980   Sex among Siblings: A Survey on Prevalence, Variety, and Effects. *Archives of Sexual Behavior* 9:171–193.

FISHER, R. A.

1930   *The Genetical Theory of Natural Selection.* Oxford: Clarendon Press.

FODOR, JERRY A.

1983   *The Modularity of Mind: An Essay on Faculty Psychology.* Cambridge: MIT Press.

FOOTE, RUSSELL, AND JACK WOODWARD

*1973   A Preliminary Investigation of Obscene Language. *Journal of Psychology* 83:263–275.
[Suggest that tabooed utterances—obscenity is an example—are universal.]

FORGE, ANTHONY

*1973   Introduction. In Forge, ed., pp. xiii–xxii.
[Art and the transformation and elaboration of the human body are universals.]

FORGE, ANTHONY, ED.

*1973   *Primitive Art and Society.* London: Oxford University Press.

FORTES, MEYER

1969   *Kinship and the Social Order: The Legacy of Lewis Henry Morgan.* Chicago: Aldine.

FOSTER, GEORGE M.

*1972   The Anatomy of Envy: A Study in Symbolic Behavior. *Current Anthropology* 13:165–202.
[Envy is present in all societies and all individuals. Fear of the consequences of envy, and symbolic means to cope with it, are also universal.]

FOX, J. R. [ROBIN]

1962   Sibling Incest. *British Journal of Sociology* 13:128–150.

*1967   *Kinship and Marriage.* Harmondsworth: Penguin Books.
[Kinship, inheritance, succession, male predominance in public decision making, the mother-child tie, classification.]

*1971   The Cultural Animal. In *Man and Beast: Comparative Social Behavior,* edited by J. F. Eisenberg and Wilton S. Dillon, pp. 273–296. Washington, D.C.: Smithsonian Institution Press.
[Ethnocentrism, inheritance, exchange, dispute settlement, a system of social statuses and methods of indicating it, tool and weapon making, kinship groups, schizophrenia, and other items listed below in Tiger and Fox.]

*1973   *Encounter with Anthropology*. New York: Harcourt Brace Jovanovich.

*1979   Kinship Categories as Natural Categories. In Chagnon and Irons, pp. 132–144.

*1980   *The Red Lamp of Incest*. New York: Dutton.
         [In addition to incest avoidance, discusses other universals too: rules, classification, kin classification, binary distinctions, imposing order on the universe, metaphor, exchange, reciprocity, gift-giving, taxonomy, taboo, anthropomorphising, time, space, logic, and the logical notions of relationship, identity, part-whole, class-subclass, hierarchy, same, opposite, causation, and dimension.]

*1989   *The Search for Society: Quest for a Biosocial Science and Morality*. New Brunswick, New Jersey: Rutgers University Press.
         [Reprints articles, published over nearly two decades, that conceptualize universals more at the level of "process" than "substance."]

FRAKE, CHARLES O.

*1963   The Ethnographic Study of Cognitive Systems. In *Anthropology and Human Behavior*, edited by Thomas Gladwin and William C. Sturtevant, pp. 72–85. Washington, D.C.: Anthropological Society of Washington.
         [Taxonomy is fundamental to human thinking.]

FREEMAN, DEREK

1970   Human Nature and Culture. In *Man and the New Biology*, by R. O. Slatyer et al., pp. 50–75. Canberra: Australian National University Press.

*1974   Kinship, Attachment Behaviour and the Primary Bond. In *The Character of Kinship*, edited by Jack Goody, pp. 109–119. Cambridge University Press.

*1981   The Anthropology of Choice. *Canberra Anthropology* 4:82–100.

*1983   *Margaret Mead and Samoa: The Making and Unmaking of an Anthropological Myth*. Cambridge: Harvard University Press.

1989   Fa'apua'a Fa'amū and Margaret Mead. *American Anthropologist* 91:1017–1022.

FRIDLUND, ALAN J.

*n.d.   Evolution and Facial Action in Reflex, Social Motive, and Paralanguage. In *Advances in Psychophysiology*, vol. 4, edited by P. K. Ackles, J. R. Jennings, and M. G. H. Coles. London: Kingsley. (Forthcoming.)

FRIEDRICH, PAUL

*1975   The Lexical Symbol and Its Relative Non-Arbitrariness. In *Linguistics and Anthropology: In Honor of C. F. Voegelin*, edited by M. Dale Kinkade, Kenneth L. Hale, and Oswald Werner, pp. 199–247. Lisse: Peter De Ridder Press.
         [Categories of shape are probably represented in all languages.]

FROMM, ERICH

1961   *Marx's Concept of Man: With a Translation from Marx's Economic and Philosophical Manuscripts by T. B. Bottomore*. New York: Ungar.

FURST, PETER

*1976   *Hallucinogens and Culture.* San Francisco: Chandler and Sharp.

GARCIA, JOHN, AND ROBERT A. KOELLING

1966   Relation of Cue to Consequence in Avoidance Learning. *Psychonomic Science* 4:123–124. (Reprinted in Seligman and Hager.)

GARDNER, HOWARD

1974   *The Shattered Mind: The Person after Brain Damage.* New York: Vintage Books.

1985   *The Mind's New Science: A History of the Cognitive Revolution.* New York: Basic Books.

GEERTZ, CLIFFORD

*1957   Ethos, World-View and the Analysis of Sacred Symbols. *Antioch Review* 17:421–437.
        [All peoples' religions consist of an "ethos" and a "worldview"; i.e., serious moral "oughts" grounded in conceptions of the way the world is.]

*1965   The Impact of the Concept of Culture on the Concept of Man. In *New Views of the Nature of Man,* edited by John R. Platt, pp. 93–118. Chicago: University of Chicago Press.

1971   Deep Play: Notes on the Balinese Cockfight. In *Myth, Symbol, and Culture,* edited by Clifford Geertz, pp. 1–37. New York: Norton.

*1975   On the Nature of Anthropological Understanding. *American Scientist* 63:47–53.
        [All peoples have a concept of the person.]

1984   Anti Anti-Relativism. *American Anthropologist* 86:263–278.

GELL, ALFRED

1980   The Gods at Play: Vertigo and Possession in Muria Religion. *Man* 15:219–248.

GELLNER, ERNEST

*1957   Ideal Language and Kinship Structure. *Philosophy of Science* 24:235–242.

*1981   General Introduction: Relativism and Universals. In *Universals of Human Thought: Some African Evidence,* edited by Barbara Lloyd and Peter Gay, pp. 1–20. Cambridge: Cambridge University Press.

GEWERTZ, DEBORAH

1981   A Historical Reconsideration of Female Dominance among the Chambri of Papua New Guinea. *American Ethnologist* 8:94–106.

GHISELIN, M. T.

*1973   Darwin and Evolutionary Psychology. *Science* 179:964–968.

GINZBURG, CARLO

*1980   Morelli, Freud and Sherlock Holmes: Clues and Scientific Method. *History Workshop* 9:5–36.

GIPPER, HELMUT

1976   Is There a Relativity Principle? In Pinxten, ed., pp. 217–228.

GLEASON, H. A.

1961   *An Introduction to Descriptive Linguistics.* New York: Holt, Rinehart & Winston.

GLUCKMAN, MAX

*1963   Gossip and Scandal. *Current Anthropology* 4:307–316.

GOLDIN-MEADOW, SUSAN, AND HEIDI FELDMAN

1977   The Development of Language-Like Communication without a Language Model. *Science* 197:401–403.

GOLDSCHMIDT, WALTER

1960   Culture and Human Behavior. In *Men and Cultures: Selected Papers of the Fifth International Congress of Anthropological and Ethnological Sciences (1956),* edited under the chairmanship of Anthony F. C. Wallace, pp. 98–104. Philadelphia: University of Pennsylvania Press.

*1966   *Comparative Functionalism: An Essay in Anthropological Theory.* Berkeley and Los Angeles: University of California Press.
[Among the many universals mentioned are superb hand-eye coordination, individual differences, sentiments of filiation, sexual jealousy, sex temperaments, and the desire for children.]

GOLEMAN, DANIEL

*1981   The 7,000 Faces of Dr. Ekman. *Psychology Today* 15 (2):43–49.

GOODENOUGH, WARD H.

1956   Componential Analysis and the Study of Meaning. *Language* 32:195–216.

*1970   *Description and Comparison in Cultural Anthropology.* Chicago: Aldine.
[Explores the role of universals in ordering anthropological description and comparison. Marriage, rights and obligations, and other universals are discussed.]

GOUGH, KATHLEEN

*1953   Female Initiation Rites on the Malabar Coast. *Journal of the Royal Anthropological Institute* 85:45–80.

*1959   The Nayars and the Definition of Marriage. *Journal of the Royal Anthropological Institute* 89:23–34.

GOULD, JAMES L., AND PETER MARLER

1987   Learning by Instinct. *Scientific American* 256 (1):74–85.

GOULD, STEPHEN JAY

1981   *The Mismeasure of Man.* New York: Norton.

1987   Freudian Slip. *Natural History* 2:14–21.

GOULDNER, ALVIN W.

*1960   The Norm of Reciprocity: A Preliminary Statement. *American Sociological Review* 25:161–178.
       [Reciprocity is a moral universal in both positive and negative (tit-for-tat) forms.]

GREENBERG, JOSEPH H.

*1966   Language Universals: With Special Reference to Feature Hierarchies. The Hague: Mouton.
       [A seminal and wide-ranging discussion of universals in language—at phonemic, grammatical, and lexical levels.]

*1975   Research on Language Universals. *Annual Review of Anthropology* 4:75–94.

*1979   Universals of Kinship Terminology: Their Nature and the Problem of Their Explanation. In *On Linguistic Anthropology: Essays in Honor of Harry Hoijer,* edited by Jacques Maquet, pp. 9–32. Malibu, California: Undena.

*1987   The Present Status of Markedness Theory: A Reply to Scheffler. *Journal of Anthropological Research* 43:367–374.

GREENBERG, JOSEPH H., ED.

*1963   *Universals of Language.* Cambridge: MIT Press.

GREENBERG, JOSEPH H., CHARLES A. FERGUSON, AND EDITH A. MORAVCSIK, EDS.

*1978   *Universals of Human Language.* 4 vols. (1, *Method and Theory*; 2, *Phonology*; 3, *Word Structure*; 4, *Syntax*) Stanford, California: Stanford University Press.

HALE, KENNETH

*1975   Gaps in Grammar and Culture. In *Linguistics and Anthropology: In Honor of C. F. Voegelin,* edited by M. Dale Kinkade, Kenneth L. Hale, and Oswald Werner, pp. 295–315. Lisse: Peter De Ridder Press.

HALLOWELL, A. IRVING

*1943   The Nature and Function of Property as a Social Institution. *Journal of Legal and Political Sociology* 1:115–138.

*1955   The Self and Its Behavioural Environment. In *Culture and Experience,* by
        A. Irving Hallowell, pp. 75–110. Philadelphia: University of Pennsylvania
        Press. (Originally published in 1954.)
        [Morality, awareness of self as an object distinct from other objects, lin-
        guistic expressions of self-other (pronouns and personal names),
        spatiotemporal orientation, topographic and place names, motivational
        orientation, values, ideals, standards.]

*1963   Personality, Culture, and Society in Behavioral Evolution. In *Psychology: A
        Study of a Science,* edited by Sigmund Koch, pp. 429–509. New York:
        McGraw-Hill.
        [Self-awareness, self-identification, symbolizing self in time and space, self-
        objectification and role differentiation, standards of good and bad and
        true and false (applied to cognitive, appreciative, and moral values), prop-
        erty rights.]

HAMILTON, W. D.

1964   The Genetical Evolution of Social Behavior, Parts I and II. *Journal of The-
        oretical Biology* 12:1–52.

HANDWERKER, W. PENN, AND PAUL CROSBIE

1982   Sex and Dominance. *American Anthropologist* 84:97–104.

HARRELL, BARBARA B.

1981   Lactation and Menstruation in Cultural Perspective. *American Anthropol-
        ogist* 83:796–823.

HARRIS, MARVIN

1980   *Culture, People, Nature: An Introduction to Anthropology,* 3d ed. New York:
        Harper & Row.

HARWOOD, DANE L.

*1976   Universals in Music: A Perspective from Cognitive Psychology. *Ethno-
        musicology* 20:521–533.
        [Musical universals of content are unlikely, but the musical process—e.g.,
        the perception of pitch and contour—may be universal. The association
        of music with ritual is a near-universal.]

HATCH, ELVIN

1973a   The Growth of Economic, Subsistence, and Ecological Studies in Ameri-
        can Anthropology. *Journal of Anthropological Research* 29:221–243.

1973b   *Theories of Man and Culture.* New York: Columbia University Press.

*1983   *Cultures and Morality: The Relativity of Values in Anthropology.* New York:
        Columbia University Press.
        [Advocates a cross-culturally valid standard of morality.]

HAUGEN, EINAR

*1977   Linguistic Relativity: Myths and Methods. In *Language and Thought: Anthropological Issues,* edited by William C. McCormack and Stephen A. Wurm, pp. 11–28. The Hague: Mouton.

HAVILAND, WILLIAM A.

1983   *Cultural Anthropology,* 4th ed. New York: Holt, Rinehart and Winston.

HEBB, DONALD O.

*1946   On the Nature of Fear. *Psychological Review* 53:259–276.

HEELAS, PAUL

*1981   The Model Applied: Anthropology and Indigenous Psychologies. In Heelas and Lock, pp. 39–63.
[A universal model and various psychological universals. These include the experiences of self/nonself, subject/object, in control/under control (causing involuntary action, for example); conscious awareness of memory, emotions, experience of acting on the world, making decisions; self-responsibility; the distinction between public and private; and a psychological language.]

HEELAS, PAUL, AND ANDREW LOCK, EDS.

*1981   *Indigenous Psychologies: The Anthropology of the Self.* New York: Academic Press.
[Various contributors discuss psychological universals.]

HEIDER, ELEANOR ROSCH

*1972   Universals in Color Naming and Memory. *Journal of Experimental Psychology* 93:10–20.

HEMPEL, CARL G.

*1942   The Function of General Laws in History. *Journal of Philosophy* 39:35–48.
[Argues that historical explanations rest on the tacit use of "universal hypotheses," i.e., implicational universals. The argument is fully applicable to sociocultural explanations.]

HERSKOVITS, MELVILLE J.

*1940   *The Economic Life of Primitive Peoples.* New York: Knopf.

*1952   [1947] *Man and His Works.* New York: Knopf.

HERTZ, ROBERT

*1960   *Death and the Right Hand.* Translated by Rodney and Claudia Needham. Introduction by E. E. Evans-Pritchard. Aberdeen: Cohen and West.

HEWLETT, BARRY

1988   Sexual Selection and Paternal Investment among Aka Pygmies. In *Human Reproductive Behaviour: A Darwinian Perspective,* edited by Laura Betzig,

Monique Borgerhoff Mulder, and Paul Turke, pp. 263–276. Cambridge: Cambridge University Press.
[Human sex differences in parental investment.]

HOCKETT, C. F.

*1973 *Man's Place in Nature.* New York: McGraw-Hill.
[Presents the most detailed list of universals since Murdock (1945). For each universal it is indicated whether it is shared with nonhuman species and if it was part of the "human historical baseline." The universals include sociality and social structure, social structure influenced by sex and age, age grading, social structure influenced by accumulated information, leadership, collective decision making, consultation in collective decision making, informal vs. formal consultation, moderator-type leader, band (or derivative organization) distinct from family, nonlocalized social groups, intimate property vs. nonproperty, loose property, inheritance rules, equation of social and physiological maternity, prohibition of mother-son incest, other incest prohibitions that yield exogamous groups, dominant household dyad includes at least one adult, dyadic conflict, modeling transactions with remote (and larger) groupings on those in intimate (small) social groups, personality apart from social role, mutual influence of personality and social role, ascribed vs. achieved status, a pool of "state parameters" (degrees of uncertainty, freedom of choice, urgency, pleasantness, anxiety, and seriosity) that characterize or govern the actors in a dyad, quandary, boredom, sleep, dreaming, ritual, play, games, joking, affection, submissiveness, hostility, worldview, worldview involving entities not directly observed or observable, curiosity about one's nature, positive death customs, knowledge of relationship between sickness and death, care of ill or injured, creativity, and creative arts (always including literature). A number of "widespread" or "almost universal" traits are also listed. Pp. 276–279.]

HOCKETT, CHARLES F.

*1963 The Problem of Universals in Language. In Greenberg, ed., pp. 1–22.
[A general discussion of language universals, with many of them specified.]

HOEBEL, E. ADAMSON

*1954 *The Law of Primitive Man: A Study in Comparative Legal Dynamics.* Cambridge: Harvard University Press.
[Homicide and adultery are universally prohibited. Property and kinship groups are always legally recognized.]

1972 *Anthropology: The Study of Man.* New York: McGraw-Hill.

HOIJER, HARRY

1954 The Sapir-Whorf Hypothesis. In *Language in Culture*, edited by Harry Hoijer, pp. 92–105. American Anthropological Association, Memoir No. 79.

HOLMES, LOWELL D.

1958 *Ta'u: Stability and Change in a Samoan Village.* Polynesian Society Reprint, No. 7. Wellington, New Zealand.

1987 *Quest for the Real Samoa: The Mead/Freeman Controversy and Beyond.* South Hadley, Massachusetts: Bergin & Garvey.

HONIGMANN, JOHN J.

1959 *The World of Man.* New York: Harper & Brothers.

HOPKINS, KEITH

1980 Brother-Sister Marriage in Roman Egypt. *Comparative Studies in Society and History* 22:303–354.

HYMES, D. H.

*1960 Lexicostatistics So Far. *Current Anthropology* 1:3–44.
[Includes a discussion of the Swadesh list of presumably universal, or nearly universal, "basic" vocabulary words.]

1970 Linguistic Method in Ethnography: Its Development in the United States. In *Method and Theory in Linguistics,* edited by Paul L. Garvin, pp. 249–325. The Hague: Mouton.

IRONS, WILLIAM

1979 Natural Selection, Adaptation, and Human Social Behavior. In Chagnon and Irons, pp. 4–39.

IZARD, CARROLL E.

*1971 *The Face of Emotion.* New York: Appleton-Century-Crofts.

IZARD, CARROLL E., AND O. MAURICE HAYNES

*1988 On the Form and Universality of the Contempt Expression: A Correction for Ekman and Friesen's Claim of Discovery. *Motivation and Emotion* 12:1–16.

JAKOBSON, ROMAN, C. GUNNAR M. FANT, AND MORRIS HALLE

*1967 Preliminaries to Speech Analysis: The Distinctive Features and Their Correlates. Cambridge: MIT Press.

JONES, ERNEST

*1925 Mother-Right and the Sexual Ignorance of Savages. *International Journal of Psychoanalysis* 6:109–130.

KAFFMAN, MORDECAI

1977 Sexual Standards and Behavior of the Kibbutz Adolescent. *Orthopsychiatry* 47:207–216.

KAPLAN, HELEN SINGER

1981 Interview. *Omni* (August):73–77, 92.

KEARNEY, MICHAEL

*1984   *World View.* Novato, California: Chandler & Sharp.
[Presents a universalistic framework for the comparative analysis of worldview.]

KEESING, ROGER M.

1989   Exotic Readings of Cultural Texts. *Current Anthropology* 30:459–479.

KEVLES, DANIEL J.

1985   *In the Name of Eugenics: Genetics and the Uses of Human Heredity.* New York: Knopf.

KIDDER, A. V.

*1940   Looking Backward. Proceedings of the American Philosophical Society 83:527–537.

KIMURA, DOREEN, AND RICHARD A. HARSHMAN

1984   Sex Differences in Brain Organization for Verbal and Non-Verbal Functions. In *Progress in Brain Research,* vol. 61, edited by G. J. de Vries et al., pp. 423–441. Amsterdam: Elsevier.

KITCHER, PHILIP

1985   *Vaulting Ambition: Sociobiology and the Quest for Human Nature.* Cambridge: MIT Press.

KLUCKHOHN, CLYDE

*1953   Universal Categories of Culture. In *Anthropology Today: An Encyclopedic Inventory,* pp. 507–523. Chicago: University of Chicago Press.

*1959   Common Humanity and Diverse Cultures. In *The Human Meaning of the Social Sciences,* edited by Daniel Lerner, pp. 245–284. New York: Meridian. [Emphasizes the importance of a common human nature for understanding people of other cultures. Universals mentioned: binary distinctions; the feelings of hostility, altruism, pride, shame, sorrow, and need; logic (modes of interpreting relationships between phenomena); prohibitions of murder and untruth (under certain circumstances); restitution; and reciprocity. No society values suffering as an end in itself.]

KOEPPING, KLAUS-PETER

*1983   *Adolf Bastian and the Psychic Unity of Mankind: The Foundations of Anthropology in Nineteenth Century Germany.* St. Lucia: University of Queensland Press. [The idea of extension of the human body underlies tool making. Space, time, and number are elementary ideas.]

KONNER, MELVIN J.

*1982a *The Tangled Wing: Biological Constraints on the Human Spirit.* New York: Holt, Rinehart & Winston.

[A lengthy essay on the biology of human behavior, pursuant to the development of a science of human nature. Fire, cooking, homicide, smiling in greeting, fear suppression, childhood fears, and greater male violence and homicide.]

*1982b Biological Aspects of the Mother-Infant Bond. In *Development of Attachment and Affiliation Systems*, edited by Robert N. Emde and Robert J. Harmon, pp. 137–59. New York: Plenum.
[The evidence suggests that in early infancy, when a child becomes more able to move about autonomously, it simultaneously develops a strong attachment to its mother (or other primary caretaker) and a fear of strangers. The pattern is universal, and at least partly genetically determined.]

KOTTAK, CONRAD

1978 *Anthropology: The Exploration of Human Diversity*. New York: Random House.

KRAUSS, ROBERT M.

1968 Language as a Symbolic Process in Communication. *American Scientist* 56:265–278.

KROEBER, A. L.

*1901 Decorative Symbolism of the Arapaho. *American Anthropologist* 3:308–336. (Partly reprinted in Kroeber 1952.)
[Art is universally conventionalized.]

*1909 Classificatory Systems of Relationship. *Journal of the Royal Anthropological Institute* 39:77–84.

1915 Eighteen Professions. *American Anthropologist* 17:283–288.

1917 The Superorganic. *American Anthropologist* 19:163–213. (Reprinted in Kroeber 1952.)

1923 *Anthropology*. New York: Harcourt, Brace & Company. (Revised and expanded in 1948.)

1928 Sub-human Culture Beginnings. *Quarterly Review of Biology* 3:325–342.

1935 History and Science in Anthropology. *American Anthropologist* 37:539–569. (Partly reprinted in Kroeber 1952.)

*1949 The Concept of Culture in Science. *Journal of General Education* 3:182–196. (Reprinted in Kroeber 1952.)

*1952 *The Nature of Culture*. Chicago: University of Chicago Press.

1955 On Human Nature. *Southwestern Journal of Anthropology* 11:195–204.

1960 Evolution, History, and Culture. In *Evolution after Darwin*. Vol. II, *The Evolution of Man: Man, Culture and Society*, edited by Sol Tax, pp. 1–16. Chicago: University of Chicago Press.

LA BARRE, WESTON

1947 The Cultural Basis of Emotions and Gestures. *Journal of Personality* 16:49–68.

*1954   *The Human Animal.* Chicago: University of Chicago Press.
        [Beliefs in spiritual entities, such as the soul, are universal or nearly so.
        Personification. No one is ever wholly satisfied with his culture. Universal
        experiences include birth, death, dreaming, seeing, memory, thought, con-
        science, language, culture.]

*1980   Anthropological Perspectives on Hallucination, Hallucinogens, and the
        Shamanic Origins of Religion. In *Culture in Context: Selected Writings of
        Weston La Barre,* pp. 37–92. Durham, North Carolina: Duke University Press.
        [The Freudian defense mechanisms, such as denial of unwelcome facts,
        are universal. So too are mood-altering drugs and the resulting altered
        states of consciousness.]

 1984   *Muelos: A Stone Age Superstition about Sexuality.* New York: Columbia Uni-
        versity Press.

LA FONTAINE, J. S.

 1988   Child Sexual Abuse and the Incest Taboo: Practical Problems and Theo-
        retical Issues. *Man* 23:1–18.

LAKOFF, GEORGE, AND MARK JOHNSON

*1980   *Metaphors We Live By.* Chicago: University of Chicago Press.

LANGLOIS, JUDITH H., AND LORI A. ROGGMAN

*1990   Attractive Faces Are Only Average. *Psychological Science* 1:115–121.
        [The evidences suggests universality in facial attractiveness; specifically,
        that humans may possess an innate preference for faces that are average
        in their dimensions.]

LARSEN, JACK LENOR (WITH BETTY FREUDENHEIM)

*1986   *Interlacing: The Elemental Fabric.* Tokyo: Kodansha International.
        [Interlacing, the generic fabric construction "in which each element passes
        over and under elements that cross its path," and that includes knotting,
        plaiting, and weaving, "is not only ancient, but universal" (pp. 10, 17).]

LASHLEY, K. S.

 1929   *Brain Mechanisms and Intelligence: A Quantitative Study of Injuries to the
        Brain.* Chicago: University of Chicago Press.

LEACH, EDMUND R.

*1958   Magical Hair. *Journal of the Royal Anthropological Institute* 88:147–164.
        [Hairdressing rituals are nearly universal, and anthropologists assume that
        hair universally possesses symbolic value.]

*1967   Virgin Birth. Proceedings of the Royal Anthropological Institute of Great
        Britain and Ireland for 1966, pp. 39–49.
        [A nearly obsessional interest in sex and kinship is universal.]

*1973   Levels of Communication and Problems of Taboo in the the Appreciation of Primitive Art. In Forge, ed., pp. 221–234.
[In all societies men judge women in terms of visual attractiveness.]

*1982   *Social Anthropology*. New York: Oxford University Press.
[Contains an ambivalent discussion of "possible" universals.]

LENNEBERG, ERIC H.

*1967   *Biological Foundations of Language*. New York: Wiley.
[In all languages one can give directions, describe past events, describe other persons' behavior, etc. All languages change through time, but an underlying structure is universal. At the appropriate age, any normal child can learn any language (or any two languages simultaneously). Pp. 364, 377, 381.]

LESSER, ALEXANDER

*1952   Evolution in Social Anthropology. *Southwestern Journal of Anthropology* 8:134–146.

LÉVI-STRAUSS, CLAUDE

 1953   In Results of the Conference of Anthropologists and Linguists. Indiana University Publications in Anthropology and Linguistics. Memoir 8. By Claude Lévi-Strauss, Roman Jakobson, C. F. Voegelin, and Thomas A. Sebeok, pp. 1–10. (Supplement to *International Journal of American Linguistics*, vol. 19, no. 2.) Baltimore: Waverly.

*1960   On Manipulated Sociological Models. *Bijdragen tot de Taal-, Land- en Volkenkunde* 116:45–64.
[Universal pools may lie behind the "bewildering diversity" of ethnographic data (p. 52).]

*1962   *The Savage Mind*. London: Weidenfeld and Nicholson.
[Says that all peoples tend to overestimate the objectivity of their thought.]

*1969   [1949] *The Elementary Structures of Kinship*. Boston: Beacon Press.
[Prohibition of incest, nature/culture, reciprocity, exchange, kinship, rules.]

LEVY, JERRE

*1976   A Review of the Evidence for a Genetic Component in the Determination of Handedness. *Behavior Genetics* 6:429–451.

LEWIN, ROGER

 1989   Inbreeding Costs Swamp Benefits. *Science* 243:482.

LINTON, RALPH

*1942   Age and Sex Categories. *American Sociological Review* 7:589–603.

*1952   Universal Ethical Principles: An Anthropological View. In *Moral Principles of Action: Man's Ethical Imperative*, edited by Ruth Nanda Anshen, pp. 645–669. New York: Harper & Brothers.

[Universals of ethics include the distinction between good and bad, between in-group and out-group, and between the family and others; the regulation of sexual behavior; some form of prohibition of rape, murder, and other violence; regulation of relationships between family members; prohibition of sex between mother and son; the expectation of parental care and training of children; some provision for the poor and unfortunate; the concept of property; the recognition of economic obligations in relationship to exchanges of goods and services; and a demand for truthfulness in certain conditions. Also notes that there are no economically egalitarian societies and gives a number of near-universals.]

LLOYD, BARBARA, AND JOHN GAY, EDS.

*1981 *Universals of Human Thought: Some African Evidence.* Cambridge: Cambridge University Press.
[Several authors explore the issues involved in conceptualizing and discovering universals. A distinction is made between process universals and product universals (universal processes may not result in universal products).]

LOMAX, ALAN

*1962 Song Structure and Social Structure. *Ethnology* 1:425–451.
[Melody is found in all musical systems.]

LONNER, WALTER J.

*1980 The Search for Psychological Universals. In *Handbook of Cross-Cultural Psychology.* Vol. 1, *Perspectives,* edited by Harry C. Triandis and William Wilson Lambert, pp. 143–204. Boston: Allyn and Bacon.
[A broad overview that includes anthropological, linguistic, and ethological materials as well. Provides various classifications of universals, e.g., simple, variform, functional, diachronic, ethologically oriented, systematic behavioral, and "cocktail party" universals (the latter are untestable, such as a hypothetical inability to transcend guilt). Aggression, hope, forgetting, anxiety, aesthetics, problem solving, rank, solidarity, an occasional need for privacy and silence, and the need to explain the world are among the many specific universals mentioned. An extensive discussion of universal models of interpersonal psychology.]

LOPREATO, JOSEPH

*1984 *Human Nature & Biocultural Evolution.* Boston: Allen & Unwin.
[Relates universals to genetic predispositions on the one hand and sociocultural variants on the other. Specific universals: self-sacrifice for one's group and "consuming substances to partake of their properties."]

LOWIE, ROBERT H.

1966 *Culture and Ethnology.* New York: Basic Books. (First published in 1917.)

MALINOWSKI, BRANISLAW

*1960   [1944] *A Scientific Theory of Culture and Other Essays.* New York: Oxford University Press.

 1961   [1927] *Sex and Repression in Savage Society.* Cleveland: World.

MALOTKI, EKKEHART

*1983   *Hopi Time: A Linguistic Analysis of the Temporal Concepts in the Hopi Language.* Berlin: Mouton.

MANN, ALAN

*1972   Hominid and Cultural Origins. *Man* 7:379–385.
        [Tool dependence.]

MAQUET, JACQUES

*1986   *The Aesthetic Experience: An Anthropologist Looks at the Visual Arts.* New Haven, Connecticut: Yale University Press.
        [Argues that contemplation is an innate human capacity that underlies the universality or near-universality of an aesthetic sense and its products.]

MARCOVIĆ, MIHAILO

*1983   Human Nature. In *A Dictionary of Marxist Thought,* edited by Tom Bottomore, pp. 214–217. Cambridge: Harvard University Press.

MARSHACK, ALEXANDER

*1972   *The Roots of Civilization: The Cognitive Beginnings of Man's First Art, Symbol and Notation.* New York: McGraw-Hill.
        [Provides evidence that "notation" (for example, notches on bone that may have counted the passage of time) began among humans in the Palaeolithic and may lie at the root of arithmetic, writing, and the calendar. If so, notation in one form or another may well be universal.]

MARTIN, LAURA

 1986   "Eskimo Words for Snow": A Case Study in the Genesis and Decay of an Anthropological Example. *American Anthropologist* 88:418–423.

MAURER, DAPHNE

 1985   Infants' Perception of Facedness. In Field and Fox, pp. 73–100.

MAY, ROBERT M.

 1979   When to Be Incestuous. *Nature* 279:192–194.

MAYER, NANCY KOZAK, AND EDWARD Z. TRONICK

*1985   Mothers' Turn-Giving Signals and Infant Turn-Taking in Mother-Infant Interaction. In Field and Fox, pp. 73–100.

MAYNARD SMITH, J.

1964   Group Selection and Kin Selection. *Nature* 20:1145–1147.

1976   Group Selection. *Quarterly Review of Biology* 5: 277–283.

MAYR, E.

1961   Cause and Effect in Biology. *Science* 134:1501–1506.

1974   Behavior Programs and Evolutionary Strategies. *American Scientist* 62:650–659.

MCCABE, JUSTINE

*1983   FBD Marriage: Further Support for the Westermarck Hypothesis of the Incest Taboo? *American Anthropologist* 85:50–69.

MEAD, MARGARET

1928   *Coming of Age in Samoa.* New York: Morrow.

1935   *Sex and Temperament in Three Primitive Societies.* New York: Morrow.

*1968   *Male and Female: A Study of the Sexes in a Changing World.* New York: Dell. (First published in 1949.)
[In all societies there is a division of labor by sex, the care of children is more women's than men's work, the sexes are thought to be different in more than procreative ways, and a male need for achievement is recognized.]

1969   *The Social Organization of Manua.* 2d ed. Honolulu: Bishop Museum Press.

MEISELMAN, KARIN C.

1978   *Incest: A Psychological Study of Causes and Effects with Treatment Recommendations.* San Francisco: Jossey-Bass.

MELTZOFF, ANDREW N., AND RICHARD W. BORTON

*1979   Intermodal Matching by Human Neonates. *Nature* 282: 403–404.

MICHELS, ROBERTO

*1915   *Political Parties: A Sociological Study of the Oligarchical Tendencies of Modern Democracy.* Translated by Eden and Cedar Paul. New York: Hearst's International Library Co.
[Argues that no society is ever a complete democracy or ever a complete autocracy; something less than everybody and more than one person always rules. Hence Michels's "iron law of oligarchy."]

MINDERHOUT, DAVID J.

1986   Introductory Texts and Social Science Stereotypes. *Anthropology Newsletter* 27 (3):14–15, 20.

MITCHELL, W. J. T., ED.

*1981   *On Narrative.* Chicago: University of Chicago Press.
[Some contributors assert the universality of narrative.]

MITCHELL, WILLIAM E.

*1988   The Defeat of Hierarchy: Gambling as Exchange in a Sepik Society. *American Ethnologist* 15:638–657.
["The penchant to rank and grade is intrinsic to the human condition."]

MOERMAN, MICHAEL

*1988   *Talking Culture: Ethnography and Conversation Analysis.* Cambridge: Cambridge University Press.
[A comparison of Thai and American conversations suggests universals of conversation structures.]

MUNDKUR, BALAJI

*1983   *The Cult of the Serpent: An Interdisciplinary Survey of Its Manifestations and Origins.* Albany: State University of New York Press.

MURDOCK, GEORGE PETER

 1932   The Science of Culture. *American Anthropologist* 34:200–215.

*1945   The Common Denominator of Cultures. In *The Science of Man in the World Crisis*, edited by Ralph Linton, pp. 123–142. New York: Columbia University Press.

 1972   Anthropology's Mythology. Proceedings of the Royal Anthropological Institute of Great Britain and Ireland for 1971, pp. 17–24.

 1975   *Outline of World Cultures.* 5th ed. New Haven, Connecticut: Human Relations Area Files. (First published in 1954.)

MURDOCK, GEORGE P. ET AL.

*1971   *Outline of Cultural Materials.* 4th ed., rev. New Haven, Connecticut: Human Relations Area Files. (First published in 1961.)

MURPHY, JANE

 1976   Psychiatric Labelling in Cross-Cultural Perspective. *Science* 191:1019–1028.
[The evidence suggests that some mental illnesses are cross-culturally valid whether indigenously labeled or not.]

NACHMAN, STEVEN R.

*1984   Lies My Informants Told Me. *Journal of Anthropological Research* 40:536–555.
[Lying is universal.]

NADEL, SIEGFRIED

*1957   *The Theory of Social Structure.* Glencoe, Illinois: Free Press.
[Asserts the universality of statuses/roles.]

NADER, LAURA

*1965   The Anthropological Study of Law. In *The Ethnography of Law*, edited by Laura Nader, pp. 3–32. Menasha, Wisconsin: American Anthropologi
[Summarizes discussions of universals in law.]

NADER, LAURA, AND JUNE STARR

*1973   Is Equity Universal? In *Equity in the World's Legal Systems: A Comparative Study,* edited by Ralph A. Newman, pp. 125–137. Brussels: Bruylant.
[The concept of equity, and most of the West's other general legal concepts, are "probably present in some form...throughout all societies."]

NEEDHAM, RODNEY

1967   Percussion and Transition. *Man* 2:606–614.

*1972   *Belief, Language, and Experience.* Oxford: Basil Blackwell.
[Intention, the promise, and various inner states that are shown by external expression are universals.]

*1978   *Primordial Characters.* Charlottesville: University Press of Virginia.

*1981   *Circumstantial Deliveries.* Berkeley and Los Angeles: University of California Press.
[Chapter 3 (originally published in Heelas and Lock 1981) discusses "inner states" as universals.]

NEEDHAM, RODNEY, ED.

*1973   *Right & Left: Essays on Dual Symbolic Classification.* Chicago: University of Chicago Press.
[Wide-ranging studies of the symbolism accompanying handedness.]

NETTL, BRUNO

*1983   *The Study of Ethnomusicology: Twenty-nine Issues and Concepts.* Urbana: University of Illinois Press.
[Chapter 3 is a concise conceptual discussion of universals in music. Music is a universal. Every musical "utterance" has a beginning, end, some repetition, some redundancy, some variation, and some rhythmic structure based on note length and dynamic stress. Music is always seen as an art, a creation. There is always some association of music with dance and ritual. Singing is universal, and always includes the use of words (poetry). Children's music is universal. There are limits to what is musical in each tradition, and certain entirely possible elements, e.g., using only notes of equal length, occur in no musical traditions.]

NIDA, EUGENE A.

1959   Principles of Translation as Exemplified by Bible Translating. In *On Translation,* edited by Reuben A. Brower, pp. 11–31. Cambridge: Harvard University Press.

NIMMO, ARLO

*1972   *The Sea People of Sulu: A Study of Social Change in the Philippines.* San Francisco: Chandler.
[Even Sea Gypsies are territorial.]

OCHS, ELINOR, AND BAMBI B. SCHIEFFELIN

1984　Language Acquisition and Socialization: Three Developmental Stories and Their Implications. In Shweder and LeVine, pp. 276–320.

OGBU, JOHN U.

*1978　African Bridewealth and Women's Status. *American Ethnologist* 5:241–262. [Universal definition of marriage.]

O'MEARA, J. TIM

1989　Anthropology as Empirical Science. *American Anthropologist* 91:354–369.

O'NEIL, JOHN

*1985　*Five Bodies: The Human Shape of Modern Society.* Ithaca, New York: Cornell University Press. [Anthropomorphism is an indispensable and creative element in human affairs.]

O'NELL, C. W.

*1976　*Dreams, Culture, and the Individual.* Novato, California: Chandler and Sharp. [Dream universals.]

OPLER, MORRIS E.

1948　Some Implications of Culture Theory for Anthropology and Psychology. *American Journal of Orthopsychiatry* 18:611–621.

ORIANS, GORDON H.

*1980　Habitat Selection: General Theory and Applications to Human Behavior. In *The Evolution of Human Social Behavior,* edited by Joan S. Lockard, pp. 49–66. New York: Elsevier. [Suggests that humans may have a universal predilection for certain kinds of landscapes—an example of Darwinian psychology.]

ORTNER, SHERRY

*1974　Is Female to Male as Nature Is to Culture? In *Woman, Culture, and Society,* edited by Michelle Zimbalist Rosaldo and Louise Lamphere, pp. 67–87. Stanford: Stanford University Press.

OSGOOD, CHARLES E., WILLIAM H. MAY, AND MURRAY S. MIRON

*1975　*Cross-Cultural Universals of Affective Meaning.* Urbana: University of Illinois Press. [Various statistical universals.]

OTTERBEIN, KEITH F.

*1987　*The Ultimate Coercive Sanction: A Cross-Cultural Study of Capital Punishment.* New Haven, Connecticut: HRAF Press. [Capital punishment is universal or nearly so.]

PALMER, CRAIG

*1989   Is Rape a Cultural Universal? A Re-examination of the Ethnographic Data. *Ethnology* 28:1–16.
[Finds no evidence against the universality of rape or against the universal disapproval of rape.]

PARKER, HILDA, AND SEYMOUR PARKER

1986   Father-Daughter Sexual Abuse: An Emerging Perspective. *American Journal of Orthopsychiatry* 56:531–549.

PARSONS, TALCOTT

*1964   Evolutionary Universals in Society. *American Sociological Review* 29:339–357.

PAULME, DENISE

*1973   Adornment and Nudity in Tropical Africa. In Forge, ed., pp. 11–24.
[Ornamentation is universal, all humans own ornaments, in each society there are special occasions when people try to look their best, all people "wish to allure," everyone wishes to stand out from others, and aesthetic considerations influence hairstyles everywhere.]

PIATELLI-PALMARINI, MASSIMO, ED.

1980   *Language and Learning: The Debate between Jean Piaget and Noam Chomsky.* Cambridge: Harvard University Press.

PINXTEN, RIK

*1976   Epistemic Universals: A Contribution to Cognitive Anthropology. In Pinxten, ed., pp. 117–175.
[Universals in the cognition of space.]

PINXTEN, RIK, ED.

*1976   *Universalism versus Relativism in Language and Thought: Proceedings of a Colloquium on the Sapir-Whorf Hypotheses.* The Hague: Mouton.

POLLNAC, RICHARD B.

*1978   Problems in Determining the Universality of Inference-Making. In *Discourse and Inference in Cognitive Anthropology: An Approach to Psychic Unity and Enculturation,* edited by Marvin D. Loflin and James Silverberg, pp. 229–237. The Hague: Mouton.

POSPISIL, LEOPOLD

*1964   *The Kapauku Papuans and Their Law.* Yale University Publications in Anthropology, no. 54. [New Haven, Connecticut]: Human Relations Area Files. (Reprinted from the 1958 edition.)
[Identifies four universal attributes of law: authority, intention of universal application, *obligatio,* and sanction. (The second is related to or the same as the concept of precedent.)]

POWELL, H. A.

*1957   Analysis of Present-Day Social Structure in the Trobriands. Ph.D. diss., University of London.

*1969   Genealogy, Residence, and Kinship in Kiriwina. *Man* 4:177–202.

QUINN, NAOMI

*1977   Anthropological Studies on Women's Status. *Annual Review of Anthropology* 6:181–225.
[Men are physically and verbally more aggressive than women. Women everywhere predominate in child care. An extensive list of negative universals: productive activities in which women never predominate.]

RADCLIFFE-BROWN, A. R.

*1935   Patrilineal and Matrilineal Succession. *Iowa Law Review* 20:286–303.

*1952   *Structure and Function in Primitive Society*. Glencoe, Illinois: Free Press.

RALLS, KATHERINE, JONATHON D. BALLOU, AND ALAN TEMPLETON

  1988   Estimates of Lethal Equivalents and the Cost of Inbreeding in Mammals. *Conservation Biology* 2:185–193.

RATLIFF, FLOYD

*1976   On the Psychophysiological Bases of Universal Color Names. *Proceedings of the American Philosophical Society*. 120:311–330.

RAY, VERNE F.

  1952   Techniques and Problems in the Study of Human Color Perception. *Southwestern Journal of Anthropology* 8:251–259.

REDFIELD, ROBERT

*1950   Social Science among the Humanities. *Measure* 1:60–74.
[The feelings of pride, shame, amusement, and shock; forgoing present pleasure for a deferred good.]

*1953   *The Primitive World and Its Transformations*. Ithaca, New York: Cornell University Press.
[Presents a universalistic framework for the analysis of worldview.]

REYNOLDS, VERNON, VINCENT FALGER, AND IAN VINE, EDS.

*1987   *The Sociobiology of Ethnocentrism: Evolutionary Dimensions of Xenophobia, Discrimination, Racism and Nationalism*. London: Croom Helm.

RICHARDS, CARA E.

  1972   *Man in Perspective*. New York: Random House.

ROBERTS, JOHN M., AND BRIAN SUTTON-SMITH

1962   Child Training and Game Involvement. *Ethnology* 1:166–185.

ROHNER, RONALD P.

*1975   *They Love Me, They Love Me Not: A Worldwide Study of the Effects of Parental Acceptance and Rejection.* New Haven, Connecticut, HRAF Press.
[Humans have a need for a positive response from persons who are important to them; when parents reject their children, it has "malignant" effects on their personalities.]

ROSCH, ELEANOR

*1975   Universals and Cultural Specifics in Human Categorization. In *Cross-Cultural Perspectives on Learning*, edited by Richard W. Brislin, Stephen Bochner, and Walter J. Lonner, pp. 177–206. New York: Wiley.
[In three apparently "biologically given" domains—color, facial expression, and geometric forms—the processes and content of category formation appear to be universal, and to involve classifications structured by "prototypes," which are "rather like Platonic forms." (The focal colors of the basic color categories are examples of prototypes.)]

1983   Prototype Classification and Logical Classification: The Two Systems. In *New Trends in Conceptual Representation: Challenges to Piaget's Theory.* edited by Ellin Kofsky Scholnick, pp. 73–86. Hillsdale, New Jersey: Lawrence Erlbaum Associates.

ROSENBLATT, PAUL C., R. PATRICIA WALSH, AND DOUGLAS A. JACKSON

*1976   Grief and Mourning in Cross-Cultural Perspective. New Haven, Connecticut: Human Relations Area Files.
[People everywhere perceive the death of close kin as a loss and feel grief.]

ROSS, DOROTHY

1979   The Development of the Social Sciences. In *The Organization of Knowledge in Modern America, 1860–1920*, edited by Alexandra Oleson and John Voss, pp. 107–138. Baltimore: Johns Hopkins University Press.

ROSSI, INO

*1978   Toward the Unification of Scientific Explanation: Evidence from Biological, Psychic, Linguistic, Cultural Universals. In *Discourse and Inference in Cognitive Anthropology: An Approach to Psychic Unity and Enculturation*, edited by Marvin D. Loflin and James Silverberg, pp. 199–228. The Hague: Mouton.
[Binary discriminations.]

RUSSELL, FINDLAY E.

*1983   *Snake Venom Poisoning.* Philadelphia: Lippincott.
[Even peoples with great reverence for snakes fear them.]

SACKETT, GENE P.

1966 Monkeys Reared in Isolation with Pictures as Varied Input: Evidence for an Innate Releasing Mechanism. *Science* 154:1468–1473.

SACKS, OLIVER

1985 *The Man Who Mistook His Wife for a Hat, and Other Clinical Tales.* New York: Summit Books.

SAHLINS, MARSHALL

*1976 Colors and Culture. *Semiotica* 16:1–22.

THE SAMOA CONTROVERSY

1983 The Samoa Controversy: A Select Bibliography. *Canberra Anthropologist* 6:86–97.

SAMUELSON, FRANZ

1981 Struggle for Scientific Authority: The Reception of Watson's Behaviorism, 1913–1920. *Journal of the History of the Behavioral Sciences* 37:399–425.

SAPIR, EDWARD

1929 The Status of Linguistics as a Science. *Language* 5:207–214.

SCARR, SANDRA, AND KATHLEEN MCCARTNEY

1983 How People Make Their Own Environments: A Theory of Genotype → Environment Effect. *Child Development* 54:424–435.

SCHEFF, THOMAS J.

*1983 Toward Integration in the Social Psychology of Emotions. *Annual Review of Sociology* 9:333–354.
[A review of the arguments on behalf of cultural and biological bases of emotions that supports the universality of "coarse" emotions.]

*1985 Universal Expressive Needs: A Critique and a Theory. *Symbolic Interaction* 8:241–262.

*1986 Micro-Linguistics and Social Structure: A Theory of Social Action. *Sociological Theory* 4:71–83.
[Argues that turn-taking is a genetically programmed universal.]

SCHNEIDER, DAVID M.

*1972 What Is Kinship All About? In *Kinship Studies in the Morgan Centennial Year,* edited by Priscilla Reining, pp. 32–63. Washington, D.C.: Anthropological Society of Washington.

SCHWARTZ, LINDA J.

*1980 Syntactic Markedness and Frequency of Occurrence. In *Evidence and Argumentation in Linguistics,* edited by Thomas A. Perry, pp. 315–333. New York: Walter de Gruyter.

SEKULAR, ROBERT, AND RANDOLPH BLAKE

1990 *Perception.* New York: McGraw-Hill.

SELBY, HENRY A.

1974 *Zapotec Deviance: The Convergence of Folk and Modern Sociology.* Austin: University of Texas Press.

SELBY, HENRY, AND LUCY GARRETSON

1981 *Cultural Anthropology.* Dubuque, Iowa: Brown.

SELIGMAN, MARTIN

*1971 Phobias and Preparedness. *Behavior Therapy* 2:307–320.

SELIGMAN, MARTIN E. P., AND JOANNE L. HAGER

1972 *Biological Boundaries of Learning.* New York: Appleton-Century-Crofts.

SHEPHER, JOSEPH

*1983 *Incest: A Biosocial View.* New York: Academic Press.

SHOTTER, JOHN

*1981 Vico, Moral Worlds, Accountability and Personhood. In Heelas and Lock, eds., pp. 265–284.
[Universals of common sense.]

SHWEDER, RICHARD A., AND EDMUND J. BOURNE

*1984 Does the Concept of the Person Vary Cross-Culturally? In Shweder and LeVine, eds., pp. 158–199.
[Compares universalism, evolutionism, and relativism. Asserts that all societies confront the following existential issues: the haves versus have nots, our way of life against theirs, and the relationship of nature to culture.]

SHWEDER, RICHARD A., AND ROBERT A. LEVINE, EDS.

*1984 *Culture Theory: Essays on Mind, Self, and Emotion.* Cambridge: Cambridge University Press.

SILK, JOAN B.

1980 Adoption and Kinship in Oceania. *American Anthropologist* 82:799–820.

SLOBIN, DAN I.

*1978 Developmental Psycholinguistics. In *A Survey of Linguistic Science*, 2d ed., edited by William Orr Dingwall, pp. 267–311. Stamford, Connecticut: Greylock.
[Sets forth a series of universal features of language (e.g., universal "communicative functions," such as asserting, requesting, etc.), but primary emphasis is to suggest a series of universals in the order in which linguistic features are acquired by children in the course of language acquisition.]

SMITH, M. G.

*1956   On Segmentary Lineage Systems. *Journal of the Royal Anthropological Institute* 86:39–80.
[Government, authority, power.]

  1983   Ethnicity and Sociobiology. *American Ethnologist* 10:364–367.

SPAIN, DAVID H.

*1987   The Westermarck-Freud Incest-Theory Debate. *Current Anthropology* 28:623–645.

SPAULDING, ALBERT C.

  1988   Distinguished Lecture: Archaeology and Anthropology. *American Anthropologist* 90: 263–271.

SPERBER, DAN

*1974   *Rethinking Symbolism.* Cambridge: Cambridge University Press.
[Universal properties of understanding. Rational thought occurs among all peoples.]

  1982   Apparently Irrational Beliefs. In *Rationality and Relativism*, edited by Martin Hollis and Steven Lukes, pp. 149–180. Cambridge: MIT Press.

  1985   Anthropology and Psychology: Towards an Epidemiology of Representations. *Man* 20:73–89.

  1986   Issues in the Ontology of Culture. In *Logic, Methodology and Philosophy of Science VII.* Proceedings of the Seventh International Congress of Logic, Methodology and Philosophy of Science, Salzburg, 1983, edited by Ruth Barcan Marcus, Georg J. W. Dorn, and Paul Weingartner, pp. 557–571. Amsterdam: North-Holland.

SPIRO, MELFORD

*1954a Is the Family Universal? *American Anthropologist* 56: 839–846.

*1954b Human Nature in Its Psychological Dimensions. *American Anthropologist* 56:19–29.
[Universals mentioned include worldview; morally right and wrong methods of satisfying needs; a personality structure that integrates needs (id), values (superego), and executive-response processes (ego); the inability of any society to prevent threat or danger to its members; psychological self-defense mechanisms; and the psychological processes of projection, displacement, rationalization, sublimation, etc.]

  1958   *Children of the Kibbutz.* Cambridge: Harvard University Press.

*1979   *Gender and Culture: Kibbutz Women Revisited.* Durham, North Carolina: Duke University Press.

[Presents evidence for a "female parenting need" that is "precultural," and that contributes to the sex role assignments that are at least nearly universal.]

*1982   *Oedipus in the Trobriands.* Chicago: University of Chicago Press.

*1984   Some Reflections on Cultural Determinism and Relativism with Special Reference to Emotion and Reason. In Shweder and LeVine, eds., pp. 323–346.

 1986   Cultural Relativism and the Future of Anthropology. *Cultural Anthropology* 1:259–286.

STAAL, FRITS

*1988   *Universals: Studies in Indian Logic and Linguistics.* Chicago: University of Chicago Press.
         [Explores the basic commonalities between Indian and Western logic and linguistics to conclude that wherever logic and linguistics develop they are fundamentally the same (as in mathematics also). Negation, the principle of noncontradiction, rule, and rationality; also music, song, and ritual.]

*1989   *Rules without Meaning: Ritual, Mantras and the Human Sciences.* New York: Lang.
         [Ritual and "the urge to attach meanings to what is essentially meaningless."]

STEADMAN, LYLE B.

 1971   Neighbours and Killers: Residence and Dominance among the Hewa of New Guinea. Ph.D. diss. Australian National University.

STEINER, GEORGE

*1975   *After Babel.* London: Oxford University Press.
         [Linguistic universals, pronouns, proper names, subject, subject-verb-object combinations, differences of stress, organized sequence, relations of hierarchy (as between general and particular, sum and part), metaphor, the contrast between white-positive and black-negative, concept of future and other "alternities."]

STERN, DANIEL

*1977   *The First Relationship: Mother and Infant.* Cambridge: Harvard University Press.

 1985   *The Interpersonal World of the Infant: A View from Psychoanalysis and Developmental Psychology.* New York: Basic Books.

STERN, DANIEL N., AND JOHN DORE

 1985   Affect Attunement: The Sharing of Feeling States between Mother and Infant by Means of Inter-Modal Fluency. In Field and Fox, pp. 249–268.

STOCKING, GEORGE W., JR.

1968 *Race, Culture, and Evolution: Essays in the History of Anthropology.* New York: Free Press.

SWARTZ, M. J.

*1961 Negative Ethnocentrism. *Journal of Conflict Resolution* 5:75–81.

SUGGS, ROBERT C.

1971 Sex and Personality in the Marquesas: A Discussion of the Linton-Kardiner Report. In *Human Sexual Behavior,* edited by Donald S. Marshall and Robert C. Suggs, pp. 163–186. New York: Basic Books.

SUMNER, WILLIAM GRAHAM

*1906 *Folkways: A Study of the Sociological Importance of Usages, Manners, Customs, Mores, and Morals.* Boston: Ginn.
[The classic statement on the universality of ethnocentrism and its correlates.]

SUTTON-SMITH, BRIAN, AND JOHN M. ROBERTS

*1981 Play, Games, and Sports. In *Handbook of Cross-Cultural Psychology.* Vol. 4, *Developmental Psychology,* edited by Harry C. Triandis and Alastair Heron, pp. 425–471. Boston: Allyn and Bacon.
[Suggests that games may be universal.]

SYMONS, DONALD

*1979 *The Evolution of Human Sexuality.* New York: Oxford University Press.
[Sexual attractiveness.]

1987a If We're All Darwinians, What's the Fuss About? In *Sociobiology and Psychology: Ideas, Issues and Findings,* edited by Charles Crawford, Marilyn Smith, and Dennis Krebs, pp. 121–146. Hillsdale, New Jersey: Erlbaum.

1987b Detecting Mr. Right. *Natural History* 96 (7):4.

1989 A Critique of Darwinian Anthropology. *Ethology and Sociobiology* 10:131–144.

*n.d. On the Use and Abuse of Darwinism in the Study of Human Behavior. In *The Adapted Mind,* edited by Jerome Barkow, Leda Cosmides, and John Tooby. New York: Oxford University Press. (In press.)

TALMON, YONINA

1964 Mate Selection in Collective Settlements. *American Sociological Review* 29:491–508.

TIGER, LIONEL

*1969 *Men in Groups.* New York: Random House.

TIGER, LIONEL, AND ROBIN FOX

*1971   *The Imperial Animal.* New York: Holt, Rinehart & Winston.
[Among the numerous possible universals that are mentioned: adornment (of young females); adultery; children's play; courtship; culture; dance; dominant individuals a focus of attention; flirting; games of skill and chance; homicide; homosexuality; incest regulation; juvenile delinquency; loyalty; male activities that exclude females and/or are secret; male dominance (in political arena); marriage; myths and legends; obligations to give, receive, and repay; persons who attempt (or pretend) to cure the ill; property; psychoses and neuroses; rules; self-deception; senility; sexual division of labor; statuses; suicide; supernatural (deference to and attempts to control); taboos (and avoidances); and traditional restraints on the rebelliousness of young men.]

TOOBY, JOHN

1985   The Emergence of Evolutionary Psychology. In *Emerging Syntheses in Science,* edited by David Pines, pp. 1–6. Santa Fe: Santa Fe Institute.

TOOBY, JOHN, AND LEDA COSMIDES

*1989a The Innate Versus the Manifest: How Universal Does Universal Have to Be? *Behavioral and Brain Sciences* 12:36–37.

*1989b On the Universality of Human Nature and the Uniqueness of the Individual: The Role of Genetics and Adaptation. Typescript.

1989c Evolutionary Psychologists Need to Distinguish between the Evolutionary Process, Ancestral Selection Pressures, and Psychological Mechanisms. *Behavioral and Brain Sciences* 12:724–725.

1989d Evolutionary Psychology and the Generation of Culture, Part I. Theoretical Considerations. *Ethology and Sociobiology* 10:29–49.

TOOBY, JOHN, AND IRVEN DEVORE

1987   The Reconstruction of Hominid Behavioral Evolution through Strategic Modeling. In *The Evolution of Human Behavior: Primate Models,* edited by Warren G. Kinzey, pp. 183–237. Albany: State University of New York Press.

TRIVERS, R. L.

*1971   The Evolution of Reciprocal Altruism. *Quarterly Review of Biology* 46:35–57.

*1972   Parental Investment and Sexual Selection. In *Sexual Selection and the Descent of Man, 1871–1971,* edited by B. H. Campbell, pp. 136–179. Chicago: Aldine.

TURNER, FREDERICK, AND ERNST PÖPPEL

*1983   The Neural Lyre: Poetic Meter, the Brain, and Time. *Poetry* 72:277–309. (Reprinted in *Natural Classicism: Essays on Literature and Science*, by Frederick Turner, pp. 61–108. New York: Paragon House.)
[Metered poetry is universal; its fundamental unit is the "line." Lines, varying within narrow limits around an average of 3 seconds in length, are demarcated by pauses and marked by repetition of one or more elements (e.g., the acoustic element of rhyme). Line length and repetition match the rhythm with which the brain processes information. All poetry allows some free variation. The association of poetry with ritual is a near-universal. The sense of time is linked to the perception of time. Humans are inveterate predictors.]

*1985   Performed Being: Word Art as a Human Inheritance. In *Natural Classicism: Essays on Literature and Science*, by Frederick Turner, pp. 3–57. New York: Paragon House.

TURNER, VICTOR W.

*1966   Colour Classification in Ndembu Ritual: A Problem in Primitive Classification. *Anthropological Approaches to the Study of Religion*. ASA Monograph No. 3, edited by Michael Banton, pp. 47–84. London: Tavistock.
[Universality or near-universality of red-white-black symbolism.]

 1983   Body, Brain, and Culture. *Zygon* 18:221–245.

TUZIN, DONALD

*1984   Miraculous Voices: The Auditory Experience of Numinous Objects. *Current Anthropology* 25:579–596.
[Argues for the virtual universality of sound as a medium of ritual communication or experience.]

TYLOR, EDWARD B.

*1870   Researches into the Early History of Mankind. 2d ed. London: Murray.

*1891   [1874] *Primitive Culture: Researches into the Development of Mythology, Philosophy, Religion, Language, Art, and Custom*. 3d ed., rev. Vol. I. London: Murray.

*1898   *Anthropology: An Introduction to the Study of Man and Civilization*. New York: Appleton.
[Universals mentioned include fire, cooking, group living, social life, families or households, marriage, ties of parent-child, rules of right and wrong, and some form of prohibition of murder.]

ULLMANN, STEPHEN

*1963   Semantic Universals. In Greenberg, ed., pp. 172–207.
[All languages contain both "transparent" and "opaque" words (i.e., words in which there is or is not a relationship between sound and sense). Yet

words as generally understood are not universal (morphemes are). Polysemy.]

VAN DEN BERGHE, PIERRE

*1981 *The Ethnic Phenomenon.* New York: Elsevier.
[Ethnocentrism, mating regulations, cheating, kinship.]

*1983 Human Inbreeding Avoidance: Culture in Nature. *Behavioral and Brain Sciences* 6:91–123.

*1986 Skin Color Preference, Sexual Dimorphism and Sexual Selection: A Case of Gene Culture Co-evolution? *Ethnic and Racial Studies* 9:87–113.

WALLACE, ANTHONY F. C.

*1961 The Psychic Unity of Human Groups. In *Studying Personality Cross-Culturally,* edited by Bert Kaplan, pp. 129–163. Evanston, Illinois: Row, Peterson.
[Elementary logical concepts: not, and, and/or, identically equal, equivalent, order, etc.; psychic functions of discrimination, conditioning, and generalization; psychological defense mechanisms.]

1962 The New Culture and Personality. In *Anthropology and Human Behavior,* edited by Thomas Gladwin and William C. Sturtevant. Washington, D.C.: Anthropological Society of Washington.

WARD, BARBARA E.

*1963 Men, Women and Change: An Essay in Understanding Social Roles in South and South-East Asia. In *Women in the New Asia: The Changing Social Roles of Men and Women in South and South-East Asia,* edited by Barbara E. Ward, pp. 25–99. Paris: UNESCO.

WARDEN, CARL J.

*1936 *The Emergence of Human Culture.* New York: Macmillan.
[In a section entitled "The Universal Cultural Pattern," he discusses Wissler's scheme and then provides his own: a list of universal "needs" and "traits" under the heading of "human nature," followed by a corresponding list of "primary pattern factors" that constitute "classes or types of cultural activities" that result from the various human needs and traits (p. 141). This framework is probably the prototype of Malinowski's (1960 [1944]). Among the specific universals mentioned: use of hands to eat, twisted string.]

WASHBURN, S. L.

1959 Speculations on the Interrelations of the History of Tools and Biological Evolution. In *The Evolution of Man's Capacity for Culture,* arranged by J. N. Spuhler, pp. 21–31. Detroit: Wayne State University Press.

WATSON, JOHN B.

1925 *Behaviorism.* New York: Norton.

WEIL, ANDREW

*1972   *The Natural Mind: A New Way of Looking at Drugs and the Higher Consciousness.* Boston: Houghton Mifflin.
[Proposes a universal drive for altered states of consciousness.]

WEINBERG, KIRSON S.

1963   *Incest Behavior.* New York: Citadel Press.

WEINER, ANNETTE B.

*1985   Oedipus and the Ancestors. *American Ethnologist* 12:758–762.

WESTERMARCK, EDWARD

*1922   *The History of Human Marriage.* 5th ed. Vol. II. New York: Allerton.

WHITE, GEOFFREY M.

*1980   Conceptual Universals in Interpersonal Language. *American Anthropologist* 82:759–781.
[A comparative study suggests that the contrasts between solidarity and conflict and between dominance and submission universally structure terms for describing personality].

WHITE, LESLIE

*1948   The Definition and Prohibition of Incest. *American Anthropologist* 50:416–435.

WHITING, B. B., AND C. P. EDWARDS

*1973   A Cross-Cultural Analysis of Sex Differences in the Behavior of Children Aged Three through Eleven. *Journal of Social Psychology* 91:171–188.
[Describe playfighting as very likely to be innate in humans.]

WIERZBICKA, ANNA

*1980   *Lingua Mentalis: The Semantics of Natural Language.* London: Academic Press.
[Argues that all languages employ thirteen semantic primes: I, you, someone, something, world, this, want, not want, think of, say, imagine, be a part of, become.]

*1986   Human Emotions: Universal or Culture-Specific? *American Anthropologist* 88:584–594.

WILLIAMS, ELGIN

1947   Anthropology for the Common Man. *American Anthropologist* 49:84–90.

WILLIAMS, GEORGE C.

1966   *Adaptation and Natural Selection: A Critique of Some Current Evolutionary Thought.* Princeton, New Jersey: Princeton University Press.

1985   A Defense of Reductionism in Evolutionary Biology. *Oxford Surveys in Evolutionary Biology* 2:1–27.

WILLNER, DOROTHY

1983   Definition and Violation: Incest and the Incest Taboos. *Man* 18:134–159.

WILSON, E. O.

1975   *Sociobiology: The New Synthesis.* Cambridge: Belknap Press of Harvard University Press.

*1978   *On Human Nature.* Cambridge: Harvard University Press.

WISSLER, CLARK

*1923   *Man and Culture.* New York: Crowell Company.

WITKOWSKI, STANLEY R., AND CECIL H. BROWN

*1977   An Explanation of Color Nomenclature Universals. *American Anthropologist* 79:50–57.

*1978   Lexical Universals. *Annual Review of Anthropology* 7:427–451.

*1982   Whorf and Universals of Color Nomenclature. *Journal of Anthropological Research* 38:411–420.

WOLF, ARTHUR P.

*1966   Childhood Association, Sexual Attraction, and the Incest Taboo: A Chinese Case. *American Anthropologist* 68:883–898.

*1968   Adopt a Daughter-in-Law, Marry a Sister: A Chinese Solution to the Problem of the Incest Taboo. *American Anthropologist* 70:864–874.

*1970   Childhood Association and Sexual Attraction: A Further Test of the Westermarck Hypothesis. *American Anthropologist* 72:503–515.

WOLF, ARTHUR, AND C. S. HUANG

*1980   *Marriage and Adoption in China, 1845–1945.* Stanford, California: Stanford University Press.

WOODBURN, JAMES

*1982   Egalitarian Societies. *Man* 17:431–441.
        [The most aggressively and successfully egalitarian societies provide only the "closest approximation to equality." Also, they only minimize emphasis on formal meal times.]

THE WORLD OF MUSIC

*1977   Universals. Vol. 19, no. 1/2.
        [This issue is devoted to discussions of the possibility of universals in music.]

*1984   Universals II. Vol. 26, no. 2.
        [This issue is also devoted to discussions of the possibility of universals in music.]

YENGOYAN, ARAM A.

*1978 Culture, Consciousness, and Problems of Translation: The Kariera System in Cross-Cultural Perspective. In *Australian Aboriginal Concepts*, edited by L. R. Hiatt, pp. 146–155. Canberra: Australian Institute of Aboriginal Studies.
[The logical concepts of hierarchy, equality, and part-whole relationships.]

YOUNG, MICHAEL

*1988 *The Metronomic Society: Natural Rhythms and Human Timetables.* Cambridge: Harvard University Press.
[Cyclicity.]

ZIPF, GEORGE KINGSLEY

*1949 *Human Behavior and the Principle of Least Effort: An Introduction to Human Ecology.* Cambridge, Massachusetts: Addison-Wesley.

INDEX

Abortion, 140–141, 166
Absent father pattern, 33, 35–36
Abstraction, 131
Acquisition (opposed to learning), 84, 144
Actions under/not under control, 135, 175
Adaptation(s), 100, 111
  aesthetics and religion as, 114
  clues to, 104
  obligate and facultative, 103
  phylogenetic, 101, 107, 115
  playfighting as, 148n
  universality as a clue to, 105
  as used by sociocultural anthropologists,
    101
Address terms, 75–76
Adolescent stress(lessness), 9, 15, 17, 143,
    144, 154
Adoption, 105
Adornment, 188
  of body, 69, 140, 167, 169, 196
  personal, 166
    special occasions for, 188
Adultery, prohibition of, 176, 196
Aesthetics, 52, 71, 114, 140, 157, 158, 161, 182,
    183, 188
  partial explanations of, 113, 115–116
  (See also Adornment; Art)
Affecting things or people (semantic cate-
    gory), 133
Affection, 134
After Babel, 110, 114
Age:
  differences, 145
  division of labor by (see Division of labor)
  grades, 69–70, 133, 176, 181
  limits of Westermarck effect, 122–123, 128

  at marriage, sex differences, 109
  organization, 137, 164, 176, 181
  study of, 150
Aggression, 182
Aggressiveness (male mating strategy), 109n,
    110
Aginsky, Burt W., 77
Aginsky, Ethel G., 77
Alexander, Richard, 111
Allure, wish to, 188
Alternities, 110, 194
Altruism, 178, 182
  evolution of, 105–108
Ambivalence, 135, 161, 167
  anthropological (see Universals)
Amusement (feeling), 189
Anger, 26, 134, 165
Animal behavior, study of, 101
  relevance to study of humans, 72, 82n
Animal communication, compared to speech,
    131
Animal counterparts, 74, 95, 104, 145
  of facial recognition, 112
  of fear of snakes, 115
  of incest avoidance, 118, 124, 128
  Murdock's views against, 63
Animism, 159
Anthropologists:
  acceptance of exaggerations of impor-
    tance of culture, 64
  distortions by, rooted in reward struc-
    tures, 155
  emphasis and exaggeration of differences,
    154–155
    self-serving nature of, 154–155
    (See also Differences)

Anthropologists (*Cont.*):
  as intercultural brokers, 154
  myths of [*see* Myth(s), anthropological]
  physical, 41, 149
  refutations of studies of, 9–10, 14–23, 27–31, 64*n*
  reliance on human similarities of, 154, 178
  skepticism toward (Freudian) psychology, 38
  skepticism toward universals, 1, 5, 6, 26, 54, 58, 64, 73, 75, 81, 82
  as specialists in the study of hunters and gatherers, 86, 150
  taboos of [*see* Taboo(s)]
Anthropology:
  aim of, 80–81, 142
  assumptions of, 6, 156
  contradictions in, 149
  dominant paradigm in, 149
  handicapped by its assumptions, 156
  and human evolution, 86
  impressionism of, 155
  influence of, on moral philosophy, 154
  and problem of separating nature from culture, 147
  propositions informing, 145–149
  and psychology, 26, 38, 87, 110, 150, 156
  role of, in determining what is universal, 149–150
  special role of, 153–154
  and study of human mind, 150, 156
  and study of mental mechanisms, 86
  unconcern of, with origins and evolution, 55, 56, 143, 144
Anthropomorphisation, 139, 168, 170, 180, 187
Antinomous thinking (*see* Binary distinctions)
Antireductionism, 56–58, 60, 72*n*, 73*n*, 120, 143–146
  (*See also* Reductionism)
Antonyms, 133
Appell, George N., 47–48
Arbitrariness, cultural and linguistic, 6, 24, 25, 65, 77, 131, 146
  of color classification, 11–13
  as hallmark of culture, 148
  limits on, 98
  overstatement of, 148–149
Archaeology, 150
Archoses, 96–97, 117
Arens, William, 118, 119*n*, 123*n*, 124–125

Art, 59, 158, 165, 166, 169, 176
  associated with ritual, 167
  decorative, 69, 140, 162
  literary, 162, 176
  themes in, 158
  (*See also* Aesthetics; Adornment)
Artificial intelligence, 85, 144
Associationism, 84
Athletic sports, 69
Attractiveness, 180, 181
Authority, legal, 188

Bagish, Henry, 155
Bamberger, Joan, 23
Basic Color Terms, 10–14, 37–38, 80, 81
Basic colors, 13, 133
Basic vocabulary words, 177
Bastian, Adolph, 54*n*, 55
Beauty, standards of, 161
Behavior:
  genetics, 147*n*
  interpretation of, 134, 168
  sociocultural and biological meanings of, 101
Behavioral propensities, 133
Behaviorism, 60–61, 73, 77, 83, 85, 143, 144
Beliefs, 59, 139
Benedict, Ruth, 1, 14*n*, 64–66, 69, 143
  (*See also Patterns of Culture*)
Berlin, Brent, 10–14, 37–38
  (*See also Basic Color Terms*)
Bidney, David, 70–71, 86*n*, 149, 155
  on human nature and universals, 71
Binary distinctions, 90, 92, 99, 150, 166, 170, 178, 190
Biogrammar, 81
Biography/hagiography, 152
Biological and ontogenetic explanations, 113
Biological clocks, 93
Biological givens, 92, 117
Biological sciences:
  earlier turmoil in, 60, 62, 143
  impact of, in understanding incest avoidance, 128
  recent influence on anthropology, 82–83, 87
  theoretically organized by evolutionary theory, 144
Biological universals, 49
  Kluckhohn on, 72
  Kroeber on, 64
  Wissler on, 59

Biology:
  as basis for universals, 59, 70, 72, 149
  and language, 77–78
  shapes human behavior, denied, 19
Biology/culture, contrast of, 40–41, 56, 62–
  64, 88, 102, 143
Biology/psychology as basis or explanation
  of universals, 6, 62, 71, 88, 94, 97,
  117
Biology/society, contrast of (see Biology/
  culture)
Biophobia, 155
Birdwhistell, Ray L., 23–24
Birth and death, consciousness of, 167
Birth customs and practices, 69, 136
Black and white, 13–14, 133, 134, 161, 167
  valuation of, 194
Black, white, and red, 12, 14, 161
Bloch, Maurice, 72, 82, 86, 92–94, 153, 155
Bloom, Allan, 155
Boas, Franz, 14, 19, 31, 60, 65, 86
  culture concept of, 55
  on universals, 55–56, 58
  on race, 55
Boasians, 63, 65, 68, 72n
  Murdock not among, 63
  particularism of, 1
  reactions to, 68–69
  in study of race/culture, 54, 55, 57, 60
Body:
  classification of parts of, 133
  decoration (see Adornment)
  size, sex differences in, 110
Brain, 82, 86–87 98–99, 113, 144
  complexity of, 148
  holistic view of, 61
  lateral specialization of, 90, 157
  lesions and deficits, 82, 85, 99, 144, 150
  localization of faculties in, 61n, 85
    (See also Localizers)
  and poetic line, 116, 150
  and religion, 114–115
Brain cell specialization, 85, 144
British social anthropology, 66–68
Brown, Cecil H., 14

Calendar, 69, 133
  Hopi, 28, 30, 31
Capital punishment, 141, 187
Categorization, 14
  (See also Classification)
Causal thinking, 99, 166, 170

Causation in explanation of universals, 89,
  117
Cheating, 198
Childcare, 136, 182
  sex differences in providing, 109, 137, 184,
    189
Childrearing, 16, 21, 137
  (See also Socialization)
Children, 136–137
Chimpanzee Politics, 111
Choice making, 135
Chomsky, Noam, 42–43, 47, 50, 77, 84, 113,
  144, 155n, 164
  criticizes learning theory, 147
  on innateness as a defense against tyr-
    anny, 155n
Classification, 14, 133, 167, 169, 170
  and aesthetics, 116
  of age, 94, 133, 137, 162, 181
  and art, 116
  of behavioral propensities, 133
  of body parts, 133
  of color, 77, 200
  of flora and fauna, 14, 46, 69, 133
  of inner states, 133, 175
  of kin, 69, 137, 162, 165, 170
  of personality, 199
  of sex (gender), 94, 137, 162, 181
    fundamental duality, 133–134
  of space, 133
  of tools, 133
  of weather conditions, 133
Class-subclass (logic), 170
Coalitions, 107, 138
Coevolution, 74
Cognitive development, stages of, 166
Cognitive imperative, 99
Collective decisions, 138
Collective identities, 137
Color, 167, 190
  classification of, 77, 200
Color terms (see Basic Color Terms)
Coming of Age in Samoa, 9, 14–21, 60, 61, 65,
  81, 143, 144
  (See also Mead, Margaret)
"Common Denominator of Cultures, The,"
  69–70
Common sense, 192
Communication (facial, nonverbal, and sym-
  bolic), 134
Comparative Functionalism, 76
Comparative perspective, 145, 156

Complementary filiation, 105
Componential analysis, 46, 48n, 75–76, 80, 133
  (*See also* Ethnosemantics)
Conceptualization, 166
Conceptualizing universals, 39–42
Concomitant variation, method of, 89
Conditional statements, 161
Conditional universals (*see* Universals)
Confessions of a Former Cultural Relativist, 155
Conflict, 59, 138, 176, 178
  ways of dealing with, 138
Conjectural reasoning, 134, 150
Consciousness, altered states of, 136, 199
Conservation of energy, 98, 117
Containers, 135, 165
Contempt (and facial expression of), 26, 134, 168, 177
Conversation structure, 185
Cooking, 50, 69, 136, 179, 197
  uses of, 95
Coon, Carleton, 71–72
Cooperation, 69, 138, 139, 161, 165
Cosmides, Leda, 83, 85, 86, 103n, 106, 147n, 148
Cosmology (*see* Worldview)
Counting, 46, 133, 157, 178
Courtship, 69
Coyness display, 48, 52, 83, 85, 101, 134
Cradle traits, 56, 63–64, 71, 95, 159, 164
Critical period, 104, 113, 123, 128, 181
Cross-cultural comparison and generalization, 27, 75, 82
Cross-species studies (*see* Animal counterparts; Interspecific comparison)
Crying, 83, 134
Cultural and noncultural, difficulty of distinguishing between, 64
Cultural anthropology:
developed by Tylor, 54–56
  and explanation of universals, 149–150
  not concerned with universals, 64
Cultural determinism, 3, 6, 19, 61, 62, 75, 143, 146, 148
Cultural evolutionists, 73n
Cultural explanations, 88, 97, 103n, 113, 117, 127
Cultural processes, 95
Cultural reflection or recognition, 92–94, 117
Cultural relativism (*see* Relativism)
Cultural scheme, 71
  (*See also* "The Universal Pattern")
Cultural traditions rich for humans, 145

Cultural universals, 39–40, 63, 142
  as determinants of human nature, 81
  (*See also* Universals, cultural)
Cultural variability, 65, 143, 146
  overstatement of, 148–149
Culture, 141, 180, 196
  as autonomous level or phenomenon, 6, 56, 58, 60, 62–65, 143–144, 146
  criticisms of, 71, 74, 149, 155
  comes from nature, 147
  concept and dilemma of universals, 62–63
  concept in middle-level propositions, 146
  definition of, 40, 130
  evolution of, 68–69
  as exclusive subject of ethnology, 57
  and explanation of differences, 146–148
  expressive, 153
  and the human mind, 72
  and language, 40, 98
  as locus of universals, 39–42, 50
  Malinowski on, 67
  material, 40, 58
  material determinants of, 68, 144
  as principal determinant of human behavior, 6, 62, 75, 143, 146
   absence of way to quantify, 148
  as product of human action, 99
  role of universals in, 150–151
  universal model for analysis of, 71
  universals as deep syntax and lexicon of, 153
Culture/biology (*see* Biology/culture; Nature/culture; Nature/nurture)
Culture/nature (*see* Biology/culture; Nature/culture; Nature/nurture)
Cultures or societies as focus of study, 143
Curiosity, 99, 167, 176
Cutters, 135
Cyclicity, 201
  of time, 133

Daily routines, 139, 165
Daly, Martin, 86, 105, 107, 109, 155
Dance, 69, 140, 162, 186, 196
Danger, inability of society to prevent, 193
D'Aquili, Eugene G., 99, 111
Dark and light, 33
Darwin, on emotions, 24
Darwinian evolution as inclusive theoretical framework, 6, 144
Darwinian thought, 62, 143
  synthesized with Mendelism, 62, 144
Darwinian view of Westermarck, 120

De Waal, Franz, 111
Deaf language, 41n, 113
Death customs (see Treatment, of the dead)
Death related to sickness, 176
Decision making, 135, 175
  collective, 138, 170
Deep and shallow, 132
Deep-noted instruments, 114
Deep processes, structures, universals, 44, 77, 113, 156, 171, 181
Defense mechanisms, 180, 193, 196, 198
Definitions, universally valid, 80
Determinism, sociocultural (see Cultural determinism; Culture)
Differences, emphasis and exaggeration of, 2, 3, 5, 23, 31, 38, 66n, 73, 76, 82, 154–156
  self-serving nature of, 154–155
Diffusion, diffusionist explanations, 95, 117
  (See also Cradle traits)
Dimension, 133
  (See also Measure)
Directions, giving, 133, 181
Discrepancies between talk, thought, and action, 130
Disgust, 26, 134
Displacement, 34, 193
Display rules, 25, 26
Dispositions, 110–111
Dispute settlement, 169
  consultation and mediation in, 138
Dissanayake, Ellen, 114–116
Diurnality, 139
Divination, 69, 139, 153n
Division of labor, 39, 69, 161
  by sex and age, 48, 137, 157, 165, 184, 196
Dog, 44, 50
Dominance, 2, 159, 161, 196
Dominants as focus of attention, 196
Douglas, Mary, 64
Dream interpretation, 69, 139
Dreaming, 139, 157, 176, 180, 187
Dress, 58
Drill, 59
Dualistic thought (see Binary distinctions)
Durkheim, Émile, 60

Education, 67, 69
Effects (as opposed to functions), 101–102, 111
Eibl-Eibesfeldt, Irenäus, 52, 83, 101
"Eighteen Professions," 56, 57
Ekman, Paul (and associates), 10, 24–27, 51–52, 98
Elementary ideas, 54n, 55, 97, 114, 178

The Elementary Structures of Kinship, 64n, 72, 98–99
Emic/etic, 76, 80–81, 91n, 131, 140
  defined, 48
  universals, 48–49
Emotion(s), 23–27, 39, 75, 113, 115, 116, 135, 165, 175, 199
  and aesthetics, 116
  basic, coarse, elementary, or primary, 26, 52, 191
  as basis for exceptions to universality, 36
Empathy, 134, 135, 139–141, 159, 165, 168
Endorphins and ritual, 115
Entification, 137, 158
Environment, humans' adjustment to, 136
Environment, of human evolutionary history, 50, 86
Environmentalism, arch, 62
  (See also Cultural determinism; Relativism, extreme cultural)
Envy, 139, 169
Equality (logic), 201
Eschatology, 69
Ethics (see Morality)
Ethnicity, 138
Ethnocentrism, 79, 107n, 138–139, 158, 163, 169, 189, 195, 198
  ethical dualism of, 139
  and sense of being a distinct people, 136
  (See also In-group/out-group)
Ethnoscience, 82, 92
Ethnosemantics, 82, 92
  (See also Componential analysis)
Ethological perspective, 129
Ethology, 78, 81, 82, 101, 144
  and explanation of incest avoidance, 129
  lessons drawn from, 81n
  recent influence on anthropology, 83
Ethos, 171
Etic grid, 48n
Etiquette, 69, 139, 162, 167
Eugenics, 55, 62
Evolution:
  accident in, 103–104
  of basic color terms, 11, 13–14
  compromise in, 103–104
  conservatism in, 103–104
  cultural, 68–69, 73n
  of human species, 145
  ignored in British social anthropology, 66
  natural selection in, 83n, 100
  of racial differences, 101n

Evolutionary biology:
  basic elements of, 99–105
  design and function in, 100–102
  after World War II, decreased interest in, 73
Evolutionary perspective and incest avoidance, 129
Evolutionary psychology, 6, 83, 84, 115, 165, 187
Evolutionary sequence of basic color terms, 11, 13–14
Evolutionary sequences as implicational universals, 46
Evolutionary theory, 81, 85, 99–111, 117, 143, 144
  conservation of energy in, 98
  alternatives to, in explaining universals, 117
  presumed, 110–111
  recent influence on anthropology, 82
  (*See also* Natural selection)
Evolutionary universals, 188
Evolutionists, cultural, 68–69
Exchange, 59, 138, 169, 170, 181, 182
Experiential universals, 47, 180, 192
Explanation(s):
  no zero-sum game between biology and culture, 156
  proximate/ultimate, 104
  of religion and aesthetics, 71
  of universals, 14, 44, 45, 52, 72, 80, 83, 88–117, 141, 142, 149–151, 153, 164
    alternatives for, 117
    formal or methodological, 116–117
Expressive culture, 153
Extrinsic universals, 49–50

Face:
  recognition of individual by, 135
  word for, 78
Facial affect program, 25, 26, 98
Facial expressions (of emotion), 10, 23–27, 38, 39, 51–52, 83, 85, 101, 134, 168, 177, 190
  indicating basic emotions, 26–27
  masking, mimicking, and modifying, 134
  as universals of content, 48
Facial recognition, ontogeny of, 112
Facultative adaptation, 103
Faculty psychology, 61n
Family, 47, 59, 69, 136, 137, 141, 165, 182, 197
  male involvement in, 136
  mother and children as basis of, 136
  regulation of members of, 182
Family complex, 10, 32

Fear(s), 26, 134, 161, 169
  childhood, 135, 179
  overcoming, 135
  of snakes, 135, 190
  of strangers, 107n, 135
  suppression of, 179
Feasting, 69, 139
Female:
  attractiveness, 181
  orgasm, 102
Fighting with hands, 165
Figurative language, 132, 162
Fire, 44, 50, 69, 135, 136, 164, 165, 179, 197
  uses of, 95
"First Contact," 3, 4, 52
Fisher, R. A., 62
Fitness, 100, 106–107
Fixed action patterns, 101, 146, 147
  (*See also* Instincts)
Fodor, Jerry A., 85
Folklore, 69, 139
Followers, dispositions of, 158
Food, 69, 138–139
Forgetting, 182
Formal universals, 43, 49, 50, 164
Fox, Robin, 42–43, 47, 49, 81, 118, 120, 124, 140
  on how to identify the inhuman, 155
  on secular social ideology of our time, ix, 154
Framework or model, universal, 158, 165, 178
  defined, 47–48
Freeman, Derek, 9, 10, 16–20, 31, 38, 61
Freud, Sigmund, 32, 33, 38, 119, 120
Fridlund, Alan J., 26
Function, sociocultural and biological definitions of, 101–102
Functions, universal, 76
Funeral rites (*see* Treatment, of the dead)
Future, past, and present, 133, 194

Games, 43, 59, 69, 163, 165, 167, 176, 190, 195, 196
Garcia, John (and associates), 84
Gardner, Howard, 61n, 85, 150
Geertz, Clifford, 3–5, 54, 74–75, 86, 114n, 151, 156
Gender (*see* Division of labor; Female; Male; Sex)
Gene mutation, 104
General and particular, 134, 194
  distinguishing between, 157
Generalization, 198
Generation, semantic component of, 80, 133

Generosity admired, 138
Genes plus environment in explanation of
  human affairs, 145–147
Genetical Theory of Natural Selection, The, 62
Genitals, explanation for sexual dimorphism
  of, 109n
Genotype, 100
Gestures, 23, 52, 54, 69, 134, 179
Gewertz, Deborah, 10, 21–23, 38
Gift giving, 69, 138, 170
Givens (biological), 117
Giving, 133
Goldschmidt, Walter, 66n, 76, 154, 155
Good and bad, 132, 134, 158, 161, 167, 174,
  182
Goodenough, Ward H., 75, 80–81, 142
Gossip, 131, 172
Government, 48, 59, 67, 69, 138
Gradation, 134
Grammar:
  universality of, 41
  universals of, 131–132, 164, 173
  (*See also* Universal grammar)
Greenberg, Joseph, 78–80, 164
Greetings, 69, 139, 173
Grief, 26, 70, 139
  as response to death of close kin, 190
Group(s), 161, 165
  local or territorial, 136, 186
  nonlocalized, 136, 170
  other than family, 176
  (*See also* Kin groups)
Group competition, 161
Group living, 105, 111, 136, 197
Group selection, 82, 103, 123n, 144

HRAF (*see* Human Relations Area Files)
Habitat selection and landscape prefer-
  ences, 116, 187
Hairstyles, 69, 140, 180, 188
Hallowell, A. Irving, 74–75, 155
Hamilton, W. D., 82, 105
Hand, word for, 133
Handedness, 89, 91, 94, 98, 99, 157, 181, 186
Hand-eye coordination, 172
Hands used to eat, 198
Happiness, 26, 134
Hatch, Elvin, 62, 68, 69
Hate, 161
Haugen, Einar, 31
Hempel, Carl G., 45, 151
Herskovits, Melville J., 68, 71
Hertz, Robert, 90, 92

Hierarchy:
  institutionalized, 92
  in language or logic, 170, 194, 201
  (*See also* Inequality)
Historic phenomena, 71
  (*See also* Cradle traits)
History/myth, 93, 151–153
Hockett, Charles F., 49, 140
Homicide (*see* Murder)
Homo sapiens, characteristics of, 94
Homosexuality, 196
Hope, 161, 182
Hopi Time, 29–31, 38, 144
Hopi verb (tense), 28, 30, 31
Hopkins, Keith, 125–127
Hospitality, 69, 139
Hostility (*see* Conflict)
Household, 197
  (*See also* Family)
Human affairs, 144–146, 148, 153
Human biology, and practical affairs, 93
Human body, 90, 98–99, 178
Human condition, 53, 145
Human evolution, as anthropological spe-
  cialization, 86
Human mind, 6, 32, 46, 60, 74–75, 84, 86–87,
  142–145, 149, 163
  complexity of, 148
  as disparate collection of adaptations, 106
  faculty or modular view of, 61
  Geertz on, 74
  as general fitness calculator, 106
  Hallowell on evolution of, 73
  how evolution acts on, 101
  importance in human nature, 145
  innate tendencies of, according to
    Malinowski, 68
  Lévi-Strauss on, 72, 142
  and mind-altering drugs, 115
  and mystical states, 115
  role of anthropology in studying, 150, 156
  as shaper of culture, 144
  as tabula rasa, 60, 85, 144, 146, 148, 154, 155
  tendencies inherent in, according to
    Kroeber, 57–58
  (*See also* Brain; Mental mechanisms)
Human nature, ix, 19, 53, 83n, 86–87, 145,
  148, 150, 163, 198
  American anthropologists' attitude to-
    ward, 68, 156
  as basis of universals, 71, 146, 148, 152
  Benedict on, 65–66
  Bidney on, 70–71

Human nature (*Cont.*):
  as capacity for culture, 146
  complexity of, 1, 5, 6, 149
  cultural conceptions of, 152–153
  defined, 50
  in defining marriage, 80
  environment of evolution of, 50, 86, 100,
    115, 116
  functions and effects as part of, 102
  Geertz on, 75
  Goldschmidt on, 66*n*
  Goodenough on, 81
  implicit assumptions about, 1, 5, 151
  importance of human mind in, 145
  and incest avoidance, 119
  malleability of, 20, 62, 66, 155
    as Mead's research problem, 14
  need for discovery by comparative stud-
    ies, 81, 156
  racial conceptions of, 152–153
  Tylor on, 55
  understanding of, in social science, 81
  in understanding other cultures, impor-
    tance of, 154, 178
  as unfinished business in social science, 142
  and universals, according to Boas, 59
  variousness as essence of, 74
  (*See also* Human mind; Mental mecha-
    nisms)
Human physiology:
  and marking, 98
  and the use of fire and cooking, 95
Human psyche (*see* Human mind)
Human psychology, implicit assumptions
  about, 1, 5, 151
Human Relations Area Files (HRAF), 51, 70
Human similarities, anthropological reli-
  ance on, 154
Human universals (*see* Universals)
Humanistic anthropology, 71
Humanities and universals, 149, 153–154, 156
Hunters and gatherers as anthropological
  specialty, 86, 150
Hygiene, 69, 140

Iconography/realistic portraiture, 152–153
Identity (logic), 170
Identity, collective, 137
  (*See also* Statuses)
Ideology/knowledge, 92–93, 153
Imagination, 161, 199
Implicational universals (*see* Universals)
Implicature, 2

Imposing meaning on the world, 99, 182
  (*See also* Worldview)
Imprinting, 78, 84–85, 123–125, 128–129
Inbreeding, costs of, 123–124
Inbreeding avoidance mechanisms, 123–124
Incest:
  in Ancient Egypt, 125–127
  avoidance, 49, 112, 118–129, 137
  cases of, 121, 124–125
  concerns sex, not marriage, 118
  functional, 125
  parent-child, 119, 124, 125, 137, 176, 182
  prohibitions, 124, 181
  regulation, 42, 176, 181, 182, 196
  royal, 119
  sibling, 121, 124, 125
  taboo, 49, 64*n*, 69, 72, 118–129, 137, 139
    as cultural invention, 118
    functional or sociological explanation
     of, 124–125
    nonuniversality of, 128
Indebtedness, 165, 182, 196
Individual:
  character, 135
  concept of, 135
  as distinct from social status, 135, 137
  facial recognition of, 135
  as locus of universals, 39–42, 50, 142
  motivation, and explanation of incest
    avoidance, 123*n*, 129
  neither wholly passive nor wholly auton-
    omous, 134–135
  as source of society, culture, and lan-
    guage, 39, 40
  as unit of selection, 82, 103, 123*n*
Individual/society/culture, artificial boundaries between, 40, 43
Inequality, 2, 76, 92, 137, 159, 161, 167, 176,
  182, 192, 199, 200
  as a topic of interest, 152
In-group/out-group, 134, 138–139, 182
  (*See also* Ethnocentrism)
Inheritance, 59, 69, 140, 169, 176
Inhibition (incest avoidance mechanism), 124
Innateness, 46–47, 83*n*, 85, 141, 180, 199
  of aesthetic principles, 157
  Chomsky on, 77, 155*n*
  as defense against totalitarianism, 155*n*
  Durkheim on, 60
  of facial recognition, 112
  of habitat preferences, 116
  Kroeber on, 57–58
  of language, 113, 164

Innateness (*Cont.*):
  of reciprocity, 108
  of triangular awareness, 111
Inner life, privacy of, 135
Inner states, 130, 133, 175, 186
  intentional altering, 136, 180
Instinct to learn, 84–85
Instincts, 62, 70–71, 77–78, 81n, 95, 101, 146,
  147
Insulting, 131
Institutions, Malinowski on, 67
Intellectual neutron bomb, 56–57
Intelligence, general purpose, 85
Intention, 134, 139, 186
Interactionism, 19, 42, 58, 62–63, 73–75, 86,
  88, 93, 98, 113, 117, 149
Interlacing, 135, 180
  (*See also* String)
Internal states (*see* Inner states)
International phonetic alphabet, 46
Interpreting behavior, 134, 168
Intersexual selection, 103
Interspecific comparison, 111–112, 116, 117,
  124, 145
  (*See also* Animal counterparts)
Intonation units, 163
Intrasexual selection, 103
Intrinsic universals, 49–50
Invention, 95, 118
Israeli *kibbutzim* (communes), 35, 120–123,
  127–128
Izard, Carroll E., 10, 24

Jealousy, 15, 165
  (*See also* Male sexual jealousy; Sexual
    jealousy)
John Wayne effect, 25–26
Joking, 69, 131, 165, 176
Jones, Ernest, 34–35
Joy, 26

Kay, Paul, 10–14, 37–38
  (*See also Basic Color Terms*)
Kidder, A. V., 68–69, 72, 73
Kin, close distinguished from distant, 137
Kin groups, 69, 137, 169
  legally recognized, 176
Kin recognition, 112
Kin selection theory, 82–83, 105–107
Kin terms (and terminologies), 40, 46, 69, 79–
  80, 93–94 133, 137, 165, 167, 170, 173
  translatable by reference to procreative
    relationships, 133

Kin terms (and terminologies) (*Cont.*):
  for mother and father, 133
  (*See also* Classification)
Kinship, 59, 150, 169, 181, 198
  as basis of solidarity, 108
  and evolution, 105–108
  explanation for universality of, 105
  genealogical core to, 163
  interest in, 180
  and marriage, 47
  sentiments, 107, 172, 190
  (*See also* Classification; Nepotism)
Kluckhohn, Clyde, 72–73, 80, 149, 155
Knowledge, 59
  ease of acquiring, 104
  as opposed to ideology, 92–93
  as opposed to magic, 37
Kroeber, A. L., 46, 56–58, 64, 70–74, 114, 149,
  155
  dismisses universals, 64
  on "no-man's land," 57, 64, 143
  on psychological reductionism, 57–58
  on racial explanations, 57
  and semantic components of kin terms,
    48n
  on innate tendencies, 57
  on "X," 58, 86, 87

La Barre, Weston, 10, 23, 96–97
Landscapes, innate preferences for, 116, 187
Language, 58, 69, 92–94, 98, 110, 130, 141, 157,
  164
  acquisition, 84, 144, 181
  and biology, 77–78
  and constant change, 33
  and culture, 27, 76–77, 98
  exemplifies relativism, 77
  functional requirements of, 164
  hereditary roots of, 62
  Hopi, 27–31, 155
  as locus of universals, 39–42, 142, 173, 176
  to manipulate others, 130, 131
  to misinform and mislead, 131
  not learned, 77–78, 84, 144
  not a simple reflex of real world, 131
  ontogeny of, 113
  prestige from proficient use of, 131
  role of universals in, 150–151
  thinking without, 130
  universal functions of, 192
  universal structure of, 181
Language Universals, 78
Lashley, Karl, 61

Laughing, 83
Laughlin, Charles D., 99, 111
Law, 59, 69, 138, 172, 176, 185, 188
Leadership, 138, 158, 165, 176
  (*See also* Government; Oligarchy)
Learned behavior, 143, 146, 147
Learning:
  critique of, 77
  ease and difficulty of, 84–85
    (*See also* Preparedness)
  generalized, 84, 143
  by instinct, 84–85
  of language, 113
  one-trial, 85
  theory, 85
  trial-and-error, 137
Legend, 196
  [*See also* Myth(s)]
Lending, 133
Lenneberg, Eric, 77, 85, 113
Lever, 135, 157
Lévi-Strauss, Claude, 64n, 72, 98–99, 142–143
Lexical universals, 162, 173, 200
Life force, interest in, 97
Life forms, 14, 46, 133
Linguistic domain, 75, 93
Linguistic universals, 77–80, 164, 194
  examples of, 41, 46, 47
  kinds of, 164
  (*See also* Grammar; Tendencies; Universals)
Linguistics, 76–80
  and anthropology, relationships between, 76–80
  influence of, on anthropology, 80, 82
  and ontogenetic studies, 113
  popularized by Whorf, 31
  (*See also* Relativism)
Literary art, 153, 162, 176
Localizers, 61n
  (*See also* Brain, localization of faculties in)
Location, 133
Logic, 170, 178, 194, 201
  elementary concepts of, 198
  of explanation, 116
  Indian and Western, 54n
  of sociocultural integration and development, 50
Logical extension, 94, 117
Losing temper, 165
Lowie, Robert, 57n, 63
Luck superstitions or theories, 69, 139
Lying (and watching for), 131, 161
  prohibited, 178, 182

McCabe, Justine, 122, 124
Magic, 69, 70, 139
Male:
  dominance, 20, 22–23, 50, 80, 91–92, 110, 137, 158, 169, 196
  exclusion of females from activities, 196
  and female temperaments, 10, 20–23, 86, 135, 136, 144, 172
    (*See also* Sex differences)
  involvement in family, 136
  male competition, 80, 103
  orgasm, 102, 115
  sexual jealousy, 107, 109
  violence and aggression, 110
    greater than female, 137, 179, 189
Male and Female, 21, 81n
Malinowski, Bronislaw, 9, 32–38, 47, 66–68, 71, 94
  on concept of needs, 67, 94
  on framework for analyzing culture, 76
  on institutions, 67
  on universal functions, 76
  includes biological universals, 49
Malleability of human nature, 20, 62, 66, 155
Malotki, Ekkehart, 10, 28–31, 38
Man and Culture, 58–59
Man and His Works, 71
Man Who Mistook His Wife for a Hat, The, 150
Manifest universals, 47
Manipulation, 138, 158
  with language, 130, 131
Margaret Mead and Samoa, 9, 16–20
  condemnation of, 19n
Marking, 41, 77n, 78–79, 98
Marriage, 59, 69, 105, 136, 141, 165, 166, 172, 187, 196, 197
  defining, 80
  hereditary roots of, 62–63
  rules, 118
  between siblings, 125–127
  usually a part of kinship, 93
Marxism, 60, 73n
Mate selection, 105
Material culture and traits, 40, 58
Material determinants of culture, 68, 144
Materialism, 139
Maternity, equation of social and physiological, 176
Maynard Smith, J., 82, 103, 105
Mead, Margaret, 9, 10, 14–23, 31, 38, 55, 61, 65, 81, 87, 143, 144, 149, 154–155
  (*See also* Coming of Age in Samoa)
Mealtimes, 69, 139, 200

Meaning, urge to attach to the meaningless, 194
Measure, 167, 170
Medicine, 69, 139
Melody, 140, 182
Memory, 135, 175, 180
Mental illness, 135, 185, 196
Mental organ, 113
Mental mechanisms, 39, 84–86, 98–99 106–107, 141, 144, 148, 156
  for incest avoidance, 129
  for language, 113
Mental structures, 98–99
Metal tools, 50
Metaphor, 28, 29, 94, 113, 132, 133, 150, 161, 167, 170, 180, 194
Metaphors We Live By, 94
Methodology, methods, 25, 89, 145*n*
  analysis of design, 102
  for distinguishing nature from culture, 144, 147, 148
  exemplified by Ekman et al., 26–27
  natural experiments, 101, 129
  for quantifying cultural determination, 148
Metonymy, 132, 133
Mind (*see* Human mind)
Mind of Primitive Man, The, 55, 58
Misinforming, misleading, 131
Model, universal (*see* Universal framework)
Modesty concerning natural functions, 69, 139
(*See also* Sexual modesty)
Mood altering, 136, 180
Moral philosophy, influence of anthropology on, 154
Morality, 55, 69, 139, 159, 161, 165, 171, 174, 181
Morphemes, 41, 132, 198
Mother, biological, as social mother, 136
Mother-infant bond, 107, 112–113, 135, 169, 179, 194
Motion, 133
Mourning, 69, 139
Muelos belief, 96
Mundkur, Balaji, 115, 116
Murder, 43, 105 161, 179, 196
  committed more by males, 179
  prohibition of, 138, 176, 178, 182, 197
Murdock, George Peter, 62–63, 65, 69–71
  on antireductionism, 120

Murdock, George Peter (*Cont.*):
  article on universals by, 73, 140
  on distinguishing culture from biology in behavior, 64
  founder of Human Relations Area Files, 51
  list of universals by, x, 41, 69–70, 82, 153
  recants earlier views, 63*n*, 149
Muscle, words for, 44–45
Music, 50, 59, 69, 174, 186, 194, 200
  as art, a creation, 140, 186
  children's, 140
  melody in, 140, 182
  redundancy and repetition in, 140, 182
  related to dance and ritual, 140, 186
  rhythm in, 140, 186
  vocals and words in, 140
Myth(s), 59, 69, 139, 166, 196
  anthropological, 9, 14, 19, 23, 29, 30, 33, 37, 38, 64, 149
  explanation of, 99
  linguistic, 14, 29, 30

Names, 133, 167
  personal, 69, 174
  topographic and place, 174
Narrative, 132, 184
Natural environment of *Homo sapiens*, 50, 86, 100, 115, 116
  (*See also* Palaeolithic)
Natural experiments, 101, 129
Natural selection, 83*n*, 100
  unit of, 103
Nature/culture, 56, 86, 91–92, 130, 134, 146, 147, 149, 181, 192
  in adolescent stress, 15
  difficulty of distinguishing, 64, 144
  traced to flesh/spirit, 86*n*
Nature/nurture:
  controversy, 16, 77
  in Western thought, 86*n*
Nature of human organism as explanation, 98–99, 117
Nazism, 73
Near universals (*see* Universals)
Need(s):
  to explain the world, 99, 182
  expressive, 191
  Malinowskian, 67, 94
  for positive response from significant others, 190
  universal, 67, 94, 198

Needham, Rodney, 114
Negative (negation, not), 194
  (*See also* Logic)
Negative imprinting (*see* Imprinting)
Negative universals, 50, 164, 186, 189
Nepotism, 105, 108, 137, 165, 172
Neuro-cultural theory, 25
New universals, 50
New World–Old World parallels, 68–69,
  72
1984, 155n
No-man's land, 57, 64, 143
Nonconditional universals (*see* Universals)
Noncontradiction, 194
  (*See also* Logic)
Normal/abnormal mental states, 135
  (*See also* Mental illness)
Noun, 132, 167
Novel environments, 100–101
Nuclear family, 47
  complex, 10, 32
  (*See also* Family)
Numbers, 46, 69, 133, 157, 178

Obligate adaptation, 103
Obligation (*see* Rights and obligations)
Obscenity, 169
Oedipus and the Trobriands, 32–38
Oedipus complex, 9–10, 32–38, 50, 135
  ontogeny of, 112
Old World–New World parallels, 68–69, 72
Oligarchy, 138, 184
Omenry, 69, 139, 153n
On Human Nature, x, 82
One (numeral), 133
One-trial learning, 85, 147
Onomatopoeia, 132
Ontogeny, 112–113, 116, 117
Opposite (logic), 170
Optimism about practical applications of
  social science, 62
Order, need to impose, 167, 170
Ordering and aesthetics, 116
Ordering continua, 134
Orgasm, 102, 115
Orians, Gordan H., 115
Orientation, spatiotemporal, 174
Origins, ignored by anthropologists, 55, 66,
  143, 144
Ornamentation (*see* Adornment)
Ortner, Sherry, 91–92
Outline of Cultural Materials, 71

Pain, 134, 135
Palaeolithic, 96, 100–101, 107, 116
Parental care and investment, 82, 108–110,
  176, 182, 197
Parent-child ties, 197
  (*See also* Mother-infant bond)
Partial explanations, 113–117
Particularism, anthropological, 1
Part-whole (logic), 134, 170, 194, 201
Past:
  describing, 4n, 181
  present and future, 133
Patterns of Culture, ix, 1, 65–66, 69
  (*See also* Benedict, Ruth)
"People' as ethnocentric autonym, 79
Percussion, 114
Person, concept of, 134, 171
Person (grammatical), 164, 199
Personality terms and structure, 193, 199
Personification, 159, 161, 180
Phenotype, 100, 101
Phobias, 85
Phonemes, 41, 131, 173
Phylogenetic adaptation(s), 107, 115
Phylogenetic constraints, 104
Physical anthropologists, 41, 149
Piaget, Jean, 166
Plan, make plans, 135
Platonic forms, 54n, 190
Play, 116, 167, 168, 140
  children's, 196
  as training in skills, 140
Playfighting, 140, 148n, 199
Pleasure, partial explanations of, 115–116
Poetry, 132, 140, 186
  beats and lines in, 163, 197
  characterized by repetition, 132, 197
  line length of, 116, 132, 150, 197
Politeness, 162
Polyandry, 75
Polysemy, 133, 198
Pool, universal, 46
Pöppel, Ernst, 116
Possessions, loose/intimate, alienable/
  inalienable, 132
  (*See also* Property)
Possessive (grammar), 132
Pounders, 135
Practice to improve skill, 137
  (*See also* Play, as training in skills)
Pragmatic choices, 158
Precedent, 161, 188

Prediction, 138, 197
Preparedness, 85, 104, 115, 147
Prestige, differences of, 137
Presumed evolutionary theory, 110–111
Prevention as incest avoidance mechanism, 124
Pride, 178, 189
Primary factors, 114
Primate studies influence anthropologists, 72, 81n
Primitive Culture, 54–55
Principle of least effort, 98
Privacy, 157, 166, 182
  of inner life, 135
Problem solving, 182
Process universals, 43, 47, 81, 141, 156, 182
Product universals, 182
Production and reproduction, 93
Prohibition as incest avoidance mechanism, 124
Projection, 193
  (*See also* Psychological defense mechanisms)
Promise, 139, 186
Pronouns, 133, 164, 174, 194
Proper names, 69, 133
Property, 48, 59, 69, 132, 158, 174, 176, 182, 196
  alienable/inalienable, 132
  intimate/loose, 132, 139–140, 176
Proximate causes, explanations, and mechanisms, 104, 117, 129
Psyche (*see* Human mind)
Psychic unity of humanity, 54, 55, 58, 73, 87, 146, 147, 152
  a concept to stimulate, not to eliminate research, 156
Psychological anthropology, 82, 110
Psychological defense mechanisms, 180, 193, 196, 198
Psychological reductionism (*see* Kroeber, A. L.; Reductionism)
Psychology, 147n
  anthropological attitudes toward, 38
  comparative, according to Hallowell, 73–75
  in explanation of universals, 149–153
  and incest taboo, 119
  recent stimulating developments in, 87
  sidetracked by behaviorism, 143
  and social facts, 60
  (*See also* Evolutionary; Inner states; Universals)

Public/private, 175
Punishment, 69
  of acts that threaten collectivity, 138
Pupil of the eye, 44–45

Questions, word order of, 164

Race and culture, 54, 55, 57, 60
Racial differences, evolution of, 101n, 145
Racism, 143, 152–153
  as opposite of superorganicism, 70
Radcliffe-Brown, A. R., 66
Rank:
  as a focus of interest, 152, 196
  penchant to, 184
  social, 2, 76, 92, 159, 161, 167, 176, 182
Rape, 17, 161, 188
  prohibition or disapproval of, 138, 182, 188
Rationality, 193, 194
Rationalization, 193
Reasoning, 165
Reciprocal altruism, 82–83, 107–108
Reciprocity, 83, 98, 107–109, 138, 139, 150, 170, 173, 178, 181
  and morality, 139
  negative, 138, 165, 173
Red, white, and black, 12, 14, 161, 197
Redfield, Robert, 47
Redress, 138, 178
Reductionism, 70–71, 76, 120, 143, 145, 148
  (*See also* Antireductionism; Kroeber, A. L.)
Refutations, 14–23, 27–31, 64n
Reification of culture, 70–71
Relationship, logical, 170
Relationships of procreation, 133
Relativism, ix, 33, 38, 45, 83–84, 192
  critics of, 155
  cultural, 6, 9, 27, 30, 55, 62, 71–73, 76, 77n
    and antiracist morality, 55
    and arbitrariness, 77n
    Herskovits on, 71
    and tolerance, 73
  extreme cultural (and linguistic), 12, 14, 27, 31, 38, 62, 76, 81n, 82
  limits of, 151
    at present, 155–156
  as justification for research, 31
  language exemplifies, 77
  linguistic, 11, 14, 31, 77
Religion, 59, 69, 110–111, 139
  difficulty of explaining, 71, 113–114
  and the Muelos belief, 96

Religion (*Cont.*):
  partial explanations of, 113–115
  as universal of classification, 48, 64
Repression, 32, 34–36
Reproduction, 93, 106, 133
  imagery of, 115
  interest in, 97
Reproductive beliefs, 33, 35, 36, 166
Reproductive cells, sex differences in 108–
    109
Reproductive potential, 109
Reproductive success, 83*n*, 100
Residence rules, 69
Responsibility, 135, 139, 165, 175
Restitution (*see* Redress)
Revenge, 165
Rhetoric, 132, 140
Right-hand preference (*see* Right-handed-
    ness)
Right-handedness, 89–91, 94, 136
  (*See also* Handedness)
Right/wrong, 139, 165, 193, 197
Rights and obligations, 138, 172, 182, 188
Rhythm, 140, 186
Rhythmicity of time, 133
Ritual, 59, 69, 114, 116, 139, 174, 176, 194
  associated with art, dance, music, 140,
      167, 186
  deep-noted instruments in, 114
  percussion in, 114
  sound as a medium of communication in,
      197
Rohner, Ronald P., 82
Roles (*see* Statuses)
Rosch, Eleanor, 14
Rules, 98, 165, 167, 181, 194, 196
  of membership, 138
Rules of the Sociological Method, The, 60

Sacks, Oliver, 61*n*, 85, 150
Sadness, 26, 134, 178
Same (logical category), 170
Sanctions (punishment), 69, 138, 188
  by exclusion or removal, 138
Sapir, Edward, 10, 27, 155*n*
Sapir-Whorf hypothesis, 10, 27, 155*n*
Scheff, Thomas J., 2, 128
Schizophrenia, 169
"Science of Culture, The," 62–63
Scientific Theory of Culture, A, 66–68
Secularism, 153*n*
Selection, unit of, 103

Self:
  in control/under control, 135, 175
  as distinct from other(s), 165, 174, 175
  self-deception, 196
  as subject and object, 134
Semantic categories, 133
Semantic components, 75, 76, 133
  of kin terms, 46, 48*n*, 80
  of sex, 80, 133
  (*See also* Ethnosemantics)
Semantic primes, 199
Semantic universals, 11, 12, 79–80, 131–133
Senility, 196
Senses, unification of, 139
Sensitive period, 104, 113, 123, 128, 181
Sex:
  differences, 42, 75, 101–104, 106–110, 133,
      134, 144, 145, 172, 189, 196
  in age at marriage, 109
  attributed to nature, 137
  cultural conceptions of, 137, 184
  in homicide rates, 137, 165
  in providing childcare, 109, 136, 176,
      184, 189
  in reproductive cells, 108–109
  study of, 108–110, 150
  (*See also* Male)
  organization, 137, 164, 176, 181, 194
  semantic component of, 80, 133
  terminology (*see* Classification)
Sex and Repression in Savage Society, 9–10
*Sex and Temperament in Three Primitive
    Societies*, 20–23
Sexual attractiveness, 109*n*, 135, 140, 195
  and skin color, 43–44
Sexual dimorphism, 108–110
Sexual division of labor, 48, 157, 165
Sexual jealousy, 18, 20, 60, 107, 109, 135, 172
Sexual modesty, 139, 166, 167
Sexual selection, 82–83, 103, 108–110
Sexuality, 15–18, 33, 41–42, 106, 108–110, 115,
    118
  cultural expressions of, 166
  as focus of interest, 137, 180
  regulation of, 69–70, 137, 157, 165, 166, 182,
      196, 198
Shame, 178, 189
Shape, categories of, 170
Shattered Mind, The, 150
Shelter, 58, 69, 136
Shepher, Joseph, 88, 122–123, 127, 128
Shock, 189

Sickness and death related, 139, 176
Signs, 165
Similarities, human, anthropological reliance on, 154
Singing, 162, 186, 194
Skepticism, anthropological (see Anthropologists)
Skill and aesthetics, 116
Skinner, B. F., 77
Smile, 24, 83, 85, 168
  in greeting, 134, 179
Snake(s):
  in art and religion, 115, 116
  ease of acquiring fear of, 115
  emotional reaction to, 135, 190
Snow, Eskimo words for, 27
Social control, 59, 67, 157
Social Darwinism, 62
Social facts explain social facts, 60
Social personhood and identity [see Statuses (and roles)]
Social structure, 69, 137, 176
Social universals, 39–40, 42, 50, 66, 142
Sociality, 59, 116, 136, 145, 165, 167, 176, 197
Socialization, 136, 137, 157, 182
  by parents and other close kin, 136, 165
Societies:
  change with time, 157
  as focus of study, 143
Society:
  adjusts to environment, 157
  as locus of universals, 39–40, 42, 50
  Malinowski on, 67
  as product of human action, 99
  rejected as causal by Murdock, 63n
  role of universals in, 150–151
  science of, 66
  universal model for analysis of, 71
Society/culture/individual, artificial boundaries between, 40, 43
Sociobiology, x, 83n, 144
Sociobiology, 82
Solidarity, 182
  kin based, 108, 199
Someone (semantic prime), 199
Song, 162, 186, 194
Sophistry, 161
Sorrow (see Sadness)
Sound:
  as medium of ritual communication, 197
  and sense, 77, 98, 131

Space, 133, 157, 170, 178, 188
Spatial metaphors of time, 28, 29
Spatiotemporal orientation, 174
Spear, 135, 157
Special occasions to look one's best, 188
Speech, 58
  insulting with, 131
  segmentation of, 163
  special, 132
  symbolic nature of, 131
Speed, 133
Sperber, Dan, 5, 80, 94, 110, 114, 147
Spiro, Melford, 9, 10, 33–38, 49–50, 112, 120, 127–128, 155
Sport, 69
Staal, Frits, 54n
Statistical universal(s), 43n, 44–45, 93, 97, 149–150, 187
  incest taboo as, 128
Status, high, admiring signs of, 44
Status markers, 169
Statuses (and roles), 39, 48, 69, 135, 137, 139, 157, 165, 169, 174, 185, 196
  ascribed/achieved, 137, 176
  based on other than kinship, age, and sex, 137
  corporate, 138
  individual distinguished from, 135
  personality distinguished from, 176
Steadman, Lyle B., 3
Steiner, George, 110, 114
Stops/nonstops, 131
Stranger recognition mechanisms, 107n
Strangers, fear of, 107n, 135
Stress (linguistic), 194
String, 59, 135, 198
Subject/verb/object, 194
Sublimation, 193
Substance consumption to partake of its properties, 182
Substantive universals, 42–43, 49, 81, 141, 164, 170
Succession, 137, 169
Sucking reflex, 101
Supernatural, 69, 139, 159, 161, 176, 196
"Superorganic, The," 56, 57
Superorganicism, 56, 57, 70, 71, 76
Surface universals, 43, 47, 141
Surprise, 26, 134, 167
Susceptibilities, 110–111
Sweets, 139

Symbolism, 75, 94, 134, 165, 167, 180
  to cope with envy, 169
  of hands, 89–91, 94, 186
  snake as, 116
Symbols (*see* Symbolism)
Symons, Donald, 75, 83, 85, 101, 102, 106, 109
Synonyms, 133
Syntax (*see* Grammar)

Taboo(s), 137, 170, 196
  anthropological, 6, 64, 72, 144
  food, 69, 139
  incest (*see* Incest)
  speech, 139, 169
Tabula rasa, 60, 85, 144, 146, 148, 154, 155
Taxonomy, 86, 133, 170
Temperaments, human, 65–66, 159
Tendencies, 43, 44, 47, 97, 164
  classification of, 133
  dismissed as innate by Durkheim, 60
  to impose meaning on the world, 99, 182
  Kroeber on, 57
  to overestimate objectivity of thought, 134,
    181
Terminological misunderstandings, 101–102
Territoriality (*see* Groups)
Textbooks, 11–12, 16, 21, 29, 33, 61–62, 156
Theft, 161
Thinking, 157, 180
  tendency to overestimate objectivity of,
    134, 181
Thought (*see* Thinking)
Tiger, Lionel, 81, 140
Time, 10, 27–31, 82, 86, 92–94, 133, 157, 170,
    174, 178, 197
  rhythmicity of, 133
  spatial metaphors of, 28, 29
  units of, 133
Toilet training, 137
Tolerance, 65, 71, 73
Tooby, John, 83, 85, 86, 103*n*, 106, 147*n*, 148
Tool making (*see* Tools)
Tools, 40, 59, 70, 135–136, 165, 167, 169, 178
  and aesthetics, 116
  dependence on, 75, 135, 183
  permanent, 135
  relation to handedness of, 94
  stylization of, 135–136
  universal types of, 135
Trade, 69, 138, 165
Traits and complexes, 40, 43, 44, 130
Translation, 12, 132, 133

Transport, 58, 165
Treatment:
  of the dead, 59, 69, 70, 139, 176
  of the sick, 59, 69, 139, 176, 196
Trial-and-error problem solving, 165
Triangular awareness, 111, 138, 166
Trivers, R. L., 82, 107, 108
True/false, 131, 174
Turn taking, 131, 183, 191
Turner, Frederick, 116, 150, 153
Turner, Victor W., 142, 143, 155
Two (numeral), 133
Tying, 135
  (*See also* Interlacing; String)
Tylor, Edward B., 54–56
  on incest taboo, 72
  on racial explanations, 54

Ultimate explanations, 104, 129
"Universal Categories of Culture," 72–73
Universal conditions as basis of human uni-
    versals, 70
Universal framework (or model), 59, 66–67,
    71, 76, 94, 158, 165, 175, 178, 189, 198
  defined, 47–48
Universal functions of society/culture, 76,
    157
Universal grammar, 164
Universal hypotheses, 175
Universal model (*see* Universal framework)
Universal needs (*see* Needs)
"Universal Pattern, The," 48, 58–59, 71
Universal People, the (UP), 130–141
Universal pool, 46, 70, 181
Universal semantic types, 167
Universal validity (knowledge), 92
Universalist approach, 82
Universality:
  as a clue to adaptation, 105
  demonstration of, 51–53
Universals:
  absolute, 43*n*, 44, 140 164
  of accident, 49–50
  anatomical and physiological traits rarely
    included among, 39, 41
  anomalousness of, 143
  anthropological ambivalence toward, 54,
    58, 64, 73, 75, 81, 82, 145
  biological, 49
    (*See also* Biological universals; Biology/
    psychology as basis or explana-
    tion of universals)

Universals (*Cont.*):

    Boas on, 55–56, 58

    causation in explanation of, 89, 117

    classification of, 182

    of classification, 48, 59, 64, 70, 71, 73

    conceptualization of, 39–42, 141

    conditional (implicational), 45–46, 50, 80, 89–90, 103, 105, 141, 142

    of content, 48, 59, 70, 73

    of conversation structure, 185

    cultural, 39–40, 63, 142

    deep, 44, 141

        (*See also* Deep processes)

    as deep syntax and lexicon of culture, 153

    definitions of, 5, 42–50, 141

    emic/etic, 48–49

    of essence, 49–50

    evolutionary, 188

    exceptions to, 36, 127

    experiential, 47, 180, 192

    explanation of, 82–92, 116–117

    extrinsic, 49–50

    "fake," 74, 114

    formal, 43, 49, 50, 164

    functions of language, 192

    of grammar, 131–132, 164, 173

    heterogeneity of, 5–6, 142

    hierarchy of, 141

    in history of social sciences, 143

    in human affairs, importance of, 153

    on human nature and (*see* Bidney, David)

    and humanities, 149, 153–154, 156

    implicational (conditional), 45–46, 50, 78, 80, 89–90, 103, 105, 142, 149–151, 175

    implications of, 149

    implicit definition of, 42

    improbability of, if culture autonomous, 58, 63, 143

    interest in, 75, 81, 88

    intrinsic, 49–50

    kinds of, 43–50

    Kroeber dismisses, 64

    lexical, 162, 173, 200

    in language, role of, 150–151

    linguistic (*see* Language; Linguistic universals; Linguistics)

    of literary art, 153, 176

    manifest, 47

    of music, 174, 200

        (*See also* Music)

Universals (*Cont.*):

    near, 43, 44, 47, 56, 89–90, 109, 141, 176, 177, 180, 182

        examples of, 44

        incest taboo as, 118, 128

        Shepher on, 127

    negative, 50, 164, 186, 189

    never proved, 53

    new, 50

    nonconditional, 45, 164

    nonimplicational, 45, 164

    partial explanations of, 113–117

    and particulars, 149

    in personality terms, 199

    phonemic, 173

    process, 43, 47, 81, 141, 156, 170, 182

    product, 182

    proving, 38, 53

    psychological, 175

    psychological bases for, 70

    reflect human nature, 146, 148

    semantic, 11, 12, 79–80, 131–133

    skepticism toward, 1, 5, 6, 26, 54, 58, 64, 73, 75, 81, 82

    social, 39–40, 42, 50, 66, 142

    statistical, 43*n*, 44–45, 93, 97, 149–150, 187

        incest taboo as, 128

    substantive, 42–43, 49, 81, 141, 164, 170

    surface, 43, 47, 141

    tracing consequences of, 150–151, 153–154

    types of, 182

    unrestricted, 45, 78, 127, 142, 150, 164

    World War II and study of, 69, 86, 87

    World War III, threat of, and study of, 73

    (*See also* Grammar, universals of)

Unknown, proneness to explain, 97

Unrestricted universals (*see* Universals)

UP (*see* Universal People, the)

Usage of terms, misunderstanding between biological and social scientists, 101–102

Van den Berghe, Pierre, 44, 107

Variation not necessarily sociocultural, 103*n*

Variousness as essence of human nature, 74

Veblen, Thorstein, 68

Verb(s), 132, 167

Vestibular induction of trance, 114, 116

Violence, 59, 110

    proscription of, 138, 182

Visiting, 70, 139

Vocalics/nonvocalics, 131

Warden, Carl J., 66
Watson, John B., 60–61
Weaning, 70, 136
Weapons, 59, 135, 169
Weather control, 70, 139
Weiner, Annette B., 34*n*, 38
Westermarck, Edward, 119–121
Westermarck effect or hypothesis, 121–122,
128–129
  age limits of, 122–123, 128
  lessons drawn from test of, 128
What Is Art For, 116
White, black, and red, 12, 14, 161
White, Leslie, 68, 72
Whorf, Benjamin Lee, 10, 27–31, 144, 155
Williams, Elgin, 65, 69
Williams, George C., 82, 100, 103, 109*n*, 148

Wilson, E. O., x, 82
Wilson, Margo, 86, 105, 107, 109, 155
Wissler, Clark, 47, 48, 58–59, 71
Witkowski, Stanley R., 14
Wolf, Arthur P., 121–122, 124
Words, 132
  shorter if used frequently, 133
  transparent and opaque, 197
Worldview, 40, 47, 49, 69, 99, 167, 170, 171,
176, 178, 189, 193, 194
  structured by features of mind, 139
  unification of senses in constructing, 139
Writing, 58

Yengoyan, Aram, 47

Zipf, George K., 98